The
WILEY
advantage

Dear Valued Customer,

We realize you're a busy professional with deadlines to hit. Whether your goal is to learn a new technology or solve a critical problem, we want to be there to lend you a hand. Our primary objective is to provide you with the insight and knowledge you need to stay atop the highly competitive and ever-changing technology industry.

Wiley Publishing, Inc., offers books on a wide variety of technical categories, including security, data warehousing, software development tools, and networking — everything you need to reach your peak. Regardless of your level of expertise, the Wiley family of books has you covered.

- For Dummies® – The *fun* and *easy* way™ to learn
- The Weekend Crash Course® –The *fastest* way to learn a new tool or technology
- Visual – For those who prefer to learn a new topic *visually*
- The Bible – The *100% comprehensive* tutorial and reference
- The Wiley Professional list – *Practical* and *reliable* resources for IT professionals

The book you now hold, *The Semantic Web: A Guide to the Future of XML, Web Services, and Knowledge Management,* provides an authoritative introduction to the most important new development in Web technology since the Web itself. The Semantic Web is a revolutionary framework for creating intelligent Web applications—when fully realized, it will have far-reaching benefits for online commerce. The authors and contributors include key thought-leaders in developing the Semantic Web framework. The book explains what the Semantic Web is, how it works technically, and how businesses will benefit. Strategic decision-makers as well as software architects and developers will discover a blueprint for translating a Semantic Web strategy into action. Among the topics covered:

- What is the Semantic Web, and how does it work.
- The business case for implementing the Semantic Web.
- The role of RDF, XML, and Web Services in building the Semantic Web.
- The nature of taxonomies and ontologies, and why they are important building blocks in constructing the Semantic Web.
- What you can do now to prepare your company for the Semantic Web.

The book's companion Website will provide further updates on the evolution of the Semantic Web, as well as links to related sites.

Our commitment to you does not end at the last page of this book. We'd want to open a dialog with you to see what other solutions we can provide. Please be sure to visit us at www.wiley.com/compbooks to review our complete title list and explore the other resources we offer. If you have a comment, suggestion, or any other inquiry, please locate the "contact us" link at www.wiley.com.

Finally, we encourage you to review the following page for a list of Wiley titles on related topics. Thank you for your support and we look forward to hearing from you and serving your needs again in the future.

Sincerely,

Richard K Swadley

Richard K. Swadley
Vice President & Executive Group Publisher
Wiley Technology Publishing

15 HOUR WEEKEND CRASH COURSE

Visual™

Bible

DUMMIES FOR

WILEY

Wiley Publishing, Inc.

The Semantic Web:

A Guide to the Future of XML, Web Services, and Knowledge Management

The Semantic Web:

A Guide to the Future of XML, Web Services, and Knowledge Management

Michael C. Daconta
Leo J. Obrst
Kevin T. Smith

Wiley Publishing, Inc.

Publisher: Joe Wilkert
Editor: Robert M. Elliot
Developmental Editor: Emilie Herman
Editorial Manager: Kathryn A. Malm
Production Editors: Felicia Robinson and Micheline Frederick
Media Development Specialist: Travis Silvers
Text Design & Composition: Wiley Composition Services

Published by Wiley Publishing, Inc., Indianapolis, Indiana
Published simultaneously in Canada

For general information on our other products and services please contact our Customer Care Department within the United States at (800) 762-2974, outside the United States at (317) 572-3993 or fax (317) 572-4002.

Library of Congress Cataloging-in-Publication Data:

ISBN 0-471-43257-1

Printed in the United States of America

10 9 8 7 6 5 4 3

Advance Praise for
The Semantic Web

"There's a revolution occurring and it's all about making the Web meaningful, understandable, and machine-processable, whether it's based in an intranet, extranet, or Internet. This is called the Semantic Web, and it will transition us toward a knowledge-centric viewpoint of 'everything.' This book is unique in its exhaustive examination of all the technologies involved, including coverage of the Semantic Web, XML, and all major related technologies and protocols, Web services and protocols, Resource Description Framework (RDF), taxonomies, and ontologies, as well as a business case for the Semantic Web and a corporate roadmap to leverage this revolution. All organizations, businesses, business leaders, developers, and IT professionals need to look carefully at this impressive study of the next killer app/framework/movement for the use and implementation of knowledge for the benefit of all."

Stephen Ibaraki
Chairman and Chief Architect, iGen Knowledge Solutions, Inc.

"The Semantic Web is rooted in the understanding of words in context. This guide acts in this role to those attempting to understand Semantic Web and corresponding technologies by providing critical definitions around the technologies and vocabulary of this emerging technology."

JP Morgenthal
Chief Services Architect, Software AG, Inc.

*This book is dedicated to Tim Berners-Lee for crafting
the Semantic Web vision and for all the people turning that
vision into a reality. Vannevar Bush is somewhere watching—and
smiling for the prospects of future generations.*

*"The bane of my existence is doing things that
I know the computer could do for me."*
—Dan Connolly, "The XML Revolution"

N othing is more frustrating than knowing you have previously solved a complex problem but not being able to find the document or note that specified the solution. It is not uncommon to refuse to rework the solution because you know you already solved the problem and don't want to waste time redoing past work. In fact, taken to the extreme, you may waste more time finding the previous solution than it would take to redo the work. This is a direct result of our information management facilities not keeping pace with the capacity of our information storage.

Look at the personal computer as an example. With $1000 personal computers sporting 60- to 80-GB hard drives, our document storage capacity (assuming 1-byte characters, plaintext, and 3500 characters per page) is around 17 to 22 million pages of information. Most of those pages are in proprietary, binary formats that cannot be searched as plaintext. Thus, our predominant knowledge discovery method for our personal information is a haphazardly created hierarchical directory structure. Scaling this example up to corporations, we see both the storage capacity and diversity of information formats and access methods increase ten- to a hundredfold multiplied by the number of employees.

In general, it is clear that we are only actively managing a small fraction of the total information we produce. The effect of this is lost productivity and reduced revenues. In fact, it is the active management of information that turns it into knowledge by selection, addition, sequence, correlation, and annotation. The purpose of this book is to lay out a clear path to improved knowledge management in your organization using Semantic Web technologies. Second, we examine the technology building blocks of the Semantic Web to include XML, Web services, and RDF. Lastly, not only do we show you how the Semantic Web will be achieved, we provide the justifications and business case on how you can put these technologies to use for a significant return on investment.

Why You Should Read This Book Now

Events become interrelated into trends because of an underlying attractive goal, which individual actors attempt to achieve often only partially. For example, the trend toward electronic device convergence is based on the goal of packing related features together to reduce device cost and improve utility. The trend toward software components is based on the goal of software reuse, which lowers cost and increases speed to market. The trend of do-it-yourself construction is based on the goals of individual empowerment, pride in accomplishment, and reduced cost. The trend toward the Semantic Web is based on the goal of semantic interoperability of data, which enables application independence, improved search facilities, and improved machine inference.

Smart organizations do not ignore powerful trends. Additionally, if the trend affects or improves mission-critical applications, it is something that must be mastered quickly. This is the case with the Semantic Web. The Semantic Web is emerging today in thousands of pilot projects in diverse industries like library science, defense, medicine, and finance. Additionally, technology leaders like IBM, HP, and Adobe have Semantic Web products available, and many more IT companies have internal Semantic Web research projects. In short, key areas of the Semantic Web are beyond the research phase and have moved into the implementation phase.

The Semantic Web dominoes have begun to tumble: from XML to Web services to taxonomies to ontologies to inference. This does not represent the latest fad; instead, it is the culmination of years of research and experimentation in knowledge representation. The impetus now is the success of the World Wide Web. HTML, HTTP, and other Web technologies provide a strong precedent for successful information sharing. The existing Web will not go away; the introduction of Semantic Web technologies will enhance it to include knowledge sharing and discovery.

Our Approach to This Complex Topic

Our model for this book is a conversation between the CIO and CEO in crafting a technical vision for a corporation. In that model, we first explain the concepts in clear terms and illustrate them with concrete examples. Second, we make hard technical judgments on the technology—warts and all. We are not acting as cheerleaders for this technology. Some of it can be better, and we point out the good, the bad, and the ugly. Lastly, we lay the cornerstones of a technical policy and tie it all together in the final chapter of the book.

Our model for each subject was to provide straightforward answers to the key questions on each area. In addition, we provide concrete, compelling examples of all key concepts presented in the book. Also, we provide numerous illustrative diagrams to assist in explaining concepts. Lastly, we present several new concepts of our own invention, leveraging our insight into these technologies, how they will evolve, and why.

How This Book Is Organized

This book is composed of nine chapters that can be read either in sequence or as standalone units:

Chapter 1, What Is the Semantic Web?   This chapter explains the Semantic Web vision of creating machine-processable data and how we achieve that vision. Explains the general framework for achieving the Semantic Web, why we need the Semantic Web, and how the key technologies in the rest of the book fit into the Semantic Web. This chapter introduces novel concepts like the *smart-data continuum* and *combinatorial experimentation*.

Chapter 2, The Business Case for the Semantic Web.   This chapter clearly demonstrates concrete examples of how businesses can leverage the Semantic Web for competitive advantage. Specifically, presents examples on decision support, business development, and knowledge management. The chapter ends with a discussion of the current state of Semantic Web technology.

Chapter 3, Understanding XML and Its Impact on the Enterprise.   This chapter explains why XML is a success, what XML is, what XML Schema is, what namespaces are, what the Document Object Model is, and how XML impacts enterprise information technology. The chapter concludes with a discussion of why XML meta data is not enough and the trend toward higher data fidelity. Lastly, we close by explaining the new concept of *semantic levels*. For any organization not currently involved in integrating XML throughout the enterprise, this chapter is a must-read.

Chapter 4, Understanding Web Services.   This chapter covers all aspects of current Web services and discusses the future direction of Web services. It explains how to discover, describe, and access Web services and the technologies behind those functions. It also provides concrete use cases for deploying Web services and answers the question "Why use Web services?" Lastly, it provides detailed description of advanced Web service applications to include orchestration and security. The chapter closes with a discussion of grid-enabled Web services and semantic-enabled Web services.

Chapter 5, Understanding the Resource Description Framework.   This chapter explains what RDF is, the distinction between the RDF model and syntax, its features, why it has not been adopted as rapidly as XML, and why that will change. This chapter also introduces a new use case for this technology called *noncontextual modeling*. The chapter closes with an explanation of data modeling using RDF Schema. The chapter stresses the importance of explicitly modeling relationships between data items.

Chapter 6, Understanding the Rest of the Alphabet Soup.   This chapter rounds out the coverage of XML-related technologies by explaining XPATH, XSL, XSLT, XSLFO, XQuery, XLink, XPointer, XInclude, XML Base, XHTML, XForms, and SVG. Besides explaining the purpose of these technologies in a direct, clear manner, the chapter offers examples and makes judgments on the utility and future of each technology.

Chapter 7, Understanding Taxonomies.   This chapter explains what taxonomies are and how they are implemented. The chapter builds a detailed understanding of taxonomies using illustrative examples and shows how they differ from ontologies. The chapter introduces an insightful concept called the *Ontology Spectrum*. The chapter then delves into a popular implementation of taxonomies called Topic Maps and XML Topic Maps (XTM). The chapter concludes with a comparison of Topic Maps and RDF and a discussion of their complementary characteristics.

Chapter 8, Understanding Ontologies.   This chapter is extremely detailed and takes a slow, building-block approach to explain what ontologies are, how they are implemented, and how to use them to achieve semantic interoperability. The chapter begins with a concrete business example and then carefully dissects the definition of an ontology from several different perspectives. Then we explain key ontology concepts like syntax, structure, semantics, pragmatics, extension, and intension. Detailed examples of these are given including how software agents use these techniques. In explaining the difference between a thesaurus and ontology, an insightful concept is introduced called the *triangle of signification*. The chapter moves on to knowledge representation and logics to detail the implementation concepts behind ontologies that provide machine inference. The chapter concludes with a detailed explanation of current ontology languages to include DAML and OWL and offers judgments on the corporate utility of ontologies.

Chapter 9, Crafting Your Company's Roadmap to the Semantic Web.   This chapter presents a detailed roadmap to leveraging the Semantic Web technologies discussed in the previous chapters in your organization. It lays the context for the roadmap by comparing the current state of information and knowledge management in most organizations to a detailed vision of a knowledge-centric organization. The chapter details the key processes of a knowledge-centric organization to include discovery and production, search and retrieval, and application of results (including information reuse). Next, detailed steps are provided to effect the change to a knowledge-centric organization. The steps include vision definition, training requirements, technical implementation, staffing, and scheduling. The chapter concludes with an exhortation to take action.

This book is a comprehensive tutorial and strategy session on the new data revolution emerging today. Each chapter offers a detailed, honest, and authoritative assessment of the technology, its current state, and advice on how you can leverage it in your organization. Where appropriate, we have highlighted "maxims" or principles on using the technology.

Who Should Read This Book

This book is written as a strategic guide to managers, technical leads, and senior developers. Some chapters will be useful to all people interested in the Semantic Web; some delve deeper into subjects after covering all the basics. However, none of the chapters assumes an in-depth knowledge of any of the technologies.

While the book was designed to be read from cover to cover in a building-block approach, some sections are more applicable to certain groups. Senior managers may only be interested in the chapters focusing on the strategic understanding, business case, and roadmap for the Semantic Web (Chapters 1, 2, and 9). CIOs and technical directors will be interested in all the chapters but will especially find the roadmap useful (Chapter 9). Training managers will want to focus on the key Semantic Web technology chapters like RDF (Chapter 5), taxonomies (Chapter 7), and ontologies (Chapter 8) to set training agendas. Senior developers and developers interested in the Semantic Web should read and understand all the technology chapters (Chapters 3 to 8).

What's on the Companion Web Site

The companion Web site at http://www.wiley.com/compbooks/daconta contains the following:

Source code.   The source code for all listings in the book are available in a compressed archive.

Errata.   Any errors discovered by readers or the authors are listed with the corresponding corrected text.

Code appendix for Chapter 8.   As some of the listings in Chapter 8 are quite long, they were abbreviated in the text yet posted in their entirety on the Web site.

Contact addresses.   The email addresses of the authors are available, as well as answers to any frequently asked questions.

Feedback Welcome

This book is written by senior technologists for senior technologists, their management counterparts, and those aspiring to be senior technologists. All comments, suggestions, and questions from the entire IT community are greatly appreciated. It is feedback from our readers that both makes the writing worthwhile and improves the quality of our work. I'd like to thank all the readers who have taken time to contact us to report errors, provide constructive criticism, or express appreciation.

I can be reached via email at mike@daconta.net or via regular mail:

Michael C. Daconta
c/o Robert Elliott
Wiley Publishing, Inc.
111 River Street
Hoboken, NJ 07030

Best wishes,

Michael C. Daconta
Sierra Vista, Arizona

Writing this book has been rewarding because of the importance of the topic, the quality of my coauthors, and the utility of our approach to provide critical, strategic guidance. At the same time, there were difficulties in writing this book simultaneously with *More Java Pitfalls* (also from Wiley). During the course of this work, I am extremely grateful to the support I have received from my wife, Lynne, and kids, CJ, Samantha, and Gregory. My dear wife Lynne deserves the most credit for her unwavering support over the years. She is a fantastic mother and wife whom I am lucky to have as a partner. We moved during the writing of this book, and everyone knows how difficult moving can be. I would also like to thank my in-laws, Buddy and Shirley Belden, for their support. The staff at Wiley Publishing, Inc., including Bob Elliott, Emilie Herman, Brian Snapp, and Micheline Frederick, were both understanding and supportive throughout the process. This project would not have even begun without the efforts of my great coauthors Kevin T. Smith and Leo Obrst. Their professionalism and hard work throughout this project was inspirational. Nothing tests the mettle of someone like multiple, simultaneous deadlines, and these guys came through!

Another significant influence on this book was the work I performed over the last three years. For Fannie Mae, I designed an XML Standard for electronic mortgages that has been adopted by the Mortgage Industry Standards Maintenance Organization (MISMO). Working with Gary Haupt, Jennifer Donaghy, and Mark Oliphant of Fannie Mae was a pleasure. Also, working with the members of MISMO in refining the standard was equally wonderful. More directly related to this book was my work as Chief Architect of the Virtual Knowledge Base Project. I would like to sincerely thank the MBI Program manager, Danny Proko, and Government Program manager, Ted Wiatrak, for their support, hard work, and outstanding management skills throughout the project. Ted has successfully led the Intelligence Community to new ways of thinking about knowledge management. Additionally, I'd like to thank the members of my architecture team: Kevin T. Smith, Joe Vitale, Joe Rajkumar, and Maurita Soltis for their hard work on a slew of tough problems. I would also like to thank my team members at Northrop Grumman, Becky Smith, Mark Leone, and Janet Sargent, for their support and hard work. Lastly, special thanks to Danny Proko and Kevin Apsley, my former Vice President of the Advanced Programs Group at MBI, for helping and supporting my move to Arizona.

There are many other family, friends, and acquaintances who have helped in ways big and small during the course of this book. Thank you all for your assistance.

I would especially like to thank my colleagues and the management at McDonald Bradley, Inc.; especially, Sharon McDonald, Ken Bartee, Dave Shuping, Gail Rissler, Danny Proko, Susan Malay, Anthony Salvi, Joe Broussard, Kyle Rice, and Dave Arnold. These friends and associates have enriched my life both personally and professionally with their professionalism, dedication, and drive. I look forward to more years of challenge and growth at McDonald Bradley, Inc.

As always, I owe a debt of gratitude to our readers. Over the last 10 books, they have enriched the writing experience by appreciating, encouraging, and challenging me to go the extra mile. My goal for my books has never changed: to provide significant value to the reader—to discuss difficult topics in an approachable and enlightening way. I sincerely hope I have achieved these goals and encourage our readers to let me know if we have not. Best wishes.

Michael C. Daconta

I would like to thank my coauthors, Mike and Leo. Because of your hard work, more people will understand the promise of the Semantic Web. This is the third book that I have written with Mike, and it has been a pleasure working with him. Thanks to Dan Hulen of Dominion Digital, Inc. and Andy Stross of CapitalOne, who were reviewers of some of the content in this book. Once again, it was a pleasure to do work with Bob Elliott and Emilie Herman at Wiley. I would also like to thank Ashland Coffee and Tea, where I did much caffeine-inspired writing for this book on Saturday and Sunday afternoons.

The Virtual Knowledge Base (VKB) program has been instrumental in helping Mike and me focus on the Semantic Web and bringing this vision and a forward-thinking solution to the government. Because of the hard work of Ted Wiatrak, Danny Proko, Clay Richardson, Don Avondolio, Joe Broussard, Becky Smith, and many others, this team has been able to do great things.

I would like to thank Gwen, who is the most wonderful wife in the world!

Kevin T. Smith

I would like to express my appreciation for the encouragement and support in the writing of this book that I've received from many individuals, including my colleague David Ferrell, my wife Christy (who tolerated my self-exile well), and the anonymous reviewers. I also note that the views expressed in this paper are those of the authors alone and do not reflect the official policy or position of The MITRE Corporation or any other company or individual.

Leo J. Obrst

The World Wide Web has dramatically changed the availability of electronically accessible information. The Web currently contains around 3 billion static documents, which are accessed by over 500 million users internationally. At the same time, this enormous amount of data has made it increasingly difficult to find, access, present, and maintain relevant information. This is because information content is presented primarily in natural language. Thus, a wide gap has emerged between the information available for tools aimed at addressing these problems and the information maintained in human-readable form.

In response to this problem, many new research initiatives and commercial enterprises have been set up to enrich available information with machine-processable semantics. Such support is essential for "bringing the Web to its full potential." Tim Berners-Lee, Director of the World Wide Web Consortium, referred to the future of the current Web as the *Semantic Web*—an extended web of machine-readable information and automated services that amplify the Web far beyond current capabilities. The explicit representation of the semantics underlying data, programs, pages, and other Web resources will enable a knowledge-based Web that provides a qualitatively new level of service. Automated services will improve in their capacity to assist humans in achieving their goals by "understanding" more of the content on the Web, and thus providing more accurate filtering, categorizing, and searching of these information sources. This process will ultimately lead to an extremely knowledgeable system that features various specialized reasoning services. These services will support us in nearly all aspects of our daily life, making access to information as pervasive, and necessary, as access to electricity is today.

When my colleagues and I started in 1996 with academic prototypes in this area, only a few other initiatives were available at that time. Step by step we learned that there were initiatives like XML and RDF run by the W3C.[1] Today the situation is quite different. The Semantic Web is already established as a research and educational topic at many universities. Many conferences, workshops, and journals have been set up. Small and large companies realize the potential impact of this area for their future performance. Still, there is a long

---

[1]I remember the first time that I was asked about RDF, I mistakenly heard "RTF" and was quite surprised that "RTF" would be considered a proper standard for the Semantic Web.

way to go in transferring scientific ideas into a widely used technology— and *The Semantic Web: A Guide to the Future of XML, Web Services, and Knowledge Management* will be a cornerstone for this transmission process. Most other material is still very hard to read and understand. I remember that it took me two months of my time to understand what RDF and RDFS are about. This book will enable you to understand these technologies even more thoroughly within two hours. The book is an excellent introduction to the core topics of the Semantic Web, its relationship with Web services, and its potential in application areas such as knowledge management. It will help you to understand these topics efficiently, with minimal consumption of your limited, productive time.

Dr. Dieter Fensel
Professor
Institute for Computer Science
University of Innsbruck

CHAPTER 1

What Is the Semantic Web?

"The first step is putting data on the Web in a form that machines can naturally understand, or converting it to that form. This creates what I call a Semantic Web—a web of data that can be processed directly or indirectly by machines."

—Tim Berners-Lee, *Weaving the Web*, **Harper San Francisco, 1999**

T he goal of this chapter is to demystify the Semantic Web. By the end of this chapter, you will see the Semantic Web as a logical extension of the current Web instead of a distant possibility. The Semantic Web is both achievable and desirable. We will lay out a clear path to the vision espoused by Tim Berners-Lee, the inventor of the Web.

What Is the Semantic Web?

Tim Berners-Lee has a two-part vision for the future of the Web. The first part is to make the Web a more collaborative medium. The second part is to make the Web understandable, and thus processable, by machines. Figure 1.1 is Tim Berners-Lee's original diagram of his vision.

Tim Berners-Lee's original vision clearly involved more than retrieving Hypertext Markup Language (HTML) pages from Web servers. In Figure 1.1 we see relations between information items like "includes," "describes," and "wrote." Unfortunately, these relationships between resources are not currently captured on the Web. The technology to capture such relationships is called the Resource Description Framework (RDF), described in Chapter 5. The key point to understand about Figure 1.1 is that the original vision encompassed additional meta data above and beyond what is currently in the Web. This additional meta data is needed for machines to be able to process information on the Web.

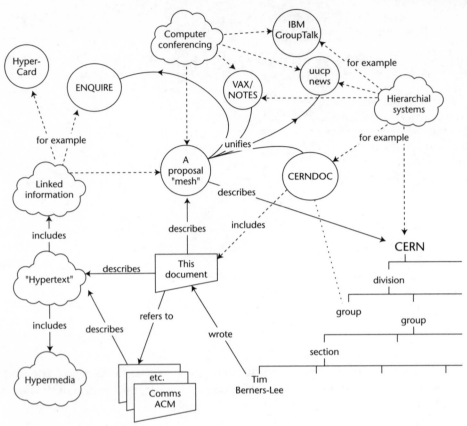

Figure 1.1 Original Web proposal to CERN.

Copyright © Tim Berners-Lee.

So, how do we create a web of data that machines can process? The first step is a paradigm shift in the way we think about data. Historically, data has been locked away in proprietary applications. Data was seen as secondary to processing the data. This incorrect attitude gave rise to the expression "garbage in, garbage out," or GIGO. GIGO basically reveals the flaw in the original argument by establishing the dependency between processing and data. In other words, useful software is wholly dependent on good data. Computing professionals began to realize that data was important, and it must be verified and protected. Programming languages began to acquire object-oriented facilities that internally made data first-class citizens. However, this "data as king" approach was kept internal to applications so that vendors could keep data proprietary to their applications for competitive reasons. With the Web, Extensible Markup Language (XML), and now the emerging Semantic Web, the shift of power is moving from applications to data. This also gives us the key to understanding the Semantic Web. The path to machine-processable data is to make the data smarter. All of the technologies in this book are the foundations of a systematic approach to creating "smart data." Figure 1.2 displays the progression of data along a continuum of increasing intelligence.

Figure 1.2 shows four stages of the smart data continuum; however, there will be more fine-grained stages, as well as more follow-on stages. The four stages in the diagram progress from data with minimal smarts to data embodied with enough semantic information for machines to make inferences about it. Let's discuss each stage:

Text and databases (pre-XML).   The initial stage where most data is proprietary to an application. Thus, the "smarts" are in the application and not in the data.

XML documents for a single domain.   The stage where data achieves application independence within a specific domain. Data is now smart enough to move between applications in a single domain. An example of this would be the XML standards in the healthcare industry, insurance industry, or real estate industry.

Taxonomies and documents with mixed vocabularies.   In this stage, data can be composed from multiple domains and accurately classified in a hierarchical taxonomy. In fact, the classification can be used for discovery of data. Simple relationships between categories in the taxonomy can be used to relate and thus combine data. Thus, data is now smart enough to be easily discovered and sensibly combined with other data.

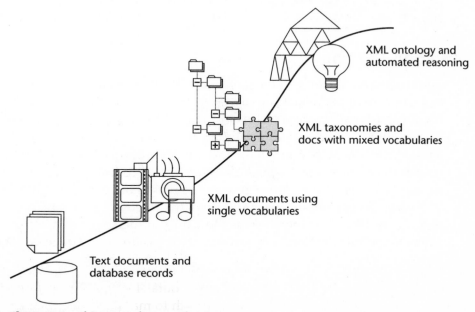

XML ontology and
automated reasoning

XML taxonomies and
docs with mixed vocabularies

XML documents using
single vocabularies

Text documents and
database records

Figure 1.2   The smart data continuum.

Ontologies and rules.   In this stage, new data can be inferred from existing data by following logical rules. In essence, data is now smart enough to be described with concrete relationships, and sophisticated formalisms where logical calculations can be made on this "semantic algebra." This allows the combination and recombination of data at a more atomic level and very fine-grained analysis of data. Thus, in this stage, data no longer exists as a blob but as a part of a sophisticated microcosm. An example of this data sophistication is the automatic translation of a document in one domain to the equivalent (or as close as possible) document in another domain.

We can now compose a new definition of the Semantic Web: a machine-processable web of smart data. Furthermore, we can further define smart data as data that is application-independent, composeable, classified, and part of a larger information ecosystem (ontology). The World Wide Web Consortium (W3C) has established an Activity (composed of several groups) dedicated to implementing the vision of the Semantic Web. See http://www.w3.org/2001/sw/.

Why Do We Need the Semantic Web?

The Semantic Web is not just for the World Wide Web. It represents a set of technologies that will work equally well on internal corporate intranets. This is analogous to Web services representing services not only across the Internet but also within a corporation's intranet. So, the Semantic Web will resolve several key problems facing current information technology architectures.

Information Overload

Information overload is the most obvious problem in need of a solution, and technology experts have been warning us about it for 50 years. In the article "Overcoming Information Overload," Paul Krill states, "This condition results from having a rapid rate of growth in the amount of information available, while days remain 24 hours long and our brains remain in roughly the same state of development as they were when cavemen communicated by scrawling messages in stone."[1] Of course, it is generally acknowledged that this problem has grown worse with the propagation of the Internet, email, and now instant messaging. Unfortunately, our bias toward production over reuse of knowledge has left this problem unresolved until it has finally hit tragic proportions.

A glaring reminder of our failure to make progress on this issue is Vannevar Bush's warning in 1945 when he said, "There is a growing mountain of

[1]Paul Krill, "Overcoming Information Overload," *InfoWorld*, January 7, 2000.

research. But there is increased evidence that we are being bogged down today as specialization extends. The investigator is staggered by the findings and conclusions of thousands of other workers—conclusions which he cannot find time to grasp, much less to remember, as they appear. Yet specialization becomes increasingly necessary for progress, and the effort to bridge between disciplines is correspondingly superficial."[2]

Stovepipe Systems

A *stovepipe system* is a system where all the components are hardwired to only work together. Therefore, information only flows in the stovepipe and cannot be shared by other systems or organizations that need it. For example, the client can only communicate with specific middleware that only understands a single database with a fixed schema. Kent Wreder and Yi Deng describe the problem for healthcare information systems as such:

> *"In the past, these systems were built based on proprietary solutions, acquired in piecemeal fashion and tightly coupled through ad hoc means. This resulted in stovepipe systems that have many duplicated functions and are monolithic, non-extensible and non-interoperable. How to migrate from these stovepipe systems to the next generation open healthcare information systems that are interoperable, extensible and maintainable is increasingly a pressing problem for the healthcare industry."[3]*

Breaking down stovepipe systems needs to occur on all tiers of enterprise information architectures; however, the Semantic Web technologies will be most effective in breaking down stovepiped database systems.

Recently, manual database coordination was successful in solving the Washington sniper case. Jonathan Alter of *Newsweek* described the success like this: "It was by matching a print found on a gun catalog at a crime scene in Montgomery, Ala., to one in an INS database in Washington state that the Feds cracked open the case and paved the way for the arrest of the two suspected snipers. . . . Even more dots were available, but didn't get connected until it was too late, like the records of the sniper's traffic violations in the first days of the spree."[4]

Lastly, the authors of this text are working on solving this problem for the intelligence community to develop a virtual knowledge base using Semantic Web technologies. This is discussed in more detail in Chapter 2.

[2]Vannevar Bush, "As We May Think," *The Atlantic*, July 1945. http://www.theatlantic.com/unbound/flashbks/computer/bushf.htm.

[3]Kent Wreder and Yi Deng, "Architecture-Centered Enterprise System Development and Integration Based on Distributed Object Technology Standard," © 1998 Institute of Electrical and Electronics Engineers, Inc.

[4]Jonathan Alter, "Actually, the Database Is God," *Newsweek*, November 4, 2002, http://stacks.msnbc.com/news/826637.asp.

Poor Content Aggregation

Putting together information from disparate sources is a recurring problem in a number of areas, such as financial account aggregation, portal aggregation, comparison shopping, and content mining. Unfortunately, the most common technique for these activities is screen scraping. Bill Orr describes the practice like this:

> *The technology of account aggregation isn't rocket science. Indeed, the method that started the current buzz goes by the distinctly low-tech name of "screen scraping." The main drawback of this method is that it scrapes messages written in HTML, which describes the format (type size, paragraph spacing, etc.) but doesn't give a clue about the meaning of a document. So the programmer who is setting up a new account to be scraped must somehow figure out that "Account Balance" always appears in a certain location on the screen. The trouble comes when the location or name changes, possibly in an attempt to foil the scrape. So this method requires a lot of ongoing maintenance.*[5]

In this section we focused on problems the Semantic Web will help solve. In Chapter 2, we will examine specific business capabilities afforded by Semantic Web technologies.

How Does XML Fit into the Semantic Web?

XML is the syntactic foundation layer of the Semantic Web. All other technologies providing features for the Semantic Web will be built on top of XML. Requiring other Semantic Web technologies (like the Resource Description Framework) to be layered on top of XML guarantees a base level of interoperability. The details of XML are explored in Chapter 3.

The technologies that XML is built upon are Unicode characters and Uniform Resource Identifiers (URIs). The Unicode characters allow XML to be authored using international characters. URIs are used as unique identifiers for concepts in the Semantic Web. URIs are discussed further in Chapters 3 and 5.

Lastly, it is important to look at the flip side of the question: Is XML enough? The answer is no, because XML only provides syntactic interoperability. In other words, sharing an XML document adds meaning to the content; however, only when both parties know and understand the element names. For

[5]Bill Orr, "Financial Portals Are Hot, But for Whom?" ABA Banking Online, http://www.banking.com/ABA/tech_portals_0700.asp.

example, if I label something a <price> $12.00 </price> and you label that field on your invoice <cost> $12.00 </cost>, there is no way that a machine will know those two mean the same thing unless Semantic Web technologies like ontologies are added (we discuss ontologies in Chapter 8).

How Do Web Services Fit into the Semantic Web?

Web services are software services identified by a URI that are described, discovered, and accessed using Web protocols. Chapter 4 describes Web services and their surrounding technologies in detail. The important point about Web services for this discussion is that they consume and produce XML. Thus, the first way that Web services fit into the Semantic Web is by furthering the adoption of XML, or more smart data.

As Web services proliferate, they become similar to Web pages in that they are more difficult to discover. Semantic Web technologies will be necessary to solve the Web service discovery problem. There are several research efforts under way to create Semantic Web-enabled Web services (like http://swws .semanticweb.org). Figure 1.3 demonstrates the various convergences that combine to form Semantic Web services.

The third way that Web services fit into the Semantic Web is in enabling Web services to interact with other Web services. Advanced Web service applications involving comparison, composition, or orchestration of Web services will require Semantic Web technologies for such interactions to be automated.

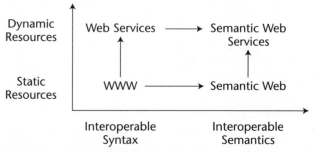

Figure 1.3   Semantic Web services.

Derived in part from two separate presentations at the Web Services One Conference 2002 by Dieter Fensel and Dragan Sretenovic.

What's after Web Services?

Web services complete a platform-neutral processing model for XML. The step after that is to make both the data and the processing model smarter. In other words, continue along the "smart-data continuum." In the near term, this will move along five axes: logical assertions, classification, formal class models, rules, and trust.

Logical assertions. An assertion is the smallest expression of useful information. How do we make an assertion? One way is to model the key parts of a sentence by connecting a subject to an object with a verb. In Chapter 5, you will learn about the Resource Description Framework (RDF), which captures these associations between subjects and objects. The importance of this cannot be understated. As Tim Berners-Lee states, "The philosophy was: What matters is in the connections. It isn't the letters, it's the way they're strung together into words. It isn't the words, it's the way they're strung together into phrases. It isn't the phrases, it is the way they're strung together into a document."[6] Agreeing with this sentiment, Hewlett-Packard Research has developed open source software to process RDF called Jena (see Chapter 5). So, how can we use these assertions? For example, it may be useful to know that the author of a document has written other articles on similar topics. Another example would be to assert that a well-known authority on the subject has refuted the main points of an article. Thus, assertions are not free-form commentary but instead add logical statements to a resource or about a resource. A commercial example that enables you to add such statements to applications or binary file formats is Adobe's Extensible Metadata Platform, or XMP (http://www.adobe.com/products/xmp/main.html).

Classification. We classify things to establish groupings by which generalizations can be made. Just as we classify files on our personal computer in a directory structure, we will continue to better classify resources on corporate intranets and even the Internet. Chapter 7 discusses taxonomy concepts and specific taxonomy models like XML Topic Maps (XTM). The concepts for classification have been around a long time. Carolus Linnaeus developed a classification system for biological organisms in 1758. An example is displayed in Figure 1.4.

The downside of classification systems is evident when examining different people's filesystem classification on their personal computers. Categories (or folder names) can be arbitrary, and the membership criteria for categories are often ambiguous. Thus, while taxonomies are extremely useful

---

[6]Tim Berners-Lee, *Weaving the Web*, Harper San Francisco, p. 13.

```
Kingdom........................Animalia
     Phylum.......................Chordata
          Class..........................Mammalia
               Order.......................Carnivora
                    Family........................Felidae
                         Genus........................Felis
                              Species........................Felis domesticus
```

Figure 1.4 Linnaean classification of a house cat.

for humans browsing for information, they lack rigorous logic for machines
to make inferences from. That is the central difference between taxonomies
and ontologies (discussed next).

Formal class models.   A formal representation of classes and relationships
between classes to enable inference requires rigorous formalisms even
beyond conventions used in current object-oriented programming languages like Java and C#. Ontologies are used to represent such formal
class hierarchies, constrained properties, and relations between classes.
The W3C is developing a Web Ontology Language (abbreviated as OWL).
Ontologies are discussed in detail in Chapter 8, and Figure 1.5 is an illustrative example of the key components of an ontology. (Keep in mind that
the figure does not contain enough formalisms to represent a true ontology.
The diagram is only illustrative, and a more precise description is provided
in Chapter 8.)

Figure 1.5 shows several classes (Person, Leader, Image, etc.), a few properties of the class Person (birthdate, gender), and relations between classes
(knows, is-A, leads, etc.). Again, while not nearly a complete ontology, the
purpose of Figure 1.5 is to demonstrate how an ontology captures logical
information in a manner that can allow inference. For example, if John is
identified as a Leader, you can infer than John is a person and that John
may lead an organization. Additionally, you may be interested in question-
ing any other person that "knows" John. Or you may want to know if
John is depicted in the same image as another person (also known as
co-depiction). It is important to state that the concepts described so far
(classes, subclasses, properties) are not rigorous enough for inference.
To each of these basic concepts, additional formalisms are added. For
example, a property can be further specialized as a symmetric property
or a transitive property. Here are the rules that define those formalisms:

If $x = y$, then $y = x$. (symmetric property)

If $x = y$ and $y = z$, then $x = z$. (transitive property)

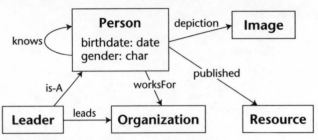

Figure 1.5 Key ontology components.

An example of a transitive property is "has Ancestor." Here is how the rule applies to the "has Ancestor" property:

If Joe hasAncestor Sam and Sam hasAncestor Jill, then Joe hasAncestor Jill.

Lastly, the Web ontology language being developed by the W3C will have a UML presentation profile as illustrated in Figure 1.6.

The wide availability of commercial and open source UML tools in addition to the familiarity of most programmers with UML will simplify the creation of ontologies. Therefore, a UML profile for OWL will significantly expand the number of potential ontologists.

Rules. With XML, RDF, and inference rules, the Web can be transformed from a collection of documents into a knowledge base. An inference rule allows you to derive conclusions from a set of premises. A well-known logic rule called "modus ponens" states the following:

If P is TRUE, then Q is TRUE.

P is TRUE.

Therefore, Q is TRUE.

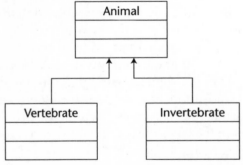

Figure 1.6 UML presentation of ontology class and subclasses.

An example of modus ponens is as follows:

An apple is tasty if it is not cooked. This apple is not cooked. Therefore, it is tasty.

The Semantic Web can use information in an ontology with logic rules to infer new information. Let's look at a common genealogical example of how to infer the "uncle" relation as depicted in Figure 1.7:

If a person C is a male and childOf a person A, then person C is a "sonOf" person A.

If a person B is a male and siblingOf a person A, then person B is a "brotherOf" person A.

If a person C is a "sonOf" person A, and person B is a "brotherOf" person A, then person B is the "uncleOf" person C.

Aaron Swartz suggests a more business-oriented application of this. He writes, "Let's say one company decides that if someone sells more than 100 of our products, then they are a member of the Super Salesman club. A smart program can now follow this rule to make a simple deduction: 'John has sold 102 things, therefore John is a member of the Super Salesman club.'"[7]

Trust.   Instead of having trust be a binary operation of possessing the correct credentials, we can make trust determination better by adding semantics. For example, you may want to allow access to information if a trusted friend vouches (via a digital signature) for a third party. Digital signatures are crucial to the "web of trust" and are discussed in Chapter 4. In fact, by allowing anyone to make logical statements about resources, smart applications will only want to make inferences on statements that they can trust. Thus, verifying the source of statements is a key part of the Semantic Web.

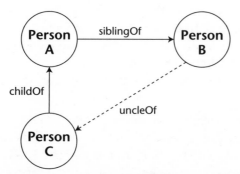

Figure 1.7   Using rules to infer the uncleOf relation.

[7]Aaron Swartz, "The Semantic Web in Breadth," http://logicerror.com/semanticWeb-long.

The five directions discussed in the preceding text will move corporate intranets and the Web into a semantically rich knowledge base where smart software agents and Web services can process information and achieve complex tasks. The return on investment (ROI) for businesses of this approach is discussed in the next chapter.

What Do the Skeptics Say about the Semantic Web?

Every new technology faces skepticism: some warranted, some not. The skepticism of the Semantic Web seems to follow one of three paths:

Bad precedent.   The most frequent specter caused by skeptics attempting to debunk the Semantic Web is the failure of the outlandish predictions of early artificial intelligence researchers in the 1960s. One of the most famous predictions was in 1957 from early AI pioneers Herbert Simon and Allen Newell, who predicted that a computer would beat a human at chess within 10 years. Tim Berners-Lee has responded to the comparison of AI and the Semantic Web like this:

A Semantic Web is not Artificial Intelligence. The concept of machine-understandable documents does not imply some magical artificial intelligence which allows machines to comprehend human mumblings. It only indicates a machine's ability to solve a well-defined problem by performing well-defined operations on existing well-defined data. Instead of asking machines to understand people's language, it involves asking people to make the extra effort.[8]

Fear, uncertainty, and doubt (FUD).   This is skepticism "in the small" or nit-picking skepticism over the difficulty of implementation details. The most common FUD tactic is deeming the Semantic Web as too costly. Semantic Web modeling is on the same scale as modeling complex relational databases. Relational databases were costly in the 1970s, but prices have dropped precipitously (especially with the advent of open source). The cost of Semantic Web applications is already low due to the Herculean efforts of academic and research institutions. The cost will drop further as the Semantic Web goes mainstream in corporate portals and intranets within the next three years.

Status quo.   This is the skeptic's assertion that things should remain essentially the same and that we don't need a Semantic Web. Thus, these people view the Semantic Web as a distraction from linear progress in current technology. Many skeptics said the same thing about the World Wide

[8]Tim Berners-Lee, "What the Semantic Web can Represent," http://www.w3.org/DesignIssues/RDFnot.html.

Web before understanding the network effect. Tim Berners-Lee's first example of the utility of the Web was to put a Web server on a mainframe and have the key information the people used at CERN (Conseil Européen pour la Recherche Nucléaire), particularly the telephone book, encoded as HTML. Tim Berners-Lee describes it like this: "Many people had workstations, with one window permanently logged on to the mainframe just to be able to look up phone numbers. We showed our new system around CERN and people accepted it, though most of them didn't understand why a simple ad hoc program for getting phone numbers wouldn't have done just as well."[9] In other words, people suggested a "stovepipe system" for each new function instead of a generic architecture! Why? They could not see the value of the network effect for publishing information.

Why the Skeptics Are Wrong!

We believe that the skeptics will be proven wrong in the near future because of a convergence of the following powerful forces:

- *We have the computing power.* We are building an always-on, always-connected, supercomputer-on-your-wrist information management infrastructure. When you connect cell phones to PDAs to personal computers to servers to mainframes, you have more brute-force computing power by several orders of magnitude than ever before in history. More computing power makes more layers possible. For example, the virtual machines of Java and C# were conceived of more than 20 years ago (the P-System was developed in 1977); however, they were not widely practical until the computing power of the 1990s was available. While the underpinnings are being standardized now, the Semantic Web will be practical, in terms of computing power, within three years.

MAXIM

Moore's Law: Gordon Moore, cofounder of Intel, predicted that the number of transistors on microprocessors (and thus performance) doubles every 18 months. Note that he originally stated the density doubles every year, but the pace has slowed slightly and the prediction was revised to reflect that.

- *Consumers and businesses want to apply the network effect to their information.* Average people see and understand the network effect and want it applied to their home information processing. Average homeowners now have

[9]Tim Berners-Lee, *Weaving the Web*, Harper San Francisco, p. 33.

multiple computers and want them networked. Employees understand that they can be more effective by capturing and leveraging knowledge from their coworkers. Businesses also see this, and the smart ones are using it to their advantage. Many businesses and government organizations see an opportunity for employing these technologies (and business process reengineering) with the deployment of enterprise portals as natural aggregation points.

MAXIM

Metcalfe's Law: Robert Metcalfe, the inventor of Ethernet, stated that the usefulness of a network equals the square of the number of users. Intuitively, the value of a network rises exponentially by the number of computers connected to it. This is sometimes referred to as the *network effect*.

- *Progress through combinatorial experimentation demands it.* An interesting brute-force approach to research called *combinatorial experimentation* is at work on the Internet. This approach recognizes that, because research findings are instantly accessible globally, the ability to leverage them by trying new combinations is the application of the network effect on research. Effective combinatorial experimentation requires the Semantic Web. And since necessity is the mother of invention, the Semantic Web will occur because progress demands it. This was known and prophesied in 1945 by Vannevar Bush.

MAXIM

The Law of Combinatorial Experimentation (from the authors): The effectiveness of combinatorial experimentation on progress is equal to the ratio of relevant documents to retrieved documents in a typical search. Intuitively, this means progress is retarded proportionally to the number of blind alleys we chase.

Summary

We close this chapter with the "call to arms" exhortation of Dr. Vannevar Bush in his seminal 1945 essay, "As We May Think":

Presumably man's spirit should be elevated if he can better review his shady past and analyze more completely and objectively his present problems. He has built a civilization so complex that he needs to mechanize his records more fully if he is to push his experiment to its logical conclusion and not merely become bogged down part way there by overtaxing his limited memory. His excursions may be more enjoyable if he can reacquire the privilege of forgetting the manifold things he does not need to have immediately at hand, with some assurance that he can find them again if they prove important.

Even in 1945, it was clear that we needed to "mechanize" our records more fully. The Semantic Web technologies discussed in this book are the way to accomplish that.

CHAPTER 2

The Business Case for the Semantic Web

"The business market for this integration of data and programs is huge . . . . The companies who choose to start exploiting Semantic Web technologies will be the first to reap the rewards."
—James Hendler, Tim Berners-Lee, and Eric Miller, "Integrating Applications on the Semantic Web"

In May 2001, Tim Berners-Lee, James Hendler, and Ora Lassila unveiled a vision of the future in an article in *Scientific American*. This vision included the promise of the Semantic Web to build knowledge and understanding from raw data. Many readers were confused by the vision because the nuts and bolts of the Semantic Web are used by machines, agents, and programs—and are not tangible to end users. Because we usually consider "the Web" to be what we can navigate with our browsers, many have difficulty understanding the practical use of a Semantic Web that lies beneath the covers of our traditional Web. In the previous chapter, we discussed the "what" of the Semantic Web. This chapter examines the "why," to allow you to understand the promise and the need to focus on these technologies to gain a competitive edge, a fast-moving, flexible organization, and to make the most of the untapped knowledge in your organization.

Perhaps you have heard about the promise of the Semantic Web through marketing projections. "By 2005," the Gartner Group reports, "lightweight ontologies will be part of 75 percent of application integration projects."[1] The implications of this statement are huge. This means that if your organization hasn't started thinking about the Semantic Web yet, it's time to start. Decision

[1] J. Jacobs, A. Linden, Gartner Group, Gartner Research Note T-17-5338, 20. August 2002.

makers in your organization will want to know, "What can we do with the Semantic Web? Why should we invest time and money in these technologies? Is there indeed this future?" This chapter answers these questions, and gives you practical ideas for using Semantic Web technologies.

What Is the Semantic Web Good For?

Many managers have said to us, "The vision sounds great, but how can I use it, and why should I invest in it?" Because this is the billion-dollar question, this section is the focus of this chapter.

MAXIM

The organization that has the best information, knows where to find it, and can utilize it the quickest wins.

The maxim of this section is fairly obvious. Knowledge is power. It used to be conventional wisdom that the organization with the most information wins. Now that we are drowning in an information glut, we realize that we need to be able to find the right information quickly to enable us to make well-informed decisions. We have also realized that knowledge (the application of data), not just raw data, is the most important. The organization that can do this will make the most of the resources that it has—and will have a competitive advantage. Knowledge management is the key.

This seems like common sense. Who doesn't want the best knowledge? Who doesn't want good information? Traditional knowledge management techniques have faced new challenges by today's Internet: information overload, the inefficiency of keyword searching, the lack of authoritative (trusted) information, and the lack of natural language-processing computer systems.[2] The Semantic Web can bring structure to information chaos. For us to get our knowledge, we need to do more than dump information into files and databases. To adapt, we must begin to take advantage of the technologies discussed in this book. We must be able to tag our information with machine-understandable markup, and we must be able to know what information is authoritative. When we discover new information, we need to have proof that we can indeed trust the information, and then we need to be able to correlate it with the other information that we have. Finally, we need the tools to take advantage of this new knowledge. These are some of the key concepts of the Semantic Web—and this book.

[2]Fensel, Bussler, Ding, Kartseva, Klein, Korotkiy, Omelayenko, Siebes, "Semantic Web Application Areas," in *Proceedings of the 7th International Workshop on Applications of Natural Language to Information Systems,* Stockholm, Sweden, June 27 to 28, 2002.

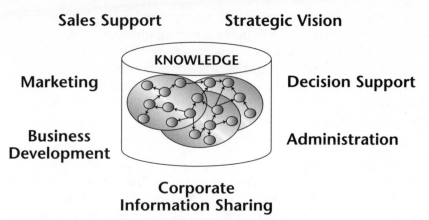

Sales Support · Strategic Vision · Marketing · KNOWLEDGE · Decision Support · Business Development · Administration · Corporate Information Sharing

Figure 2.1 Uses of the Semantic Web in your enterprise.

Figure 2.1 provides a view of how your organization can revolve around your corporate Semantic Web, impacting virtually every piece of your organization. If you can gather all of it together, organize it, and know where to find it, you can capitalize on it. Only when you bring the information together with semantics will this information lead to knowledge that enables your staff to make well-informed decisions.

Chances are, your organization has a lot of information that is not utilized. If your organization is large, you may unknowingly have projects within your company that duplicate efforts. You may have projects that could share lessons learned, provide competitive intelligence information, and save you a lot of time and work. If you had a corporate knowledge base that could be searched and analyzed by software agents, you could have Web-based applications that save you a lot of time and money. The following sections provide some of these examples.

Decision Support

Having knowledge—not just data—at your fingertips allows you to make better decisions. Consider for a moment the information management dilemma that our intelligence agencies have had in the past decade. Discussing this problem related to September 11 was FBI Director Robert Mueller. "It would be nice," he said in a June 2002 interview on *Meet the Press*, "if we had the computers in the FBI that were tied into the CIA that you could go in and do flight schools, and any report relating to flight schools that had been generated any place in the FBI field offices would spit out—over the last 10 years. What would be even better is if you had the artificial intelligence so that you don't even have to make the query, but to look at patterns like that in reports." What

Director Mueller was describing is a Semantic Web, which allows not only users but software agents to find hidden relationships between data in databases that our government already has. The FBI director's statement also touches on interoperability and data sharing. Because different organizations usually have different databases and servers, we have been bound to proprietary solutions. System integrators have struggled to make different proprietary systems "talk to each other." The advent of Web services is allowing us to eliminate this barrier.

The Virtual Knowledge Base (VKB) program in the Department of Defense aims to provide a solution to this dilemma. For the government, the VKB provides an interoperability framework for horizontally integrating producers and consumers of information using a standards-based architecture. By exposing all information sources as Web services, abstracting the details into knowledge objects, providing an ontology for mining associations between data elements, and providing a registry for the discovery of information sources, the VKB is utilizing key Semantic Web concepts and technologies to solve the information management quandary that every organization today faces.

MAXIM

If you have a lot of information, there are implied and hidden relationships in your data. Using Semantic Web technologies will help you find them.

Businesses have much the same information management dilemma as the federal government. They have suborganizations, divisions, groups, and projects that have sources of information. To tap the power of these groups, you need to combine the information of groups and understand the relationships between them. The simplest example that we are accustomed to is the status report process. Each employee writes a status report. A manager takes all the status reports and combines them into a project status report. The project manager's division director takes the project status report and creates a division status report. Finally, his or her boss compiles the division status reports into an executive summary and gives it to the president of the company. During this process, information is filtered so that the end product is an understandable report used to make decisions. Unfortunately, important information is almost always left out—especially with respect to the relationships between the work that is being accomplished in individual projects.

Work is being done in creating semantic-enabled decision support systems (DSSs) that focus on software agent analysis and interaction between the end user and computer system for decision making, in order to empower the end user to make informed decisions.[3] Even without decision support systems,

[3]M. Casey and M. Austin, "Semantic Web Methodologies for Spatial Decision Support," University of Maryland, Institute for Systems Research and Department of Civil and Environmental Engineering, November 2001.

software agents can monitor your knowledge base and provide alerts. In a 2001 article in *Information Week*, Duncan Johnson-Watt, CTO of Enigmatic Corp., provided another example, suggesting that if SEC filings contain semantic tags, regulators or investors could create programs to automatically alert them to red flags such as insider stock selling.[4] To make superior decisions, you need to have superior knowledge. The Semantic Web allows you to get there.

Business Development

It is important for members of your organization to have up-to-the minute information that could help you win business. In most cases, your organization can't afford to fly all the members of your corporate brain trust out with your sales staff. Imagine a scenario where your salesperson is in a meeting with a potential customer. During the discussion, your salesperson discovers that the customer is very interested in a certain topic. The potential customer says, "We're thinking about hiring a company to build an online e-commerce system that uses biometric identification." If your salesperson is able to reach into your corporate knowledge base quickly, he or she may be able to find important information that takes advantage of the opportunity. By quickly using your corporate knowledge base, your salesperson could quickly respond by saying, "We just wrote a white paper on that topic yesterday, and engineers prototyped an internal biometric solution last month. Would you like me to arrange a demonstration?" Because of the Semantic Web working in your organization, you are able to open the doors to new business.

Competitive proposals could be another important use of your company's Semantic Web. If you have more knowledge about potential customers, the proposed task to bid on, and what skill sets they are looking for, you have a better chance of winning. If you had a growing knowledge base where old status reports, old proposals, lessons learned, and competitive intelligence were all interconnected, there is a possibility that you may have a nugget of information that will be valuable for this proposal. If your proposal team was able to enter information in your knowledge base, and you had a software agent to analyze that information, your agents may able to "connect the dots" on information that you had but didn't realize it.

Customer relationship management (CRM) enables collaboration between partners, customers, and employees by providing relevant, personalized information from a variety of data sources within your organization. These solutions have become key in helping to retain customer loyalty, but a barrier to creating such a solution has been the speed in integrating legacy data sources, as well as the ability to compare information across domains in your

---

[4]David Ewalt, "The Next Web," *Information Week*, October 10, 2002, http://www .informationweek.com/story/IWK20021010S0016.

enterprise. Using the technologies discussed in this book will allow companies to create a smarter CRM solution.

E-commerce industry experts believe that the Semantic Web can be used in matchmaking for ebusiness. Matchmaking is a process in which businesses are put in contact with potential business partners or customers. Traditionally, this process is handled by hired brokers, and many have suggested creating a matchmaking service that handles advertising services and querying for advertised services. Experts argue that only Semantic Web technologies can sufficiently meet these requirements, and they believe that the Semantic Web can automate matchmaking and negotiation.[5]

The opportunities for maximizing your business opportunities with Semantic Web technologies are limitless.

Information Sharing and Knowledge Discovery

Information sharing and communication are paramount in any organization, but as most organizations grow and collect more information, this is a major struggle. We all understand the importance of not reinventing the wheel, but how many times have we unintentionally duplicated efforts? When organizations get larger, communication gaps are inevitable. With a little bit of effort, a corporate knowledge base could at least include a registry of descriptions of projects and what each team is building. Imagine how easy it would be for your employees to be able to find relevant information. Using Semantic Web-enabled Web services can allow us to create such a registry.

Administration and Automation

Up to this point, we've discussed the somewhat obvious examples based on sharing knowledge within an organization. A side effect of having such a knowledge base is the ability of software programs to automate administrative tasks. Booking travel, for example, is an example where the Semantic Web and Web services could aid in making a painful task easy. Making travel arrangements can be an administrative nightmare. Everyone has personal travel preferences and must take items such as the following into consideration:

- Transportation preference (car, train, bus, plane)
- Hotel preference and rewards associated with hotel
- Airline preference and frequent flyer miles

[5]Trastour, Bartolini, Gonzales-Castillo, "A Semantic Web Approach to Service Description of Matchmaking of Service," in *Proceedings of the International Semantic Web Working Symposium (SWWS)*, Stanford, California, July 2001.

- Hotel proximity to meeting places
- Hotel room preferences (nonsmoking, king, bar, wireless network in lobby)
- Rental car options and associated rewards
- Price (lodging and transportation per diem rates for your company)

Creating a flowchart of your travel arrangement decisions can be a complex process. Say, for example, that if the trip is less than 100 miles, you will rent a car. If the trip is between 100 miles and 300 miles, you will take the train or bus. If the trip is above 300 miles, you will fly. If you fly, you will look for the cheapest ticket, unless you can get a first-class seat with your frequent flyer miles from American Airlines. If you do book a flight, you want a vegetarian meal. You want to weigh the cost of your hotel against the proximity to your meeting place, and you have room preferences, and so on. As you begin mapping out the logic for simply booking travel, you realize that this could be a complex process that could take a few hours.

Information Sharing Analogy

For you Trekkies out there, an interesting analogy to the "perfect" information sharing organization can be seen in a popular television series *Star Trek: The Next Generation.* In that show, the Borg species were masters of communication and knowledge sharing. When they would assimilate a new species, they would download all the new information into their central knowledge base. All the members of the Borg would immediately be able to understand the new knowledge. As a result, they could grow smarter and quickly adapt into a dynamic, agile organization. Although we don't necessarily want to be like the Borg, it would be great to share information as effectively as they did!

When employees leave, they carry with them irreplaceable knowledge that isn't stored. Wouldn't it be great if we could retain all of an employee's work in a corporate knowledge base so that we have all of his or her documents, emails, notes, and code, and retain as much information as possible? Not only that, if this information was saved or annotated with meta data in a machine-understandable format, like RDF, the information in these documents could be assimilated into the knowledge base. If your organization could use tools that allow your employees to author their documents and tag content with annotations that contain information tied to your corporate ontology of knowledge, you could minimize the loss of data that employee turnover inevitably causes.

These are only a few ideas of how Semantic Web technologies can help you share and discover information in your business.

Finalizing your arrangements manually may take a long time. Luckily, with the Semantic Web and Web service orchestration, much of this could be accomplished by an automated process. If you have all of these rules and personal travel preferences in your corporate knowledge base, your smart travel application can choose your travel arrangements for you, using your machine-understandable rule set as the basis for conflict resolution. By accessing relatable semantic tags on online travel and hotel services, your travel application can compare, contrast, evaluate the options, and present you with a list of best matches. (A good example of this is in Chapter 4, "Understanding Web Services.")

In short, Semantic Web-enabled Web services have the potential to automate menial and complex tasks in your organization.

Is the Technology for the Semantic Web "There Yet"?

You may be thinking, "It sounds great, but is the technology really here yet?" While implementing the Semantic Web on the Internet is still a vision, the building blocks for the Semantic Web are being deployed in small domains and prototypes. Thus, the pieces are falling into place to make the promise a reality. Over the past five years, we have seen a paradigm shift away from proprietary stovepiped systems and toward open standards. The W3C, the Internet Engineering Task Force (IETF), and Organization for the Advancement of Structured Information Standards (OASIS) have had widespread support from corporations and academic institutions alike for interoperability. The support of XML has spawned support of XML-based technologies, such as SOAP-based Web services that provide interoperable interfaces into applications over the Internet. RDF provides a way to associate information. Using XML as a serialization syntax, RDF is the foundation of other ontology-based languages of the Semantic Web. XML Topic Maps (XTM) provide another mechanism for presenting taxonomies of information to classify data. Web services provide a mechanism for software programs to communicate with each other. Ontology languages (OWL, DAML+OIL) are ready for prime time, and many organizations are using these to add semantics to their corporate knowledge bases. This list could go on and on. Currently, there is an explosion of technologies that will help us reach the vision of the Semantic Web.

Helping the Semantic Web's promise is our industry's current focus on Web services. Organizations are beginning to discover the positive ROI of Web services on interoperability for Enterprise Application Integration (EAI). The next big trend in Web services will be semantic-enabled Web services, where we can use information from Web services from different organizations to perform correlation, aggregation, and orchestration. Academic research programs, such as TAP at Stanford, are bridging the gap between disparate Web service-based data sources and "creating a coherent Semantic Web from disparate chunks."[6] Among other things, TAP enables semantic search capabilities, using ontology-based knowledge bases of information.

Companies are heavily investing in Semantic Web technologies. Adobe, for example, is reorganizing its software meta data around RDF, and they are using Web ontology-level power for managing documents. Because of this change, "the information in PDF files can be understood by other software even if the software doesn't know what a PDF document is or how to display it."[7] In its recent creation of the Institute of Search and Text Analysis in California, IBM is making significant investments in Semantic Web research. Other companies, such as Germany's Ontoprise, are making a business out of ontologies, creating tools for knowledge modeling, knowledge retrieval, and knowledge integration. In the same Gartner report mentioned at the beginning of this chapter, which said Semantic Web ontologies will play a key role in 75 percent of application integration by 2005, the group also recommended that "enterprises should begin to develop the needed semantic modeling and information management skills within their integration competence centers."[8]

So, to answer the question of this section: Yes, we are ready for the Semantic Web. The building blocks are here, Semantic Web-supporting technologies and programs are being developed, and companies are investing more money into bringing their organizations to the level where they can utilize these technologies for competitive and monetary advantage.

Summary

This chapter provided many examples of the practical uses of the Semantic Web. Semantic Web technologies can help in decision support, business development, information sharing, and automated administration. We gave you examples of some of the work and investment that is occurring right now, and we briefly showed how the technology building blocks of the Semantic Web are falling into place. Chapter 9 picks up where this chapter left off, providing you with a roadmap of how your organization can begin taking advantage of these technologies.

[6]R.V. Guha, R. McCool, "TAP" presentation, WWW2002.

[7]*BusinessWeek*, "The Web Weaver Looks Forward" (interview with Tim Berners-Lee), March 27, 2002, http://www.businessweek.com/bwdaily/dnflash/mar2002/nf20020327_4579.htm.

[8]Gartner Research Note T-17-5338, 20. August 2002.

Understanding XML and Its Impact on the Enterprise

"By 2003, more than 95% of the G2000 organizations will deploy XML-based content management infrastructures."
META Group (2000)

In this chapter you will learn:

- Why XML is the cornerstone of the Semantic Web
- Why XML has achieved widespread adoption and continues to expand to new areas of information processing
- How XML works and the mechanics of related standards like namespaces and XML Schema

Once you understand the core concepts, we move on to examine the impact of XML on the enterprise. Lastly, we examine why XML itself is not enough and the current state of confusion as different technologies compete to fill in the gaps.

Why Is XML a Success?

XML has passed from the early-adopter phase to mainstream acceptance. Currently, the primary use of XML is for data exchange between internal and external organizations. In this regard, XML plays the role of interoperability mechanism. As XQuery and XML Schema (see sidebar) achieve greater maturity and adoption, XML may become the primary syntax for all enterprise data. Why is XML so successful? XML has four primary accomplishments, which we discuss in detail in the sections that follow:

- XML creates application-independent documents and data.
- It has a standard syntax for meta data.
- It has a standard structure for both documents and data.
- XML is not a new technology (not a 1.0 release).

A key variable in XML's adoption, one that possibly holds even more weight than the preceding four accomplishments, is that computers are now fast enough and storage cheap enough to afford the luxury of XML. Simply put, we've been dancing around the concepts in XML for 20 years, and it is only catching fire now because computers are fast enough to handle it. In this regard, XML is similar to the rise of virtual machine environments like .NET and Java. Both of these phenomena would simply have been rejected as too slow five years ago. The concepts were known back then, but the technology was just not practical. And this same logic applies to XML.

Now let's examine the other reasons for XML's success. XML is application-independent because it is plaintext in human-readable form. Figure 3.1 shows a simple one-line word-processing document. Figure 3.2 and Listing 3.1 contrast XML to a proprietary binary format like Microsoft Word for the one-line document shown in Figure 3.1. In contrast, Figure 3.2 is a string of binary numbers (shown in base 16, or hexadecimal, format) where only the creators of the format understand it (some companies attempt to reverse-engineer these files by looking for patterns). Binary formats lock you into applications for the life of your data. Encoding XML as text allows any program to open and read the file. Listing 3.1 is plaintext, and its intent is easily understood.

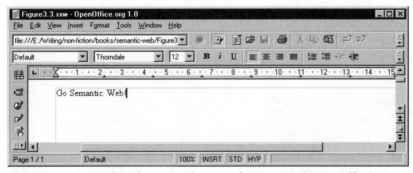

Figure 3.1 A one-line document in a word processor (Open Office).

XQuery and XML Schema in a Nutshell

XQuery is an XML-based query language for querying XML documents. A query is a search statement to retrieve specific portions of a document that conform to a specified search criterion. XQuery is defined further in Chapter 6. XML Schema is a markup definition language that defines the legal names for elements and attributes, and the legal hierarchical structure of the document. XML Schema is discussed in detail later in this chapter.

By using an open, standard syntax and verbose descriptions of the meaning of data, XML is readable and understandable by everyone—not just the application and person that produced it. This is a critical underpinning of the Semantic Web, because you cannot predict the variety of software agents and systems that will need to consume data on the World Wide Web. An additional benefit for storing data in XML, rather than binary data, is that it can be searched as easily as Web pages.

```xml
<?xml version="1.0" encoding="UTF-8"?>
<!DOCTYPE office:document-content PUBLIC "-//OpenOffice.org//DTD Office-
Document 1.0//EN" "office.dtd"><office:document-content
xmlns:office="http://openoffice.org/2000/office"
...
xmlns:script="http://openoffice.org/2000/script" office:class="text"
office:version="1.0">
<office:script/>
<office:font-decls>
...
<style:font-decl style:name="Thorndale" fo:font-family="Thorndale"
style:font-family-generic="roman" style:font-pitch="variable"/>
</office:font-decls>
<office:automatic-styles/>
<office:body>
<text:sequence-decls>
...
</text:sequence-decls>
<text:p text:style-name="Standard">Go Semantic Web!</text:p>
</office:body>
</office:document-content>
```

Listing 3.1 XML format of Figure 3.1 (portions omitted for brevity).

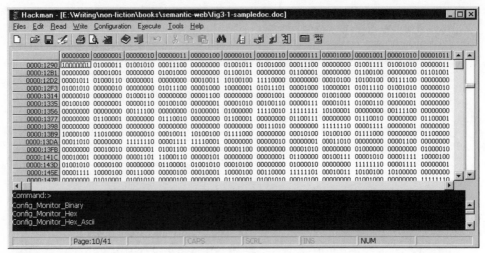

Figure 3.2 Binary MS Word format of the same one line in Figure 3.1 (portions omitted for brevity).

The second key accomplishment is that XML provides a simple, standard syntax for encoding the meaning of data values, or *meta data*. An often-used definition of meta data is "data about data." We discuss the details of the XML syntax later. For now what is important is that XML standardizes a simple, text-based method for encoding meta data. In other words, XML provides a simple yet robust mechanism for encoding semantic information, or the meaning of data. Table 3.1 demonstrates the difference between meta data and data. It should be evident that the data is the raw context-specific values and the meta data denotes the meaning or purpose of those values.

The third major accomplishment of XML is standardizing a structure suitable to express semantic information for both documents and data fields (see the sidebar comparing them). The structure XML uses is a hierarchy or tree structure. A good common example of a tree structure is an individual's filesystem on a computer, as shown in Figure 3.3. The hierarchical structure allows the user to decompose a concept into its component parts in a recursive manner.

Table 3.1 Comparing Data to Meta Data

DATA	META DATA
Joe Smith	Name
222 Happy Lane	Address
Sierra Vista	City
AZ	State
85635	Zip code

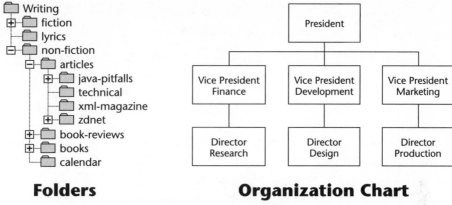

Folders   **Organization Chart**

Figure 3.3 Sample trees as organization structures.

The last accomplishment of XML is that it is not a new technology. XML is a subset of the Standardized Generalized Markup Language (SGML) that was invented in 1969 by Dr. Charles Goldfarb, Ed Mosher, and Ray Lorie. So, the concepts for XML were devised over 30 years ago and continuously perfected, tested, and broadly implemented. In a nutshell, XML is "SGML for the Web." So, it should be clear that XML possesses some compelling and simple value propositions that continue to drive its adoption. Let's now examine the mechanics of those accomplishments.

The Difference between Documents and Data Fields

An electronic document is the electronic counterpart of a paper document. As such, it is a combination of both content (raw information) and presentation instructions. Its content uses natural language in the form of sentences, paragraphs, and pages. In contrast, data fields are atomic name/value pairs processable by a computer and are often captured in forms.

Both types of information are widespread in organizations, and both have strengths and weaknesses. A significant strength of XML is that it enables meta data attachment (markup) on both of these data sources. Thus XML, bridges the gap between documents and data to enable them to both participate in a single web of information.

What Is XML?

XML is not a language; it is actually a set of syntax rules for creating semantically rich markup languages in a particular domain. In other words, you *apply* XML to create new languages. Any language created via the rules of XML, like the Math Markup Language (MathML), is called an application of XML. A markup language's primary concern is how to add semantic information about the raw content in a document; thus, the vocabulary of a markup language is the external "marks" to be attached or embedded in a document. This concept of adding marks, or semantic instructions, to a document has been done manually in the text publishing industry for years. Figure 3.4 shows the manual markup for page layout of a school newspaper.

As publishing moved to electronic media, several languages were devised to capture these marks alongside content like TeX and PostScript (see Listing 3.2).

```
\documentstyle[doublespace,12pt]{article}
\title{An Example of Computerized Text Processing}
\author{A. Student}
\date{8 June 1993}
\begin{document}
\maketitle

This is the text of your article. You can
type in the material without being
concerned about ends of lines and word
spacing. LaTeX will handle the spacing for
you.

The default type size is 10 point.

The Roman type font is used. Text is
justified and double spaced. Paragraphs are
separated by a blank line.
\end{document}
```

Listing 3.2 Markup in TeX.

Markup is separate from content.

So, the first key principle of XML is *markup is separate from content*. A corollary to that principle is that markup can surround or contain content. Thus, a markup language is a set of words, or marks, that surround, or "tag," a portion of a document's content in order to attach additional meaning to the tagged content. The mechanism invented to mark content was to enclose each word of the language's vocabulary in a less-than sign (<) and a greater-than sign (>) like this:

```
<auto>
```

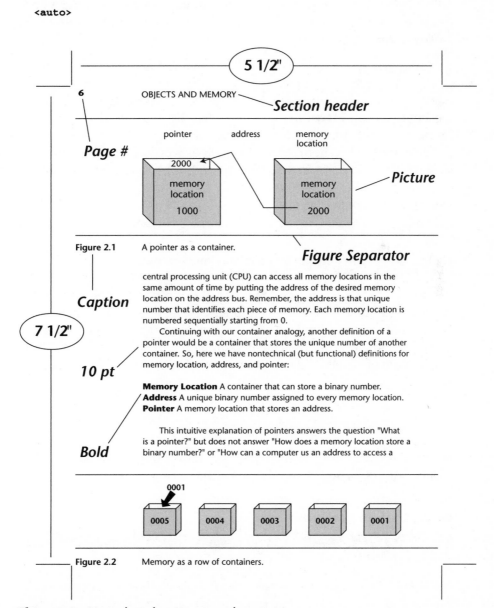

Figure 3.4 Manual markup on a page layout.

To use the < and > characters as part of a tag, these characters cannot be used in content, and therefore they are replaced by the special codes (called entities) > (for greater than) and < (for less than). This satisfies our requirement to separate a mark from content but does not yet allow us to surround, or contain, content. Containing content is achieved by wrapping the target content with a start and end tag. Thus, each vocabulary word in our markup language can be expressed in one of three ways: a start tag, an end tag, or an empty tag. Table 3.2 demonstrates all three tag types.

The start and end tags are used to demarcate the start and end of the tagged content, respectively. The empty tag is used to embed semantic information that does not surround content. A good example of the use of an empty tag is the image tag in HTML, which looks like this: <img src="apple.gif" />. An image tag does not need to surround content, as its purpose is to insert an image at the place where the tag is. In other words, its purpose is to be embedded at a specific point in raw content and not to surround content. Thus, we can now extend our first principle of XML to this: *Markup is separate from content and may contain content.*

MAXIM

Markup is separate from content and may contain content.

We can now formally introduce an XML definition for the term XML *element*. An XML element is an XML container consisting of a start tag, content (contained character data, subelements, or both), and an end tag—except for empty elements, which use a single tag denoting both the start and end of the element. The content of an element can be other elements. Following is an example of an element:

```
<footnote>
<author> Michael C. Daconta </author>, <title> Java Pitfalls </title>
</footnote>
```

Here we have one element, called "footnote," which contains character data and two subelements: "author" and "title."

Table 3.2 Three Types of XML Tags

TAG TYPE	EXAMPLE
Start tag	<author>
End tag	</author>
Empty tag	<img />

Another effect of tagging content is that it divides the document into semantic parts. For example, we could divide this chapter into <chapter>, <section>, and <para> elements. The creation of diverse parts of a whole entity enables us to classify, or group, parts, and thus treat them differently based on their membership in a group. In XML, such classification begins by constraining a valid document to be composed of a single element, called the *root*. In turn, that element may contain other elements or content. Thus, we create a hierarchy, or tree structure, for every XML document. Here is an example of the hierarchy of an XHTML document (see sidebar on XHTML):

```
<html>
   <head>
      <title> My web page </title>
   </head>
   <body>
      Go Semantic Web!!
   </body>
</html>
```

Listing 3.3 A single HTML root element.

The second key principle of XML is this: *A document is classified as a member of a type by dividing its parts, or elements, into a hierarchical structure known as a tree*. In Listing 3.3, an HTML document starts with a root element, called "html." which contains a "head" element and a "body" element. The head and body element can contain other subelements and content as specified by the HTML specification. Thus, another function of XML is to classify all parts of a document into a single hierarchical set of parts.

MAXIM

An XML document is classified as a member of a type by dividing its parts, or elements, into a hierarchical structure known as a tree.

XHTML in a Nutshell

XHTML is a reformulation of HTML as an XML application. In practical terms, this boils down to eliminating the laxness in HTML by requiring things like strict nesting, corresponding end tags with all nonempty elements, and adding the forward slash to the empty element tag.

In the discussion about empty elements, we used the <img> tag, which included a name/value pair (src = "apple.gif"). Each name/value pair attached to an element is called an *attribute*. Attributes only appear in start tags or empty element tags. It has a name (src) followed by an equal sign, followed by a value surrounded in either single or double quotes. An element may have more than one attribute. Here is an example of an element with three attributes:

```
<auto color="red" make="Dodge" model="Viper"> My car </auto>
```

The combination of elements and attributes makes XML well suited to model both relational and object-oriented data. Table 3.3 shows how attributes and elements correlate to the relational and object-oriented data models.

Overall, XML's information representation facilities of elements, attributes, and a single document root implement the accomplishments outlined in the first section in the chapter.

Why Should Documents Be Well-Formed and Valid?

The XML specification defined two levels of conformance for XML documents: *well-formed* and *valid*. Well-formedness is mandatory, while validity is optional. A well-formed XML document complies with all the W3C syntax rules of XML (explicitly called out in the XML specification as well-formedness constraints) like naming, nesting, and attribute quoting. This requirement guarantees that an XML processor can parse (break into identifiable components) the document without error. If a compliant XML processor encounters a well-formedness violation, the specification requires it to stop processing the document and report a fatal error to the calling application.

A valid XML document references and satisfies a schema. A *schema* is a separate document whose purpose is to define the legal elements, attributes, and structure of an XML instance document. In general, think of a schema as defining the legal vocabulary, number, and placement of elements and attributes in your markup language. Therefore, a schema defines a particular type or class of documents. The markup language constrains the information to be of a certain type to be considered "legal." We discuss schemas in more detail in the next section.

Table 3.3 Data Modeling Similarities

XML	OO	RELATIONAL
Element	Class	Entity
Attribute	Data member	Relation

W3C-compliant XML processors check for well-formedness but may not check for validity. Validation is often a feature that can be turned on or off in an XML parser. Validation is time-consuming and not always necessary. It is generally best to perform validation either as part of document creation or immediately after creation.

What Is XML Schema?

XML Schema is a definition language that enables you to constrain conforming XML documents to a specific vocabulary and a specific hierarchical structure. The things you want to define in your language are element types, attribute types, and the composition of both into composite types (called complex types). XML Schema is analogous to a database schema, which defines the column names and data types in database tables. XML Schema became a W3C Recommendation (synonymous with standard) on May 5, 2001. XML Schema is not the only definition language, and you may hear about others like Document Type Definitions (DTDs), RELAX NG, and Schematron (see the sidebar titled "Other Schema Languages").

As shown in Figure 3.5, we have two types of documents: a schema document (or definition document) and multiple instance documents that conform to the schema. A good analogy to remember the difference between these two types of documents is that a *schema* definition is a blueprint (or template) of a type and each *instance* is an incarnation of that template. This also demonstrates the two roles that a schema can play:

- Template for a form generator to generate instances of a document type
- Validator to ensure the accuracy of documents

Both the schema document and the instance document use XML syntax (tags, elements, and attributes). This was one of the primary motivating factors to replace DTDs, which did not use XML syntax. Having a single syntax for both definition and instance documents enables a single parser to be used for both.

Referring back to our database analogy, the database schema defines the columns, and the table rows are instances of each definition. Each instance document must "declare" which definition document (or schema) it adheres to. This is done with a special attribute attached to the root element called "xsi:noNamespaceSchemaLocation" or "xsi:schemaLocation." The attribute used depends on whether your vocabulary is defined in the context of a namespace (discussed later in this chapter).

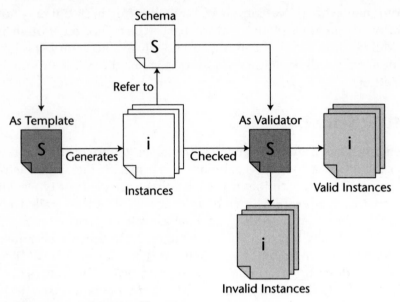

Figure 3.5 Schema and instances.

XML Schemas allow validation of instances to ensure the accuracy of field values and document structure at the time of creation. The accuracy of fields is checked against the type of the field; for example, a quantity typed as an integer or money typed as a decimal. The structure of a document is checked for things like legal element and attribute names, correct number of children, and required attributes. All XML documents should be checked for validity before they are transferred to another partner or system.

What Do Schemas Look Like?

An XML Schema uses XML syntax to declare a set of simple and complex type declarations. A *type* is a named template that can hold one or more values. Simple types hold one value. Complex types are composed of multiple simple types. So, a type has two key characteristics: a name and a legal set of values. Let's look at examples of both simple and complex types.

A simple type is an element declaration that includes its name and value constraints. Here is an example of an element called "author" that can contain any number of text characters:

```
<xsd:element name="author" type="xsd:string" />
```

The preceding element declaration enables an instance document to have an element like this:

```
<author> Mike Daconta </author>
```

Other Schema Languages

While there are dozens of schema languages (as this is a popular topic for experimentation), we will discuss the top three alternatives to XML Schema: DTD, RELAX NG, and Schematron.

Document Type Definition (DTD) was the original schema definition language inherited from SGML, and its syntax is defined as part of the XML 1.0 Recommendation released on February 10, 1998. Some markup languages are still defined with DTDs today, but the majority of organizations have switched or are considering switching to XML Schema. The chief deficiencies of DTDs are their non-XML syntax, their lack of data types, and their lack of support for namespaces. These were the top three items XML Schema set out to fix.

RELAX NG is the top competitor to the W3C's XML Schema and is considered technically superior to XML Schema by many people in the XML community. On the other hand, major software vendors like Microsoft and IBM have come out strongly in favor of standardizing on XML Schema and fixing any deficiencies it has. RELAX NG represents a combination of two previous efforts: RELAX and TREX. Here is the definition of RELAX NG from its specification: "A RELAX NG schema specifies a pattern for the structure and content of an XML document. A RELAX NG schema thus identifies a class of XML documents consisting of those documents that match the pattern. A RELAX NG schema is itself an XML document." [1] For interoperability, RELAX NG can use the W3C XML Schema data types.

Schematron is an open source XML validation tool that uses a combination of patterns, rules, and assertions made up of XPath expressions (see Chapter 6 for a discussion of XPath) to validate XML instances. It is interesting to note that rule-based validation is a different approach from the more common, grammar-based approach used in both XML Schema and RELAX NG.

Sun Microsystems, Inc. offers a free Java-based tool called the Multi-Schema Validator. This tool validates RELAX NG, RELAX Namespace, RELAX Core, TREX, XML DTDs, and a subset of XML Schema.

Notice that the type attributed in the element declaration declares the type to be "xsd:string". A *string* is a sequence of characters. There are many built-in data types defined in the XML Schema specification. Table 3.4 lists the most common. If a built-in data type does not constrain the values the way the document designer wants, XML Schema allows the definition of custom data types.

[1]James C. Clark and Murata Makoto, "RELAX NG Tutorial," December 3, 2001. Available at http://www.oasis-open.org/committees/relax-ng/tutorial.html.

Table 3.4 Common XML Schema Primitive Data Types

DATA TYPE	DESCRIPTION
string	Unicode characters of some specified length.
boolean	A binary state value of true or false.
ID	A unique identifier attribute type from the 1.0 XML Specification.
IDREF	A reference to an ID.
integer	The set of whole numbers.
long	long is derived from integer by fixing the values of maxInclusive to be 9223372036854775807 and minInclusive to be - 9223372036854775808.
int	int is derived from long by fixing the values of maxInclusive to be 2147483647 and minInclusive to be -2147483648.
short	short is derived from int by fixing the values of maxInclusive to be 32767 and minInclusive to be -32768.
decimal	Represents arbitrary precision decimal numbers with an integer part and a fraction part.
float	IEEE single precision 32-bit floating-point number.
double	IEEE double-precision 64-bit floating-point number.
date	Date as a string defined in ISO 8601.
time	Time as a string defined in ISO 8601.

A *complex type* is an element that either contains other elements or has attached attributes. Let's first examine an element with attached attributes and then a more complex element that contains child elements. Here is a definition for a book element that has two attributes called "title" and "pages":

```
<xsd:element name="book">
    <xsd:complexType>
      <xsd:attribute name="title" type="xsd:string" />
      <xsd:attribute name="pages" type = "xsd:int" />
    </xsd:complexType>
</xsd:element>
```

An XML instance of the book element would look like this:

```
<book title = "More Java Pitfalls" pages="453" />
```

Now let's look at how we define a "product" element with both attributes and child elements. The product element will have three attributes: id, title, and price. It will also have two child elements: description and categories. The categories child element is mandatory and repeatable, while the description child element will be optional:

```
<xsd:element name="product">
   <xsd:complexType>
      <xsd:sequence>
         <xsd:element name="description" type="xsd:string"
         minOccurs="0" maxOccurs = "1" />
         <xsd:element name="category" type="xsd:string"
         minOccurs = "1" maxOccurs = "unbounded" />
      </xsd:sequence>
      <xsd:attribute name="id" type="xsd:ID" />
      <xsd:attribute name="title" type="xsd:string" />
      <xsd:attribute name="price" type="xsd:decimal" />
   </xsd:complexType>
</xsd:element>
```

Here is an XML instance of the product element defined previously:

```
<product id="P01" title="Wonder Teddy" price="49.99">
    <description>
    The best selling teddy bear of the year.
    </description>
    <category> toys </category>
    <category> stuffed animals </category>
</product>
```

An alternate version of the product element could look like this:

```
<product id="P02" title="RC Racer" price="89.99">
    <category> toys </category>
    <category> electronic </category>
    <category> radio-controlled </category>
</product>
```

Schema definitions can be very complex and require some expertise to construct. Some organizations have chosen to ignore validation or hardwire it into the software. The next section examines this issue.

Is Validation Worth the Trouble?

Anyone who has worked with validation tools knows that developers are at the mercy of the maturity of the tools and specifications they implement. Validation, and the tool support for it, is still evolving. Until the schema languages mature, validation will be a frustrating process that requires testing with multiple tools. You should not rely on the results of just one tool because it may not have implemented the specification correctly or could be buggy. Fortunately, the tool support for schema validation has been steadily improving and is now capable of validating even complex schemas.

Even though it may involve significant testing and the use of multiple tools, *validation is a critical component of your data management process*. Validation is critical because XML, by its nature, is intended to be shared and processed by a large number and variety of applications. Second, a source document, if not used in its entirety, may be broken up into XML fragments and parts reused. Therefore, the cost of errors in XML must be multiplied across all the programs and partners that rely on that data. As mining tools proliferate, the multiplication factor increases accordingly.

MAXIM

Every XML instance should be validated during creation to ensure the accuracy of all data values in order to guarantee data interoperability.

The chief difficulties with validation stem from the additional complexity of new features introduced with XML Schema: data types, namespace support, and type inheritance. A robust data-typing facility, similar to that found in programming languages, is not part of XML syntax and is therefore layered on top of it. Strong data typing is key to ensuring consistent interpretation of XML data values across diverse programming languages and hardware. Namespace support provides the ability to create XML instances that combine elements and attributes from different markup languages. This allows you to reuse elements from other markup languages instead of reinventing the wheel for identical concepts. Thus, namespace support eases software interoperability by reducing the number of unique vocabularies applications must be aware of. Type inheritance is the most complex new feature in XML Schema and is also borrowed from object-oriented programming. This feature has come under fire for being overly complex and poorly implemented; therefore, it should be avoided until the next version of XML Schema.

As stated previously, namespace support is a key benefit of XML Schema. Let's examine namespaces in more detail and see how they are implemented.

What Are XML Namespaces?

Namespaces are a simple mechanism for creating globally unique names for the elements and attributes of your markup language. This is important for two reasons: to deconflict the meaning of identical names in different markup languages and to allow different markup languages to be mixed together without ambiguity. Unfortunately, namespaces were not fully compatible with DTDs, and therefore their adoption has been slow. The current markup definition languages, like XML Schema, fully support namespaces.

MAXIM

All new markup languages should declare one or more namespaces.

Other Schema-Related Efforts

Two efforts that extend schemas are worth mentioning: the Schema Adjunct Framework and the Post Schema Validation Infoset (PSVI). The Schema Adjunct Framework is a small markup language to associate new domain-specific information to specific elements or attributes in the schema. For example, you could associate a set of database mappings to a schema. Schema Adjunct Framework is still experimental and not a W3C Recommendation.

The PSVI defines a standard set of information classes that an application can retrieve after an instance document has been validated against a schema. For example, an application can retrieve the declared data types of elements and attributes present in an instance document. Here are some of the key PSVI information classes: element and attribute type information, validation context, validity of elements and attributes, identity table, and document information.

Namespaces are implemented by requiring every XML name to consist of two parts: a prefix and a local part. Here is an example of a fully qualified element name:

```
<xsd:integer>
```

The local part is the identifier for the meta data (in the preceding example, the local part is "integer"), and the prefix is an abbreviation for the actual namespace in the namespace declaration. The actual namespace is a unique Uniform Resource Identifier (URI; see sidebar). Here is a sample namespace declaration:

```
<xsd:schema xmlns:xsd="http://www.w3.org/2001/XMLSchema">
```

The preceding example declares a namespace for all the XML Schema elements to be used in a schema document. It defines the prefix "xsd" to stand for the namespace "http://www.w3.org/2001/XMLSchema". It is important to understand that the prefix is not the namespace. The prefix can change from one instance document to another. The prefix is merely an abbreviation for the namespace, which is the URI. To specify the namespace of the new elements you are defining, you use the targetNamespace attribute:

```
<xsd:schema xmlns:xsd="http://www.w3.org/2001/XMLSchema"
  targetNamespace="http://www.mycompany.com/markup">
```

There are two ways to apply a namespace to a document: attach the prefix to each element and attribute in the document or declare a default namespace for the document. A default namespace is declared by eliminating the prefix from the declaration:

```
<html xmlns="http://www.w3.org/1999/xhtml">
<head> <title> Default namespace Test </title> </head>
<body> Go Semantic Web!! </body>
</html>
```

Here is a text representation of what the preceding document is internally translated to by a conforming XML processor (note that the use of braces to off-set the namespace is an artifice to clearly demarcate the namespace from the local part):

```
<{http://www.w3.org/1999/xhtml}html>
<{http://www.w3.org/1999/xhtml}head>
<{http://www.w3.org/1999/xhtml}title> Default namespace Test
</{http://www.w3.org/1999/xhtml}title> </head>
<{http://www.w3.org/1999/xhtml}body> Go Semantic Web!!
</{http://www.w3.org/1999/xhtml}body>
</{http://www.w3.org/1999/xhtml}html>
```

This processing occurs during parsing by an application. *Parsing* is the dissection of a block of text into discernible words (also known as tokens). There are three common ways to parse an XML document: by using the Simple API for XML (SAX), by building a Document Object Model (DOM), and by employing a new technique called *pull parsing*. SAX is a style of parsing called *event-based parsing* where each information class in the instance document generates a corresponding event in the parser as the document is traversed. SAX parsers are useful for parsing very large XML documents or in low-memory environments. Building a DOM is the most common approach to parsing an XML document and is discussed in detail in the next section. Pull parsing is a new technique that aims for both low-memory consumption and high performance. It is especially well suited for parsing XML Web services (see Chapter 4 for details on Web services).

What Is a URI?

A Uniform Resource Identifier (URI) is a standard syntax for strings that identify a resource. Informally, URI is a generic term for *addresses* and *names* of objects (or resources) on the World Wide Web. A *resource* is any physical or abstract thing that has an identity.

There are two types of URIs: Uniform Resource Locators (URLs) and Uniform Resource Names (URNs). A URL identifies a resource by how it is accessed; for example, "http://www.example.com/stuff/index.html" identifies an HTML page on a server with a Domain Name System (DNS) name of www.example.com and accessed via the Hypertext Transfer Protocol (used by Web servers on standard port 80). A URN creates a unique and persistent name for a resource either in the "urn" namespace or another registered namespace. A URN namespace dictates the syntax for the URN identifier.

Pull parsing is also an event-based parsing technique; however, the events are read by the application (pulled) and not automatically triggered as in SAX. Parsers using this technique are still experimental. The majority of applications use the DOM approach to parse XML, discussed next.

What Is the Document Object Model (DOM)?

The *Document Object Model (DOM)* is a language-neutral data model and application programming interface (API) for programmatic access and manipulation of XML and HTML. Unlike XML instances and XML schemas, which reside in files on disk, the DOM is an in-memory representation of a document. The need for this arose from differences between the way Internet Explorer (IE) and Netscape Navigator allowed access and manipulation of HTML documents to support Dynamic HTML (DHTML). IE and Navigator represent the parts of a document with different names, which made cross-browser scripting extremely difficult. Thus, out of the desire for cross-browser scripting came the need for a standard representation for document objects in the browser's memory. The model for this memory representation is object-oriented programming (OOP). So, by turning around the title, we get the definition of a DOM: a data model, using objects, to represent an XML or HTML document.

Object-oriented programming introduces two key data modeling concepts that we will introduce here and visit again in our discussion of RDF in Chapter 6: classes and objects. A *class* is a definition or template describing the *characteristics* and *behaviors* of a real-world entity or concept. From this description, an in-memory instance of the class can be constructed, which is called an object. So, an *object* is a specific instance of a class. The key benefit of this approach to modeling program data is that your programming language more closely resembles the problem domain you are solving. Real-world entities have characteristics and behaviors. Thus, programmers create classes that model real-world entities like "Auto," "Employee," and "Product." Along with a class name, a class has characteristics, known as *data members*, and behaviors, known as *methods*. Figure 3.6 graphically portrays a class and two objects.

The simplest way to think about a DOM is as a set of classes that allow you to create a tree of objects in memory that represent a manipulable version of an XML or HTML document. There are two ways to access this tree of objects: a generic way and a specific way. The generic way (see Figure 3.7) shows all parts of the document as objects of the same class, called Node. The generic DOM representation is often called a "flattened view" because it does not use class inheritance. Class inheritance is where a child class inherits characteristics and behaviors from a parent class just like in biological inheritance.

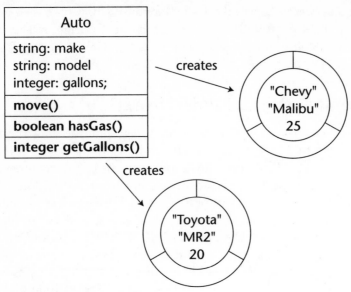

Figure 3.6 Class and objects.

The DOM in Figure 3.7 can also be accessed using specific subclasses of Node for each major part of the document like Document, DocumentFragment, Element, Attr (for attribute), Text, and Comment. This more object-oriented tree is displayed in Figure 3.8.

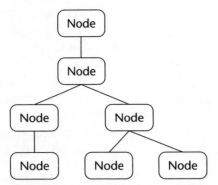

Figure 3.7 A DOM as a tree of nodes.

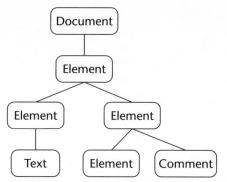

Figure 3.8 A DOM as a tree of subclasses.

The DOM has steadily evolved by increasing the detail of the representation, increasing the scope of the representation, and adding new manipulation methods. This is accomplished by dividing the DOM into conformance levels, where each new level adds to the feature set. There are currently three DOM levels:

DOM Level 1. This set of classes represents XML 1.0 and HTML 4.0 documents.

DOM Level 2. This extends Level 1 to add support for namespaces; cascading style sheets, level 2 (CSS2); alternate views; user interface events; and enhanced tree manipulation via interfaces for traversal and ranges. Cascading style sheets can be embedded in HTML or XML documents in the <style> element and provide a method of attaching styles to selected elements in the document. Alternate views allow alternate perspectives of a document like a new DOM after a style sheet has been applied. User interface events are events triggered by a user, such as mouse events and key events, or triggered by other software, such as mutation events and HTML events (load, unload, submit, etc.). Traversals add new methods of visiting nodes in a tree—specifically, NodeInterator and TreeWalker—that correspond to traversing the flattened view and traversing the hierarchical view (as diagrammed in Figures 3.7 and 3.8). A range allows a selection of nodes between two boundary points.

DOM Level 3. This extends Level 2 by adding support for mixed vocabularies (different namespaces), XPath expressions (XPath is discussed in detail in Chapter 6), load and save methods, and a representation of abstract schemas (includes both DTD and XML Schema). XPath is a language to select a set of nodes within a document. Load and save methods specify a standard way to load an XML document into a DOM and a way to save a DOM into an XML document. Abstract schemas provide classes to represent DTDs and schemas and operations on the schemas.

In summary, the Document Object Model is an in-memory representation of an XML or HTML document and methods to manipulate it. DOMs can be loaded from XML documents, saved to XML documents, or dynamically generated by a program. The DOM has provided a standard set of classes and APIs for browsers and programming languages to represent XML and HTML. The DOM is represented as a set of interfaces with specific language bindings to those interfaces.

Impact of XML on Enterprise IT

XML is pervading all areas of the enterprise, from the IT department to the intranet, extranet, Web sites, and databases. The adoption of XML technology has moved well beyond early adopters into mainstream use and has become integrated with the majority of commercial products on the market, either as a primary or enabling technology. This section examines the current and future impact of XML in 10 specific areas:

Data exchange and interoperability. XML has become the universal syntax for exchanging data between organizations. By agreeing on a standard schema, organization can produce these text documents that can be validated, transmitted, and parsed by any application regardless of hardware or operating system. The government has become a major adopter of XML and is moving all reporting requirements to XML. Companies report financial information via XML, and local governments report regulatory information. XML has been called the next Electronic Data Interchange (EDI) system, which formerly was extremely costly, was cumbersome, and used binary encoding. The reasons for widespread adoption in this area are the same reasons for XML success (listed earlier in this chapter). Easy data exchange is the enabling technology behind the next two areas: ebusiness and Enterprise Application Integration.

Ebusiness. Business-to-business (B2B) transactions have been revolutionized through XML. B2B revolves around the exchange of business messages to conduct business transactions. There are dozens of commercial products supporting numerous business vocabularies developed by RosettaNet, OASIS, and other organizations. Case studies and success stories abound from top companies like Coca-Cola, IBM, Cardinal Health, and Fannie Mae. Web services and Web service registries are discussed in Chapter 4 and will increase this trend by making it even easier to deploy such solutions. IBM's Chief Information Officer, Phil Thompson, recently stated in an interview on CNET, "We have $27 billion of e-commerce floating through our systems at an operating cost point that is giving us leverage for enhanced profitability."

Enterprise Application Integration (EAI). Enterprise Application Integration is the assembling of legacy applications, databases, and systems to work together to support integrated Web views, e-commerce, and Enterprise Resource Planning (ERP). The Open Applications Group (www .openapplications.org) is a nonprofit consortium of companies to define standards for application integration. It currently boasts over 250 live sites and more than 100 vendors (including SAP, PeopleSoft, and Oracle) supporting the Open Applications Group Integration Specification (OAGIS) in their products. David Chappell writes, "EAI has proven to be the killer app for Web services."[2]

Enterprise IT architectures. The impact of XML on IT architectures has grown increasingly important as a bridge between the Java 2 Enterprise Edition (J2EE) platform and Microsoft's .NET platform. Large companies are implementing both architectures and turning to XML Web services to integrate them. Additionally, XML is influencing development on every tier of the N-tier network. On the client tier, XML is transformed via XSLT to multiple presentation languages like Scalable Vector Graphics (SVG). SVG is discussed in Chapter 6. On the Web tier, XML is used primarily as the integration format of choice and merged in middleware. Additionally, XML is used to configure and deploy applications on this tier like Java Server Pages (JSP) and Active Server Pages (ASP). In the back-end tier, XML is being stored and queried in relational databases and native XML databases. A more detailed discussion of this is provided later in this section.

Content Management Systems (CMS). CMS is a Web-based system to manage the production and distribution of content to intranet and Internet sites. XML technologies are central to these systems in order to separate raw content from its presentation. Content can be transformed on the fly via the Extensible Stylesheet Language Transformation (XSLT) to browsers or wireless clients. XSLT is discussed in Chapter 6. The ability to tailor content to user groups on the fly will continue to drive the use of XML for CMS systems.

Knowledge management and e-learning. Knowledge management involves the capturing, cataloging, and dissemination of corporate knowledge on intranets. In essence, this treats corporate knowledge as an asset. Electronic learning (e-learning) is part of the knowledge acquisition for employees through online training. Current incarnations of knowledge management systems are intranet-based content management systems (discussed previously) and Web logs. XML is driving the future of knowledge management

[2]David Chappell, "Who Cares about UDDI?", available at http://www.chappellassoc.com/ articles/article_who_cares_UDDI.html.

in terms of knowledge representation (RDF is discussed in Chapter 5), tax-onomies (discussed in Chapter 7), and ontologies (discussed in Chapter 8). XML is fostering e-learning with standard formats like the Instructional Management System (IMS) XML standards (at www.imsproject.org).

Portals and data integration.   A portal is a customizable, multipaned view tailored to support a specific community of users. XML is supported via standard transformation portlets that use XSLT to generate specific presen-tations of content (as discussed previously under *Content Management Systems*), syndication of content, and the integration of Web services. A portlet is a dynamically pluggable application that generates content for one pane (or subwindow) in a portal. Syndication is the reuse of content from another site. The most popular format for syndication is an XML-based format called the Resource Description Framework Site Summary (RSS). RDF is discussed in Chapter 5. The integration of Web services into portals is still in its early stages but will enhance portals as the focal point for enterprise data integration. All the major portal vendors are integrating Web services into their portal products.

Customer relationship management (CRM).   CRM systems enable an organization's sales and marketing staff to understand, track, inform, and service their customers. CRM involves many of the other systems we have discussed here, such as portals, content management systems, data inte-gration, and databases (see next item), where XML is playing a major role. XML is becoming the glue to tie all these systems together to enable the sales force or customers (directly) to access information when they want and wherever they are (including wireless).

Databases and data mining.   XML has had a greater effect on relational database management systems (DBMS) than object-oriented programming (which created a new category of database called object-oriented database management systems, or OODBMS). XML has even spawned a new cate-gory of databases called native XML databases exclusively for the storage and retrieval of XML. All the major database vendors have responded to this challenge by supporting XML translation between relational tables and XML schemas. Additionally, all of the database vendors are further integrating XML into their systems as a native data type. This trend toward storing and retrieving XML will accelerate with the completion of the W3C XQuery specification. We discuss XQuery in Chapter 6.

Collaboration technologies and peer-to-peer (P2P).   Collaboration tech-nologies allow individuals to interact and participate in joint activities from disparate locations over computer networks. P2P is a specific decentralized collaboration protocol. XML is being used for collaboration at the protocol level, for supporting interoperable tools, configuring the collaboration experience, and capturing shared content. XML is the underpinning of the open source JXTA project (www.jxta.org).

XML is positively affecting every corner of the enterprise. This impact has been so extensive that it can be considered a data revolution. This revolution of data description, sharing, and processing is fertile ground to move beyond a simplistic view of meta data. The next section examines why meta data is not enough and how it will evolve in the Semantic Web.

Why Meta Data Is Not Enough

XML meta data is a form of description. It describes the purpose or meaning of raw data values via a text format to more easily enable exchange, interoperability, and application independence. As description, the general rule applies that "more is better." Meta data increases the fidelity and granularity of our data. The way to think about the current state of meta data is that we attach words (or labels) to our data values to describe it. How could we attach sentences? What about paragraphs? While the approach toward meta data evolution will not follow natural language description, it is a good analogy for the inadequacy of words alone. The motivation for providing richer data description is to move data processing from being tediously preplanned and mechanistic to dynamic, just-in-time, and adaptive.

For example, you may be enabling your systems to respond in real time to a location-aware cell phone customer who is walking by one of your store outlets. If your system can match consumers' needs or past buying habits to current sale merchandise, you increase revenue. Additionally, your computers should be able to support that sale with just-in-time inventory by automating your supply chain with your partners. Finally, after the sale, your systems should perform rich customer relationship management by allowing transparency of your operations in fulfilling the sale and the ability to anticipate the needs of your customers by understanding their life and needs. The general rule is this: The more computers understand, the more effectively they can handle complex tasks.

We have not yet invented all the ways a semantically aware computing system can drive new business and decrease your operation costs. But to get there, we must push beyond simple meta data modeling to knowledge modeling and standard knowledge processing. Here are three emerging steps beyond simple meta data: semantic levels, rule languages, and inference engines.

Semantic Levels

Figure 3.9 shows the evolution of data fidelity required for semantically aware applications. Instead of just meta data, we will have an information stack composed of semantic levels. We are currently at Level 1 with XML Schema, which is represented as modeling the properties of our data classes. We are capturing and processing meta data about isolated data classes like purchase orders, products, employees, and customers. On the left side of the diagram we associate a simple physical metaphor to the state of each level. Level 1 is analogous to describing singular concepts or objects.

In Level 2, we will move beyond data modeling (simple meta data properties) to knowledge modeling. This is discussed in detail in Chapter 5 on the Resource Description Framework (RDF) and Chapter 7 on taxonomies. Knowledge modeling enables us to model statements both about the relationships between Level 1 objects and about how those objects operate. This is diagrammed as connections between our objects in Figure 3.9.

Beyond the knowledge statements of Level 2 are the superstructures or "closed-world modeling" of Level 3. The technology that implements these sophisticated models of systems is called ontologies and is discussed in Chapter 8.

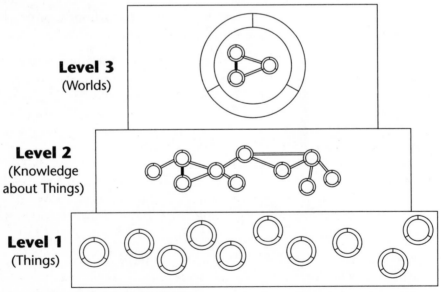

Figure 3.9 Evolution in data fidelity.

How can we be sure this evolution will happen and will deliver a return on investment? The evolution of data fidelity and realism has already occurred in many vertical industries to include video games, architecture (computer-aided drafting), and simulations (weather, military, and so on). As an analogy to the effects of realism, a simple test would be to attempt to convince a teenager to play a 1970s arcade-style game like Asteroids instead of any of the current three-dimensional first-person shooter games. Figure 3.10 displays the fidelity difference between the original action arcade game SpaceWar and a high-fidelity combat game called Halo. My 12-year-old son will eagerly discuss the advanced physics of the latest game on the market and why it blows away the competition. How do we apply this to business? High-fidelity, closed-world models allow you to know your customer better, respond faster, rapidly set up new business partners, improve efficiencies, and reduce operation costs. For dimensions like responsiveness, just-in-time, and tailored, which are matters of degree, moving beyond simple meta data will produce the same orders of magnitude improvement as demonstrated in Figure 3.10.

Rules and Logic

The semantic levels of information provide the input for software systems. The operations that a software system uses to manipulate the semantic information will be standardized into one or more rule languages. In general, a rule specifies an action if certain conditions are met. The general form is this: if (x) then y. Current efforts on rule languages are discussed in Chapters 5 and 8.

Figure 3.10 Data fidelity evolution in video games.
SpaceWar by Stern, from the Spacewar emulator at the MIT Media Lab

Inference Engines

Applying rules and logic to our semantic data requires standard, embeddable inference engines. These programs will execute a set of rules on a specific instance of data using an ontology. An early example of these types of inferencing engines is the open source software Closed World Machine (CWM). CWM is an inference engine that allows you to load ontologies or closed worlds (Semantic Level 3), then it executes a rule language on that world.

So, meta data is a starting point for semantic representation and processing. The rise of meta data is related to the ability to reuse meta data between organizations and systems. XML provides the best universal syntax to do that. With XML, everyone is glimpsing the power of meta data and the limitations of simple meta data. The following chapters examine how we move beyond meta data toward knowledge.

Summary

This chapter provided an in-depth understanding of XML and its impact on the enterprise. The discussion was broken down into four major sections: XML success factors, the mechanics of XML, the impact of XML, and why simple data modeling is not enough.

There are four primary reasons for XML's success:

XML creates application-independent documents and data. XML can be inspected by humans and processed by any application.

It has a standard syntax for meta data. XML provides an effective approach to describe the structure and purpose of data.

It has a standard structure for both documents and data. XML organizes data into a hierarchy.

XML is not a new technology (not a 1.0 release). XML is a subset of SGML, which has been around more than 30 years.

In understanding the mechanics of XML, we examined what markup is, the syntax of tags, and how start, end, and empty tags are used. We continued to explore the mechanics of XML by learning the difference between well-formed and valid documents, how we define the legal elements and attributes using XML Schema, how to use namespaces to create unique element and attribute names, and how applications and browsers represent documents internally using the Document Object Model. After understanding XML, we turned to its impact on the enterprise. XML has had considerable impact on 10 areas: data exchange, ebusiness, EAI, IT architectures, CMS, knowledge management, portals, CRM, databases, and collaboration. XML's influence will increase dramatically over the next 10 years with the advent of the Semantic Web.

Lastly, we turned a critical eye on the current state of XML meta data and why it is not enough to fulfill the goals of the Semantic Web. The evolution of meta data will expand into three levels: modeling of things, modeling of knowledge about things, and, finally, modeling "closed worlds." In addition to modeling knowledge and worlds, we will expand to model the rules and axioms of logic in order for computers to automatically use and manipulate those worlds on our behalf. Finally, to apply those rules, standard inference engines, like CWM, will be created and embedded into many of the current IT applications.

In conclusion, XML is a strong foundation for the Semantic Web. Its next significant stage of development is the advent of Web services, discussed in the next chapter.

4

Understanding Web Services

"By 2005, the aggressive use of web services will drive a 30% increase in the efficiency of IT development projects."

"The Hype Is Right: Web Services Will Deliver Immediate Benefits," Gartner Inc, October 9, 2001.

Web services provide interoperability solutions, making application integration and transacting business easier. Because it is now obvious that monolithic, proprietary solutions are barriers to interoperability, industry has embraced open standards. One of these standards, XML, is supported by all major vendors. It forms the foundation for Web services, providing a needed framework for interoperability. The widespread support and adoption of Web services—in addition to the cost-saving advantages of Web services technology—make the technologies involved very important to understand. This chapter gives an overview of Web services and provides a look at the major standards, specifications, and implementation solutions currently available.

What Are Web Services?

Web services have been endlessly hyped but sometimes badly described. "A framework for creating services for the use over the World Wide Web" is a fairly nondescriptive definition, but nonetheless, we hear marketing briefs telling us this every day. The generality of the definition and mischaracterization of "Web" to mean World Wide Web instead of "Web technologies" makes this simple definition do more harm than good. For this reason, we will give a more concrete definition of Web services here, and then explain each part in detail.

Web services are software applications that can be *discovered*, *described*, and *accessed* based on XML and standard Web protocols over intranets, extranets, and the Internet. The beginning of that sentence, "Web services are software applications," conveys a main point: Web services are software applications available on the Web that perform specific functions. Next, we will look at the middle of the definition where we write that Web services can be "discovered, described, and accessed based on XML and standard Web protocols." Built on XML, a standard that is supported and accepted by thousands of vendors worldwide, Web services first focus on interoperability. XML is the syntax of messages, and Hypertext Transport Protocol (HTTP), the underlying protocol, is how applications send XML messages to Web services in order to communicate. Web services technologies, such as Universal Description, Discovery, and Integration (UDDI) and ebXML registries, allow applications to dynamically discover information about Web services—the "discovered" part of our definition. The message syntax for a Web service is described in WSDL, the Web Service Definition Language. When most technologists think of Web services, they think of SOAP, the "accessed" part of our Web services definition. SOAP, developed as the Simple Object Access Protocol, is the XML-based message protocol (or API) for communicating with Web services. SOAP is the underlying "plumbing" for Web services, because it is the protocol that everyone agrees with.

The last part of our definition mentions that Web services are available "over intranets, extranets, and the Internet." Not only can Web services be public, they can exist on an internal network for internal applications. Web services could be used between partnering organizations in a small B2B solution. It is important to understand that there are benefits for using Web services internally as well as externally.

Figure 4.1 gives a graphical view of that definition, shown as layers. Relying on the foundation of XML for the technologies of Web services, and using HTTP as the underlying protocol, the world of Web services involves standard protocols to achieve the capabilities of access, description, and discovery.

Figure 4.2 shows these technologies in use in a common scenario. In Step 1, the client application discovers information about Web Service A in a UDDI registry. In Step 2, the client application gets the WSDL for Web Service A from the UDDI registry to determine Web Service A's API. Finally, in Steps 3 and 4, the client application communicates with the Web service via SOAP, using the API found in Step 2. We'll get more into the details of these technologies later in the chapter.

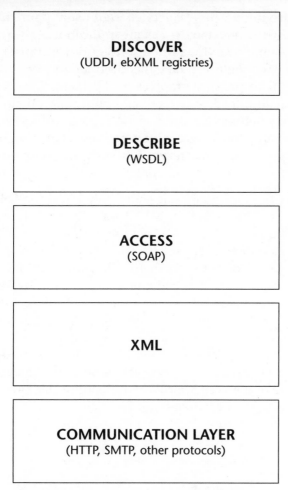

Figure 4.1 The basic layers of Web services.

Our example scenario in Figure 4.2 shows the basics of client and Web service interaction. Because of these processes, such as discovery, the client application can automate interactions with Web services. Web services provide common standards for doing business and software integration—complementing a user-driven, manual navigation architecture to one where automated business process can be the focus.

It is important to understand that Web services can be completely independent of the presentation, or the graphical user interface (GUI) of applications. Instead, Web services send data in XML format, and applications can add style and formatting when they receive the data. An example of a Web service could be a "driving directions finder" Web service that provides the capability to get text-based car directions from any address to any address, listing the driving distances and estimated driving times. The service itself usually provides no graphics; simply speaking XML messages to a client application. Any application, such as a program created in UNIX, a Microsoft Windows application, a Java applet, or server-side Web page, can take the information received from that application and style it to provide graphics and presentation. Because only XML data is sent back and forth, any front-end application that understands XML can speak to the Web service. Because a Web service does not need to focus on presentation styling, the focus for creating them is purely on business logic, making it easier to reuse Web services as software components in your enterprise.

Separating business logic from presentation is commonly known in software engineering as the Model-View-Controller (MVC) paradigm. Web services support this paradigm. Shown in Figure 4.3, the user interface details (the view) and business logic (the model) are separated in two different components, while the component layer between them (the controller) facilitates communication. This paradigm, which has had much success in software engineering, makes sense because it solves business problems. When a business decides to create a Web service, the application integrator/developer can simply focus on the business logic when designing and developing the Web service. Because the presentation is separate, the client application can present the information to the user in many different ways. This is an important concept because many browsers make it easier for you by offloading this processing with style sheets, using XSL Transformations (XSLT).

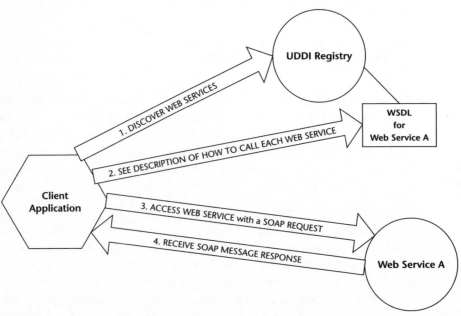

Figure 4.2 A common scenario of Web services in use.

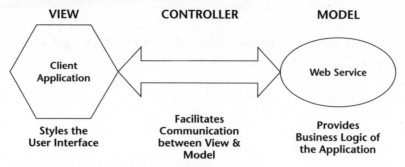

Figure 4.3 The Model-View-Controller paradigm.

In this introductory section, we have provided you with a definition of Web services and given you a taste of the technologies involved. The next sections discuss the business case for Web services, some of the technical details, and a vision for Web services in the future.

Why Use Web Services?

You've heard the hype. If you haven't already adopted a Web services-based strategy, you're probably wondering the following:

- *Do Web services solve real problems?* What problems do Web services solve?
- *Is there really a future for Web services?* That is, will this market continue to grow? Will Web services *really* play a big part in the next generation of the Web—or are we drowning in technology hype?
- *How can I use Web services?* Where exactly can my business focus to take advantage of the technology?

These questions are so fundamental that you should ask them about any candidate technology. In this section we examine each of these.

Do Web Services Solve Real Problems?

What problems do Web services have the ability to solve? Many businesses suffer from integration problems in our fast-paced world of ever-changing technologies, market conditions, and business relationships. It is vital to be able to have your internal systems communicate with your partner's internal systems, and databases. Rapid and easy integration facilitates and empowers your business processes. Yet businesses frequently experience many problems in this area. Because of different database languages, different communication protocols, and different ways of expressing problems in languages understood by computers, integrating systems is extremely difficult.

MAXIM

One of the major indicators of a successful technology is its ability to solve problems to help organizations do business.

So, we have integration problems, but we want to solve them quickly. People want to see return on their investments as soon as possible. How can you repurpose your existing assets without being disruptive to your organization's business process? How quickly can you change given new market conditions? The problem with solutions in the past is that integration efforts have taken too long, and we have created new stovepipes by creating inflexible, hard-to-change architectures.

Although it sounds like a paradox, a key reason businesses were so quick to adopt Web services was that other businesses adopted Web services. This agreement only took place because the technology can solve these integration problems by providing a common language that could be used in integration—both within and between enterprises. Without agreement on a common language, there would be no interoperability.

MAXIM

Agreement on a technology that works is more important for business than debating which technology works best.

In the past, there have been battles over what protocols and computer languages to use. At one time, there was debate over whether TCP/IP would be the dominant networking protocol. When it became the dominant protocol for the Internet, other protocols used that as a foundation for transport, including HTTP, which became the protocol for use over the Web. HTTP became a widely supported application-layer protocol, and SOAP was developed using HTTP as its foundation. Now that major businesses have adopted SOAP for the communication medium between applications and servers, this ensures that everyone's applications have a chance to speak a common language. Web services are based on SOAP and represent our current state of evolution in communication agreement.

Because there is such widespread agreement and adoption of the Web service protocols, it is now possible to leverage the work of your existing applications and turn them into Web services by using the standard Web service protocols that everyone understands. Web services allow you to change the *interfaces* to your applications—without rewriting them—using middleware. An example that should have a profound impact is that with easy-to-use middleware, .NET clients and servers can talk to J2EE servers using SOAP. The implementation of the underlying application is no longer relevant—only the communication medium.

Wasn't CORBA Supposed to Solve Interoperability Problems?

CORBA, the Common Object Request Broker Architecture, provides an object-based approach for distributing computing in a platform-independent, language-independent way. In the 1990s, CORBA's main competitor was Microsoft's DCOM. Some people believe that because of the friction between these two technologies, because of the complexities of CORBA, and because object request brokers (ORBs) were necessary for these technologies to work, there was no unanimous adoption.

SOAP is also a platform-neutral and language-neutral choice, but a major difference is that it has widespread industry support.

Today's business strategies are demanding more intercompany relationships. The broad spectrum of companies means a broad spectrum of applications and integration technology choices. Companies who succeed in this market realize that flexibility is everything. To interoperate with many companies and applications in your business, you need a common language and a way to solve problems in a dynamic environment. Web services provide this framework.

Is There Really a Future for Web Services?

This may be the most important question for you to ask. One thing that we've learned over the past 10 years is that a technology's success is not dependent on how well it works or how "cool" it is—most of the success is based on business decisions that are made by major business players. Many well-thought-out, well-designed technologies now languish in the graveyard of useless technology because they were not widely adopted. When many key businesses begin using a technology and begin touting it, there is a good possibility that the technology has a future. When all key businesses begin using it and evangelizing it, there is an even greater possibility that the technology has a future. When the technology solves key problems, is simple to understand, and is adopted by all key businesses, its success in the future is nearly ensured.

MAXIM

One of the major indicators of a successful technology is its adoption by key business players.

The maxim that we defined in this section seems to be a good way to partially predict the success of Web services. One of the main factors that is driving this market is business adoption. When giants such as Microsoft, IBM, Sun, and the open source community agree on something, it is not only a major milestone, it is a sign that whatever they have agreed on has a big future. In the Web services arena, this is exactly what has happened. The development of the open standards for Web services has been an open-industry effort, based on partnerships of vendors and standards organizations.

Of course, it is hard to predict the future, but because of the adoption of Web services protocols (SOAP in particular), the future is very bright.

How Can I Use Web Services?

Now that we have discussed the widespread adoption of Web services, as well as the problems that Web services can solve, you need to decide whether to use Web services in your business, and if so, how to use them. This section provides ideas on how Web services can be used.

If you are an application vendor, you need to have a SOAP API to your application, because it is now a common API for all platforms. If you are a business that provides services to individuals and other companies, the previous section may have provided you with new ideas. If you are an organization that has many legacy systems that work but do not interoperate, you may find that you can easily adopt the Web services model for your business. Because the value of Web services is interoperability, you can use the technologies to solve your business problems, focusing less on the technology and more on your business process. The promise of networked businesses will not be realized until we can rapidly and dynamically interoperate. Within an enterprise, this is called Enterprise Application Integration (EAI). Between enterprises, this is known as business-to-business (B2B).

EAI is currently the killer app for Web services. Because we are at the stage of Web services where legacy applications can be made Web service-enabled via SOAP, EAI is doable now—and this is currently where the real value is. Most analysts believe that organizations will adopt Web services "from the inside out." That is, *intranet* applications such as enterprise portals, where many data sources are integrated into a federation of data stores, will flourish. In your integration projects, if your systems have SOAP interfaces, integrating them will be easier. Tying together your internal infrastructure, such as Enterprise Resource Planning, customer relationship management, project management, value chain management, and accounting, all with Web services, will eventually prepare you to interoperate with business partners on a B2B basis. More importantly, Web services allow you to integrate your internal processes, saving time and money.

B2B may be the future of Web services. Currently, folks at OASIS are working on standards that provide common semantics for doing business for Web services. This will be the next step in Web services development, and most business analysts believe that organizations that deploy Web services internally will be prepared for the next boom in a mass B2B marketplace. We feel that there may be an intermediary step: As your organization uses Web service technology to integrate your processes, you may be able to use Web services to do business with your private business partners, performing B2B on a smaller scale on private extranets.

In conclusion, there is a good case for Web services in most businesses. Chances are, you will need to integrate many of your internal systems with an EAI solution, and Web services makes this easy. If your company does systems integration, your integrators should look to Web services to easily connect legacy systems. If your company develops a server software product, creating a SOAP interface to your product will absolutely be necessary, because there is such a demand for Web service-enabled products. If your company is currently pursuing small-scale or large-scale B2B solutions, you should look to Web services as the next step for doing business. Finally, we would like to underscore our point that the near-term evolution of Web services will revolve around EAI.

Understanding the Basics of Web Services

This section gives a high-level overview of some of the basic Web services technologies. In this section, we discuss the following concepts that are fundamental in understanding Web services: Web service message syntax (SOAP), Web service discovery and registration technologies, Web service orchestration, Web service security, and technologies that will undoubtedly shape the future of Web services. Although key standards and technologies will be discussed, this is not meant to present an in-depth technical study; instead, it will provide you with an understanding of how these technologies fit together to deliver the benefits of Web services.

What Is SOAP?

SOAP is the envelope syntax for sending and receiving XML messages with Web services. That is, SOAP is the "envelope" that packages the XML messages that are sent over HTTP between clients and Web services. As defined by the W3C, SOAP is "a lightweight protocol for exchange of information in a decentralized, distributed environment." (http://www.w3.org/TR/SOAP/). It provides a standard language for tying applications and services together. An application sends a SOAP request to a Web service, and the Web service returns the response in something called a SOAP response. SOAP can potentially be used in combination with a variety of other protocols, but in practice, it is used with HTTP.

TIP
SOAP used to stand for "Simple Object Access Protocol," but with the release of SOAP 1.2, its acronym status is now revoked. After the original specification was developed by Microsoft and DevelopMentor in SOAP 1.0, IBM and Lotus contributed to the specification for SOAP 1.1. Some believed that it would later be renamed "the XML Protocol." Others thought it should stand for "Service-Oriented Architecture Protocol." But instead, because developers associated the term "SOAP" with Web services, they kept the name and just dropped the acronym. This is a good decision because SOAP has nothing to do with object-oriented programming. You can very nicely create a C or Pascal SOAP-based Web service.

SOAP has been adopted as the standard for Web services, and applications from major vendors have developed SOAP APIs for their products, thus making software systems integration easier. The syntax of SOAP, in its basic form, is fairly simple, as shown in Figure 4.4. A SOAP message contains the following elements:

- A SOAP envelope that wraps the message
- A description of how data is encoded
- A SOAP body that contains the application-specific message that the back-end application will understand

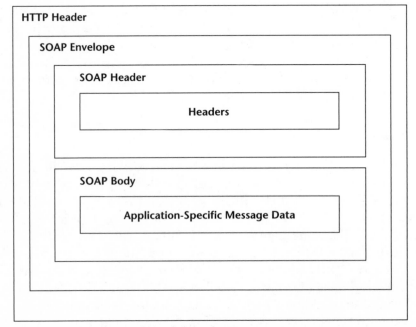

Figure 4.4 Structure of a Web-based SOAP message.

Let's look at an example of a simple SOAP message, taken from the first example in the SOAP 1.1 specification. The listing that follows shows a simple SOAP message for getting the last trade price of the "DIS" ticker symbol. The SOAP envelope wraps everything in the message. On line 3, an attribute of the SOAP envelope, encodingStyle, shows how the message is encoded, so that the Web service can read it. Finally, lines 4 to 7 are the SOAP body of the message that wraps the application-specific information (the call to GetLast-TradePrice in the SOAP body). A Web service receives this information, processes the request in the SOAP body, and can return a SOAP response.

```
<SOAP-ENV:Envelope
  xmlns:SOAP-ENV="http://schemas.xmlsoap.org/soap/envelope/"
  SOAP-ENV:encodingStyle="http://schemas.xmlsoap.org/soap/encoding/">
  <SOAP-ENV:Body>
      <m:GetLastTradePrice xmlns:m="Some-URI">
          <symbol>DIS</symbol>
      </m:GetLastTradePrice>
  </SOAP-ENV:Body>
</SOAP-ENV:Envelope>
```

The SOAP response for our example stock price request is shown in the listing that follows. Just like the request, the message is syntactically the same: It consists of an envelope that wraps the message, it describes its encoding style in line 3, and it wraps the content of the message in the SOAP body in lines 4 to 9. The message inside the body is different. On lines 5 to 7, we see that the message is wrapped in the GetLastTradePriceResponse tag, with the result price shown in line 6.

```
<SOAP-ENV:Envelope
  xmlns:SOAP-ENV="http://schemas.xmlsoap.org/soap/envelope/"
  SOAP-ENV:encodingStyle="http://schemas.xmlsoap.org/soap/encoding/"/>
  <SOAP-ENV:Body>
      <m:GetLastTradePriceResponse xmlns:m="Some-URI">
          <Price>34.5</Price>
      </m:GetLastTradePriceResponse>
  </SOAP-ENV:Body>
</SOAP-ENV:Envelope>
```

SOAP messages may look simple, but they can get complicated. Luckily, your developers don't necessarily have to understand the details of SOAP. Many tools, such as those that come with Microsoft's .NET and the Java tools for Sun's JAX-RPC, create the SOAP handlers automatically. The developer simply creates objects with methods to be invoked and transforms the object into a Web service with his or her vendor's toolkit.

Now that you've seen what a SOAP request and response look like, you may be thinking, "How will my applications know the application-specific details for talking to a Web service?" In our example, it is easy to see that the common language is SOAP, but how would your application know how to call Get-LastTradePrice, or be able to understand the result GetLastTradePriceResponse? The answer lies in the next section—describing Web services.

How to Describe Basic Web Services

Whereas SOAP is the communication language of Web services, Web Service Definition Language (WSDL) is the way we describe the communication details and the application-specific messages that can be sent in SOAP. WSDL, like SOAP, is an XML grammar. The W3C defines WSDL as "an XML format for describing network services as a set of endpoints operating on messages containing either document-oriented or procedure-oriented information." To know how to send messages to a particular Web service, an application can look at the WSDL and dynamically construct SOAP messages.

WSDL describes the operational information—where the service is located, what the service does, and how to talk to (or invoke) the service. It can be thought of as an XML form of CORBA's Interface Definition Language (IDL). The format of WSDL can look pretty scary, but it isn't really intended to be human-readable.

Developers and integrators do not have to understand WSDL and SOAP to create Web services. When you create a Web service from your enterprise applications, most toolkits create WSDL for you. Figure 4.5 shows an example of how this process works.

In Figure 4.5, the Web service developer creates a WSDL description with developer tools that inspect the Web service's SOAP interface layer in Step 1. In Step 2, the client application generates the code for handling the Web service (its SOAP handler) by looking at the WSDL. Finally, in Step 3, the client application and the Web service can communicate.

Now that we know the language that Web services speak (SOAP), and how the messages are defined (WSDL), how can we find the Web services that we need? We discuss this in the next section.

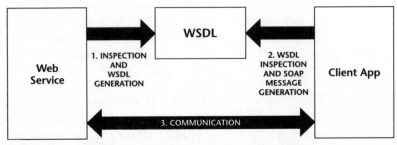

Figure 4.5 Dynamic communication by inspecting WSDL.

How to Discover Web Services

If you know where Web services are and you know what they do, you can easily get software to communicate with them. However, if you would like to search for Web services based on the features they provide and then dynamically connect to them and use them, you will need a Web service registry. Finding Web services based on what they provide introduces two key registry technologies: UDDI (Universal Description, Discovery, and Integration) and ebXML registries. UDDI, introduced in 2000 by Ariba, Microsoft, and IBM, was created to facilitate the discovery of business processes. OASIS introduced ebXML in 1999 to focus the EDI (Electronic Data Interchange) community into consistent use of XML and standard protocols. Part of this effort, ebXML registries, is used for the discovery of ebXML business details. Both of these technologies are worth discussing, and while they may seem to be competing technologies, it is possible that they may complement each other in the evolution of Web services.

What Is UDDI?

Universal Description, Discovery, and Integration is an evolving technology and is not yet a standard, but it is being implemented and embraced by major vendors. Simply put, UDDI is a phone book for Web services. Organizations can register public information about their Web services and types of services with UDDI, and applications can view information about these Web services with UDDI. UDDI allows you to discover Web services just like network discovery tools (such as "My Network Places") can discover nodes on a network.

The information provided in a UDDI business registration consists of three components: white pages of company contact information, yellow pages that categorize businesses by standard taxonomies, and green pages that document the technical information about services that are exposed. Figure 4.6 demonstrates this concept. A business's white pages may include basic business information, such as a description of the business in different languages, points of contact with email addresses and phone numbers, and links to external documents that describe the business in more detail. The yellow pages describe taxonomies of what kinds of information the services provide. Finally, the green pages show information on how to do business with the Web service, listing business rules and specifying how to invoke Web services (the WSDL).

What we have described has two functions: registration of information by a business about its Web services and discovery by organizations who would like to "browse" information about the business and the services it provides. The business can decide what it would like to register about itself in a registry, and once the information is in there, applications can discover and browse the information, getting information on how to do business with the organization.

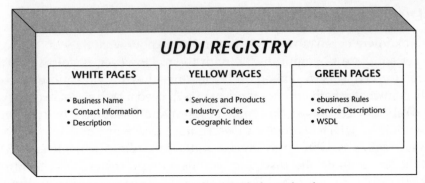

Figure 4.6 A UDDI Registry as a conceptual phone book.

Obviously, there may be security concerns about placing information in a public registry. Although it can be seen that such a technology could be very powerful in a dynamic ebusiness environment, placing information about all of your assets in a public registry may be risky. Much like your Internet's Web pages, your organization will need to decide what information it would like to publish publicly in a UDDI registry.

For internal integration, the use of UDDI private registries may be where much value is today. Within a large organization, where several large enterprise applications may need to interoperate in the future, the use of UDDI registries within the organization can be helpful for discovering how to do so. The use of such a private registry, where Web services are described with WSDL and other information, could potentially minimize the use of interoperation documentation. Using such a registry, in addition to WSDL and SOAP, could reduce integration and development time for legacy enterprise applications. Once applications have been SOAP-enabled, and once the interfaces have been described in WSDL and published in a private UDDI registry, programs and projects within your organization can dynamically connect and begin to interoperate.

Although UDDI has been embraced by major vendors, such as Microsoft and IBM, it is evolving and changing. It is not yet a standard, but it will be. Many business leaders have debated whether businesses would want to use a registry on the Internet; they might fear giving too much information by publishing descriptions of their assets on the Web. The question some critics ask is, "Do you want your technology to choose your business partners?" It remains to be seen whether or not UDDI will fully be embraced and implemented in a fully open B2B environment. Many market analysts believe that UDDI private registries, used in EAI, will provide much value.

What Are ebXML Registries?

The ebXML standard was created by OASIS to link traditional data exchanges to business applications to enable intelligent business processes using XML. Because XML by itself does not provide semantics to solve interoperability problems, ebXML was developed as a mechanism for XML-based business vocabularies. In short, ebXML provides a common way for businesses to quickly and dynamically perform business transactions based on common business practices. Figure 4.7 shows an example of an ebXML architecture in use. In the diagram, company business process information and implementation details are found in the ebXML registry, and businesses can do business transactions after they agree on trading arrangements.

Information that can be described and discovered in an ebXML architecture includes the following:

- Business processes and components described in XML
- Capabilities of a trading partner
- Trading partner agreements between companies

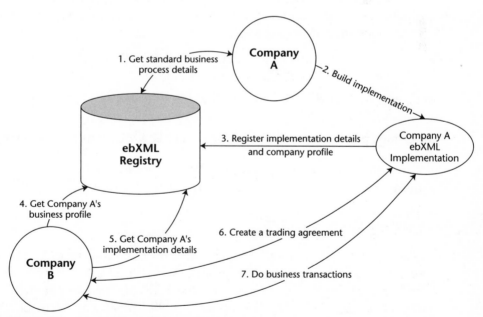

Figure 4.7 An ebXML architecture in use.

The heart of the ebXML architecture is the ebXML registry, which is the mechanism that is used to store and discover this information. Although it seems similar in purpose to UDDI, the ebXML registry contains domain-specific semantics for B2B. These domain-specific semantics are the product of agreement on many business technologies and protocols, such as EDI, SAP, and RosettaNet. Simply put, ebXML could be described as the start of a domain-specific Semantic Web.

The focus of ebXML was not initially on Web services, but it now uses SOAP as its message format. Therefore, many believe that ebXML will have a large role in the future of Web services. Unlike UDDI, ebXML is a standard. The ebXML standard does have support from many businesses, but the most influential companies in Web services, IBM and Microsoft, would like to see UDDI succeed as a registry for business information. Skeptics of ebXML suggest that its specifications have much content on business processes, but it will only be successful if businesses agree to those processes. However, it is possible that the two technologies can complement each other, and ebXML could succeed in the B2B market, while private UDDI registries succeed in the EAI market in the short term.

Although the technologies of UDDI and ebXML registries can complement each other, each will undoubtedly have its key successful areas. The following scenarios are indeed possible:

- Using the UDDI business registry to find ebXML registries and ebXML-enabled businesses for organizations that support ebXML

- Using UDDI to help businesses find other businesses to transact Web services

- Using ebXML registries for finding other ebXML-enabled businesses

It is unclear what the future holds for these technologies, because UDDI is continuing to evolve and ebXML has not yet seen widespread adoption.

Orchestrating Web Services

Orchestration is the process of combining simple Web services to create complex, sequence-driven tasks. This process, sometimes called *flow composition* or *Web service choreography*, involves creating business logic to maintain conversations between multiple Web services. Orchestration can occur between an application and multiple Web services, or multiple Web services can be chained into a workflow, so that they can communicate with one another. This section provides an example of a Web service orchestration solution and discusses the technologies available.

A Simple Example

For our example, we'll list five separate Web services within a fictional organization: a hotel finder Web service, a driving directions finder, an airline ticket booker, a car rental service, and an expense report creator:

Hotel finder Web service. This Web service provides the ability to search for a hotel in a given city, list room rates, check room availability, list hotel amenities, and make room reservations.

Driving directions finder. This Web service gives driving directions and distance information between two addresses.

Airline ticket booker. This Web service searches for flights between two cities in a certain timeframe, lists all available flights and their prices, and provides the capability to make flight reservations.

Car rental Web service. This provides the capability to search for available cars on a certain date, lists rental rates, and allows an application to make a reservation for a car.

Expense report creator. This Web service automatically creates expense reports, based on the expense information sent.

By themselves, these Web services provide simple functionality. By using them together, however, a client application can solve complex problems. Consider the following scenario:

After your first week on the job, your new boss has requested that you go to Wailea, Maui, on a business trip, where you will go to an important conference at Big Makena Beach. (We can dream, can't we?) Given a limited budget, you are to find the cheapest airline ticket, a hotel room less than $150 a night, and the cheapest rental car, and you need to provide this documentation to your internal accounting department. For your trip, you want to find a hotel that has a nonsmoking room and a gym, and you would like to use your frequent flyer account on Party Airlines. Because you don't like to drive, you would like to reduce your car driving time to a minimum.

After making a few inquiries about your travel department, you discover that your company does not have such a department, and you don't have an administrative assistant who handles these details. In addition to all the work that you have to do, you need to make these travel arrangements right away. Luckily, the software integrators at your organization were able to compose the existing Web services into an application that accomplishes these tasks. Going to your organization's internal Web site, you fill in the required information for your trip and answer a few questions online. Because the internal application resides in your organization, you have assurance of trust and can provide your credit card to the application. After you are prompted to make a few basic selections, all of your travel plans and your documentation are confirmed, and you can worry about your other work. How did this happen?

Figure 4.8 shows a high-level diagram of your application's solution. The following steps took place in this example:

1. The client application sent a message to the hotel finder Web service, looking for the name, address, and the rates of hotels (with nonsmoking rooms, local gyms, and rates below $150 a night) available in the Wailea, Maui, area during the duration of your trip.

2. The client application sent a message to the driving directions finder Web service. For the addresses returned in Step 1, the client application requests the distance to Big Makena Beach. Based on the distance returned for the requests to this Web service, the client application finds the four closest hotels.

3. After finding the four closest hotels, the client application requested the user to make a choice. Once that choice was selected, the application booked a room at the desired hotel by sending another message to the hotel finder Web service.

4. Based on the user's frequent flyer information on Party Airlines and the date of the trip to Maui, the client application sent a message to the airline ticket booker Web service, requesting the cheapest ticket on Party Airlines, as well as the cheapest ticket in general. Luckily, Party Airlines had the cheapest ticket, so after receiving user confirmation on the flight, the application booked this flight reservation.

5. The client application sent a message to the car rental Web service, requesting the cheapest rental car during the dates of the trip. Because multiple car types were available for the cheapest price, the client application prompted the user for a choice. After the user selected a car model, the client application reserved the rental car for a pickup at the airport arrival time found in Step 4, and the drop-off time at a time two hours prior to the airport departure time.

6. Sending all necessary receipt information found in Steps 1 to 5, the client application requested an expense report generated from the expense report creator Web service. The client application then emailed the resulting expense report, in the corporate format, to the end user.

Our travel example shows important concepts in orchestration. The client application must make decisions based on business logic and may need to interact with the end user. In the example, the Web services were developed internally, so the client application may know all of the Web service-specific calls. In another situation, however, the technologies of Web services provide the possibility that the client application could "discover" the available services via UDDI, download the WSDL for creating the SOAP for querying the services, and dynamically create those messages on the fly. If the client application understands the semantics of how the business process works, this is doable.

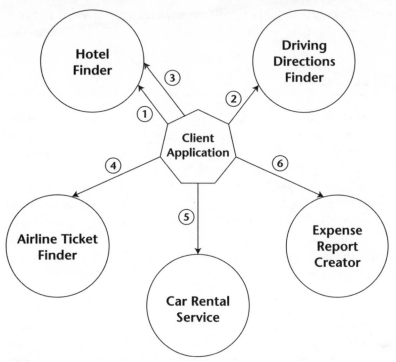

Figure 4.8 An orchestration example.

The idea of moving such an orchestration process from an intranet to an Internet environment underscores a need for the Semantic Web notion of ontologies. As the user's requirements stated that the user wanted to be "near" Makena Beach, how would you define near? Would you define near in respect to distance or time? We encounter the same problem as we mention that we want the "cheapest" ticket. "Cheap" is relative based on what is available and does not always mean the lowest price, because it must be compared to what you get for your money. Good orchestration requires good semantic understanding of the service and its parameters. The better the semantic understanding, the better the automated orchestration.

Orchestration Products and Technologies

Back in 2000, Microsoft's BizTalk Server was released for the purpose of orchestrating Web service and enterprise applications. BizTalk uses XLANG, Microsoft's XML-based orchestration language, to define process flow and conversations between Web services. At the same time, other products, such as BEA, Iona, and IBM have developed similar products. IBM later developed Web Services Flow Language (WSFL) to describe how Web services can be composed into new Web services. WSFL describes interactions between multiple Web services and is similar in purpose to XLANG. Many believe that IBM's

WSFL and Microsoft's XLANG will agree to submit a joint proposal to the W3C to create a standard orchestration language.

Securing Web Services

One of the biggest concerns in the deployment of Web services today is security. In a distributed Internet environment where portals may talk to other Web services, which in turn talk to other Web services, how can we know the identity of who's getting the information? How can we know what information that user is allowed to see? With online transactions, how can we have some assurance that the transaction is valid? How can we keep sensitive information transfers confidential? How can we prove, in a court of law, that someone accessed information? How can we know that a user's transmission hasn't been intercepted and changed? In this section we address some of these issues and discuss evolving security solutions.

Although some of the questions related to Web services and Internet security may seem troubling, the good news is that for most internal Web service architectures (intranet and, to some extent, extranet), these security issues can be minimized. This is why internal EAI projects will be the first areas of major Web service rollouts. Another good piece of news is that Web services security standards are evolving rapidly. We provide an overview in this chapter.

One of the reasons that many system integrators appreciate Web services is that SOAP rides on a standard protocol. Because SOAP lies on an HTTP transport, firewalls that accept HTTP requests into their network allow communication to happen. In the past, system integrators have had to worry about the use of specialized network ports, such as those used for CORBA IIOP and Java RMI, and networks that wanted to communicate over those mediums had to "open up" ports in their firewalls. SOAP's firewall-accepted underlying HTTP protocol presents a double-edged sword. Unfortunately, because firewalls are not necessarily smart enough to analyze SOAP requests, the security protection now lies on the implementation of the Web services themselves. Many security analysts believe that allowing SOAP procedure calls into your network, without additional security measures, opens up potential vulnerabilities. Many cryptanalysts, such as Counterpane's Bruce Schneier, argue that the mind-set of promoting SOAP specifically for "security avoidance" in firewalls, needs to go.[1] Believe it or not, this is only one of the issues involved in Web services security.

---

[1]Bruce Schneier, "Cryptogram Monthly Newsletter," February 15, 2002, http://www.counterpane.com/crypto-gram-0202.html#2.

For the purpose of simplicity, we will list a few basic terms that will establish a common vocabulary of security concerns and explain how they are related to Web services security:

Authentication. This means validating identity. In a Web services environment, it may be important to initially validate a user's identity in certain transactions. Usually, an organization's infrastructure provides mechanisms for proving a user's identity. *Mutual authentication* means proving the identity of both parties involved in communication, and this is done using special security protocols. *Message origin authentication* is used to make certain that the message was sent by the expected sender and that it was not "replayed."

Authorization. Once a user's identity is validated, it is important to know what the user has permission to do. Authorization means determining a user's permissions. Usually, an organization's infrastructure provides mechanisms (such as access control lists and directories) for finding a user's permissions and roles.

Single sign-on (SSO). Although this term may not fit with the other security terms in this list, it is a popular feature that should be discussed. SSO is a concept, or a technical mechanism, that allows the user to only authenticate once to her client, so that she does not have to memorize many usernames and passwords for other Web sites, Web services, and server applications. SSO blends the concepts of authentication and authorization; enabling other servers to validate a user's identity and what the user is allowed to do. There are many technology enablers for SSO, including Kerberos, Secure Assertion Markup Language (SAML), and other cryptographic protocols.

Confidentiality. When sensitive information is transmitted, keeping it secret is important. It is common practice to satisfy confidentiality requirements with encryption.

Integrity. In a network, making sure data has not been altered in transit is imperative. Validating a message's integrity means using techniques that prove that data has not been altered in transit. Usually, techniques such as hash codes and MAC (Message Authentication Codes) are used for this purpose.

Nonrepudiation. The process of proving legally that a user has performed a transaction is called nonrepudiation. Using digital signatures provides this capability.

In many environments, satisfying these security concerns is vital. We defined the preceding terms from the Web service's perspective, but it is important to know that these security basics may need to be satisfied between every point. That is, a user may want assurance that he's talking to the right Web service, and the Web service may want assurance that it is talking to the right user. In addition, every point in between the user and the Web service (a portal, middleware, etc.) may want to satisfy concerns of authentication, authorization, confidentiality, integrity, and nonrepudiation. Figure 4.9 shows a good depiction of the distributed nature of Web services and its impact on security.

In the figure, if the user authenticates to the portal, how do the next two Web services and the back-end legacy application know the user's identity? If there is any sort of SSO solution, you wouldn't want the user to authenticate four times. Also, between the points in the figure, do the back-end applications have to authenticate, validate integrity, or encrypt data to each other to maintain confidentiality? If messages pass through multiple points, how does auditing work? It is possible that certain organizations may have security policies that address these issues, and if the security policies exist, the ability to address them with solutions for Web services is important.

Fortunately, technologies for Web services security and XML security have been evolving over the past few years. Some of these technologies are XML Signature, XML Encryption, XKMS, SAML, XACML, and WS-Security. This section discusses these technologies, as well as the Liberty Alliance Project.

Isn't Secure Sockets Layer Enough Security?

Many people ask the question, "Since SOAP lies on HTTP, won't Secure Sockets Layer (SSL) offer Web services adequate protection?" SSL is a point-to-point protocol that can be used for mutual or one-way authentication, and it is used to encrypt data between two points. In environments with a simple client and server, an HTTPS session may be enough to protect the confidentiality of the data in the transmission. However, because SSL occurs between two points, it does little to protect every point shown in Figure 4.9.

In a multiple-point scenario, where a user's client talks to a portal, which talks to a Web service, which in turn talks to another Web service, one or more SSL connections will not propagate proof of an original user's authentication and authorization credentials between all of those nodes—and assurance of message integrity gets lost, as there is more distance between the original user and the eventual Web service. In addition, many organizations do not want SOAP method invocations coming through their firewall if they are encrypted and cannot see them. Although SSL accomplishes a piece of the security puzzle, other technologies need to be used to accomplish security goals of Web services.

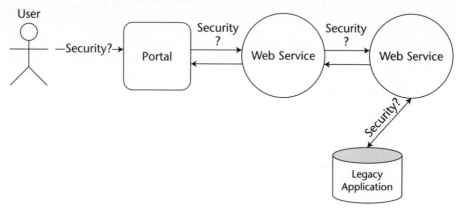

Figure 4.9　Protection at every point?

XML Signature

XML Signature is a W3C Recommendation that provides a means to validate message *integrity* and *nonrepudiation*. With XML Signature, any part of an XML document can be digitally signed. In fact, multiple parts of an XML document can be signed by different people or applications. XML Signature, sometimes called XML-DSIG or XML-SIG, relies on public key technology in which the hash (or message digest) of a message is cryptographically signed. Because of the nature of public key signatures, anyone with the signer's digital certificate (or public key) can validate that the signer indeed signed the message, providing legal proof that the signer cannot refute. A trusted third party can look at the message and validate that the message was indeed digitally signed by the sender. A digitally signed message can verify the message's origin and content, which can also serve as *authentication* of SOAP messages. For example, in Figure 4.9, the user could sign part of the message that is initially sent to the portal and that initially needs to be read by the last Web service. When that part of the message gets to the final Web service, it can validate that the user indeed sent the message.

XML digital signatures will play an important role in Web services security. If a Web service sells widgets, and a purchase order for 500 widgets is made, making sure that the message wasn't altered (for example, someone changing the purchase to 5000 widgets) will be important, as will be ensuring that the purchaser digitally signed the purchase order to provide the legal proof. In a purchasing scenario, validating the purchase order will be more important than hiding its contents (with encryption, for example).

XML Encryption

XML Encryption is a technology and W3C Candidate Recommendation that handles *confidentiality*; it can hide sensitive content, so that only the intended recipient can read the sensitive information. In an XML file, different parts of the document can be encrypted, while other parts can remain unencrypted. This can be helpful with Web services, when messages may be sent to multiple points before the receiver gets the message. Different ciphers (encryption mechanisms) can be used, including symmetric (secret key) and public key encryption. If confidentiality is a factor in Web services, a part of the application-specific SOAP message may be encrypted to the intended recipient. For example, in Figure 4.9, one of the back-end Web services may encrypt a piece of information so that only the intended user can see the contents of the message. Although the message may travel through many servers, only the intended user should be able to read the message.

XML encryption will also play an important role in Web services security. In the purchasing scenario we discussed in the previous section, on XML Signature, we provided an example of a Web service that sells widgets. While the purchase request itself may be signed, it may be important to encrypt confidential information, such as the credit card number.

XKMS

XML Key Management Specification (XKMS) is a W3C Note that was developed jointly by the W3C and the IETF, and it specifies protocols for registering and distributing public keys. It is something that is intended for use in conjunction with XML Signature and XML Encryption. XKMS is composed of the XML Key Information Service Specification (X-KISS) and the XML Key Registration Service Specification (X-KRSS). These protocols can be used with SOAP for securely distributing and finding key information.

SAML

Security Assertion Markup Language (SAML) is an OASIS standard that has received industrywide support and acceptance, and it promises to be key in the achievement of SSO in Web services. An initiative driven by OASIS that is used for passing *authentication* and *authorization* information between parties. SAML provides "assertions" of trust. That is, an application can *assert* that it authenticated a user, and that the user has certain privileges. A SAML document can be digitally signed using XML Signature, providing *nonrepudiation* of a user's original authentication, identity, and authorization credentials. Because SAML is used to distribute information between platforms and organizations, regardless of how many points it crosses, it can solve tough challenges in Web services security. In Figure 4.9, for example, if the portal authenticates the user "Alice" and knows that Alice has the "Producer" role, the portal application will attach this assertion to a SOAP message with the request to the next Web service. The next Web service, seeing that it can validate the portal's identity by validating its digital signature, can then grant or deny access to the user based on the user's role. SAML is an OASIS standard, and it has industrywide support. It is a key technology enabler in SSO initiatives such as the Liberty Alliance Project, and a working draft of a WS-Security profile of SAML has been recently released. Vendors are releasing toolkits for developers to use, and SAML shows much promise.

XACML

Extensible Access Control Markup Language (XACML) is an initiative driven by OASIS that expresses access control policy (*authentication* and *authorization* information) for XML documents and data sources. It is currently under development. In simple terms, it relates to SAML in the sense that SAML provides the mechanism of propagating authentication and authorization information between services and servers, and XACML *is* the authentication and authorization information. The idea of XACML is that XML documents (or SOAP messages themselves) can describe the policy of who can access them, which has interesting potential. It remains to be seen whether XACML will play a major role in Web services.

WS-Security

The WS-Security specification was released in April 2002 by Microsoft, IBM, and VeriSign, and is a specification that describes enhancements to SOAP messaging to provide protection through *integrity*, *confidentiality*, and *message authentication*. It combines SOAP with XML Encryption and XML Signature, and is intended to complement other security models and other security technologies. WS-Security also includes a family of specifications, including specifications unveiled in December 2002: WS-Policy, WS-Trust, and WS-SecureConversation. Because the corporate sponsors of this specification are so influential, the future may be bright for these specifications.

Liberty Alliance Project

The Liberty Alliance Project was established by a group of corporations with the purpose of protecting consumer privacy and establishing an open standard for achieving "federated network identity" for SSO across multiple networks, domains, and organizations. Using the specifications of this project, organizations have the potential to partner in a "federation" so that the credentials of users can be trusted by a group. Federated SSO enables users to sign on once to one site and subsequently use other sites within a group without having to sign on again. The Liberty Alliance released specifications in the summer of 2002, and these specifications include protocols that use XML Encryption, XML Signature, and SAML.

Where Security Is Today

Currently, security is a major hole in Web services, but the good news is that standards organizations and vendors, realizing the promise of these services, are frantically working on this problem. At this writing, XML Encryption, XML Signature, and SAML seem to hold the most promise from a standards perspective; these standards have been developed for quite a while, and software products are beginning to support their usage. At the same time, WS-Security and the Liberty Alliance Project are embracing some of these core standards and marrying them with SOAP-based Web services. Much of the growth, development, and future of Web services security is happening with WS-Security and the Liberty Alliance camps, and technologists should keep an eye on their progress.

Because of the changes occurring in these security drafts related to Web services, much emphasis today is being placed on EAI in internal deployments of Web services. Many organizations are exposing their internal applications as Web services to allow interoperability within their enterprise, rather than opening them up to external B2B applications that may make them vulnerable to security risks. Organizations and programs that need to focus on the security of Web services have been early adopters of SAML, XML Encryption, and XML Signature with Web services, and have been presenting their solutions, findings, and lessons learned to groups and standards bodies.[2]

What's Next for Web Services?

As Web services evolve, there is great potential in two major areas: grid computing and semantics. This section briefly discusses these two areas.

Grid-Enabled Web Services

Grid computing is a technology concept that can achieve flexible, secure, and coordinated resource sharing among dynamic collections of individuals, institutions, and resources.[3] One popular analogy of grid computing is the electric

---

[2]Kevin T. Smith, "Solutions for Web Services Security: Lessons Learned in a Department of Defense Program," Web Services for the Integrated Enterprise-OMG's Second Workshop on Web Services, Modeling, Architectures, Infrastructures and Standards, April 2003, http://www.omg.org/news/meetings/webservices2003usa/.

[3]Foster, Kesselman, Tuecke, "The Anatomy of the Grid: Enabling Scalable Virtual Organizations," *International J. Supercomputer Applications* 15, no.3, (2001).

utility grid, which makes power available in our homes and businesses. A user connects to this system with a power outlet, without having to know where the power is coming from and without scheduling an appointment to receive power at any given instant. The power amount that the user requires is automatically provided, the power meter records the power consumed by the user, and the user is charged for the power that is used. In a grid-computing environment, a user or application can connect to a computational grid with a simple interface (a Web portal or client application) and obtain resources without having to know where the resources are. Like the electricity grid, these resources are provided automatically.

A *computational grid* is a collection of distributed systems that can perform operations. Each individual system may have limitations, but when hundreds, thousands, or millions of systems work together in a distributed environment, much computing power can be unleashed. In a Web services environment, such a concept brings more distributed power to the network. If you want an online production system based on Web services that serves millions of customers, you will need load balancing and fault tolerance on a massive scale. The marriage of grid computing to Web services may bring stability in such a dynamic environment. When a Web service shuts down, the network grid should be able to route a request to a substitute Web service. Web services could use a distributed number of machines for processing power. Distributing Web services can create large groups of collaborating Web services that could solve problems on a massive scale.

Work being done by the Globus Project (http://www.globus.org/) will allow grids to offer computing resources as Web services to open up the next phase of distributed computing. Globus will add tools to its Open Grid Services Architecture (OGSA) that deliver integration with Web services technologies. Vendors such as Sun, IBM, and The Mind Electric will be implementing grid-enabled Web services as products.

A Semantic Web of Web Services

The Semantic Web and Web services go hand in hand. XML, a self-describing language, is not enough. WSDL, a language that describes the SOAP interfaces to Web services, is not enough. Automated support is needed in dealing with numerous specialized data formats. In the next 10 years, we will see semantics to describe problems and business processes in specialized domains. Ontologies will be this key enabling concept for the Semantic Web, interweaving human understanding of symbols with machine processibility.[4]

[4]Dieter Fensel, "Semantic Enabled Web Services," XML-Web Services ONE Conference, June 7, 2002.

Much effort is going into ontologies in Web services. DARPA Agent Markup Language Services (DAML-S) is an effort that is specifically addressing this area. Built on the foundation of Resource Description Framework (RDF), RDF Schema, and DAML+OIL, DAML-S provides an upper ontology for describing properties and capabilities of Web services in an unambiguous, computer-interpretable markup language.[5] Simply put, DAML-S is an ontology for Web services. In addition, Semantic Web Enabled Web Services (SWWS) was developed in August 2002 to provide a comprehensive Web service description framework and discovery framework, and to provide scalable Web service mediation. Together, both of these technologies have the potential to increase automated usability of Web services.

As we build ontologies (models of how things work), we will be able to use this common language to describe Web services and the payloads they contain in much more detail. The rest of this book focuses on this vision.

Summary

In this chapter, we have given you a high-level introduction to Web services. In defining Web services, we gave business reasons and possible implementations of Web service technologies. We provided an overview of the basic technologies of Web services, we discussed orchestration and security in Web services, and we provided a vision of where we believe Web services will be tomorrow.

Web services have become the standardized method for interfacing with applications. Various software vendors of new and legacy systems are beginning to provide Web services for their application platforms, and this trend is leading to quick and inexpensive application integration across platforms and operating systems. Businesses are currently deploying internal Web services-related projects, creating powerful EAI processes, and the development of B2B Web services in extranet environments and global Internet environments is on the horizon. We are currently at the beginning of the evolution of Web services. As ontologies are developed to provide richer descriptive content, and as distributed technologies such as grid computing merge with Web services, the future is very bright.

[5]Sheila McIllraith, "Semantic Enabled Web Services," XML-Web Services ONE Conference, June 7, 2002.

CHAPTER 5

Understanding the Resource Description Framework

*"In short, the Semantic Web offers powerful new possi-
bilities and a revolution in function. These capabilities
will arrive sooner if we stop squabbling and realize that
the rift between XML and RDF-based languages is now
down to the minor technical details easily ironed out in
the standards process or kludged by designing interoperable tools."*

**—James Hendler and Bijan Parsia,
"XML and the Semantic Web,"** *XML-Journal*

I n this chapter, you will learn what the Resource Description Framework (RDF) is, why it has not yet been widely adopted and how that will change, how RDF is based on a simple model that is distinct from the RDF syntax, and how RDF Schema is layered on top of RDF to provide support for class modeling. We then examine some current applications of RDF, including noncontextual modeling and inference. We conclude the chapter by examining some of the current tools for editing and storing RDF. After reading this chapter, you should have a firm understanding of how RDF provides the logical underpinnings of the Semantic Web.

What Is RDF?

At the simplest level, the Resource Description Framework is an XML-based language to describe resources. While the definition of "resource" can be quite broad, let's begin with the common understanding of a resource as an electronic file available via the Web. Such a resource is accessed via a Uniform Resource Locator (URL). While XML documents attach meta data to parts of a document, one use of RDF is to create meta data about the document as a standalone entity. In other words, instead of marking up the internals of a document, RDF captures meta data about the "externals" of a document, like the author, the creation date, and type. A particularly good use of RDF is to describe resources, which are "opaque" like images or audio files. Figure 5.1 displays an application, which uses RDF to describe an image resource.

The RDFPic application is a demonstration application developed by the W3C to embed RDF meta data inside JPEG images. The application can work in conjunction with the W3C's Jigsaw Web server to automatically extract the RDF meta data from images stored on the server. As you see in Figure 5.1, the application loads the image on the right side and allows data entry in a form on the left side. The tabbed panels on the left side allow you to load custom RDF schemas to describe the image. The two built-in schemas available for describing an image are the Dublin Core (www.dublincore.org) elements and a technical schema with meta data properties on the camera used. Besides embedding the meta data in the photo, you can export the RDF annotations to an external file, as shown in Listing 5.1.

```xml
<?xml version='1.0' encoding='ISO-8859-1'?>
  <rdf:RDF xmlns:rdf="http://www.w3.org/1999/02/22-rdf-syntax-ns#"
      xmlns:rdfs="http://www.w3.org/TR/1999/PR-rdf-schema-19990303#"
      xmlns:s0="http://www.w3.org/2000/PhotoRDF/dc-1-0#"
      xmlns:s1="http://sophia.inria.fr/~enerbonn/rdfpiclang#"
      xmlns:s2="http://www.w3.org/2000/PhotoRDF/technical-1-0#">
    <rdf:Description
rdf:about="http://www.c2i2.com/~budstv/images/shop1.jpg">
      <s0:relation>part-of Store Front</s0:relation>
      <s0:type>image</s0:type>
      <s0:format>image/jpeg</s0:format>
      <s1:xmllang>en</s1:xmllang>
      <s0:description>Buddy Belden's work bench for
TV/VCR repair</s0:description>
      <s2:camera>Kodak EasyShare</s2:camera>
      <s0:title>TV Shop repair bench</s0:title>
    </rdf:Description>
  </rdf:RDF>
```

Listing 5.1 RDF generated by RDFPic.

The first thing you should notice about Listing 5.1 is the consistent use of namespaces on all elements in the listing. In the root element <rdf:RDF>, four namespaces are declared. The root element specifies this document is an RDF document. An RDF document contains one or more "descriptions" of resources. A *description* is a set of statements about a resource. The <rdf: Description> element contains an rdf:about attribute that refers to the resource being described. In Listing 5.1, the rdf:about attribute points to the URL of a

JPEG image called shop1.jpg. The rdf:about attribute is critical to understanding RDF because all resources described in RDF must be denoted via a URI. The child elements of the Description element are all properties of the resource being described. Two properties are bolded, one in the Dublin Core namespaces and one in the technical namespace. The values of those properties are stored as the element content. In summary, Listing 5.1 has demonstrated a syntax where we describe a resource, a resource's properties, and the property values. This three-part model is separate from the RDF syntax. The RDF syntax in Listing 5.1 is considered to be one (of many) serializations of the RDF model. Now let's examine the RDF model.

The RDF model is often called a "triple" because it has three parts, as described previously. Though described in terms of resource properties in the preceding text, in the knowledge representation community, those three parts are described in terms of the grammatical parts of a sentence: subject, predicate, and object. Figure 5.2 displays the elements of the tri-part model and the symbology associated with the elements when graphing them.

Figure 5.1 RDFPic application describing an image.

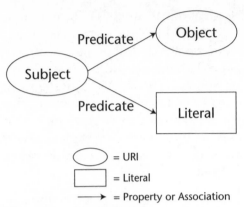

Figure 5.2 The RDF triple.

The key elements of an RDF triple are as follows:

Subject.   In grammar, this is the noun or noun phrase that is the doer of the action. In the sentence "The company sells batteries," the subject is "the company." The subject of the sentence tells us what the sentence is about. In logic, this is the term about which something is asserted. In RDF, this is the resource that is being described by the ensuing predicate and object. Therefore, in RDF, we want a URI to stand for the unique concept "company" like "http://www.business.org/ontology/#company" to denote that we mean a form of business ownership and not friends coming for a visit.

NOTE   An RDF resource stands for either electronic resources, like files, or concepts, like "person." One way to think of an RDF resource is as "anything that has identity."

Predicate.   In grammar, this is the part of a sentence that modifies the subject and includes the verb phrase. Returning to our sentence "The company sells batteries," the predicate is the phrase "sells batteries." In other words, the predicate tells us something about the subject. In logic, a predicate is a function from individuals (a particular type of subject) to truth-values with an arity based on the number of arguments it has. In RDF, a predicate is a relation between the subject and the object. Thus, in RDF, we would define a unique URI for the concept "sells" like "http://www.business.org/ontology/#sells".

Object.   In grammar this is a noun that is acted upon by the verb. Returning to our sentence "The company sells batteries," the object is the noun "batteries." In logic, an object is acted upon by the predicate. In RDF, an object is either a resource referred to by the predicate or a literal value. In our example, we would define a unique URI for "batteries" like "http://www.business.org/ontology/#batteries".

Statement. In RDF, the combination of the preceding three elements, subject, predicate, and object, as a single unit. Figure 5.3 displays a graph representation of two RDF statements. These two statements illustrate the concepts in Figure 5.2. Note that the object can be represented by a resource or by a literal value. The graphing is done via a W3C application called IsaViz available at http://www.w3.org/2001/11/IsaViz/.

We should stress that resources in RDF must be identified by resource IDs, which are URIs with optional anchor IDs. This is important so that a unique concept can be unambiguously identified via a globally unique ID. This is a key difference between relying on semantics over syntax. The syntactic meaning of words is often ambiguous. For example, the word "bark" in the sentences "The bark felt rough" and "The bark was loud" has two different meanings; however, by giving a unique URI to the concept of tree bark like "www.business.org/ontology/plant/#bark", we can always refer to a single definition of bark.

Capturing Knowledge with RDF

There is wide consensus that the triple-based model of RDF is simpler than the RDF/XML format, which is called the "serialization format." Because of this, a variety of simpler formats have been created to quickly capture knowledge expressed as a list of triples. Let's walk through a simple scenario where we express concepts in four different ways: as natural language sentences, in a simple triple notation called N3, in RDF/XML serialization format, and, finally, as a graph of the triples.

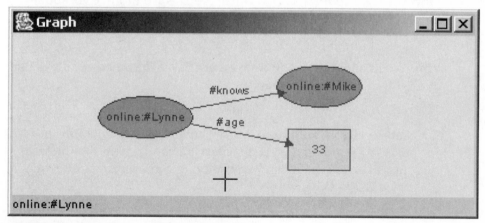

Figure 5.3 A graph of two RDF statements.

IsaViz is copyrighted by the W3C. All Rights Reserved.
http://www.w3.org/Consortium/Legal/.

Following the linguistic model of subject, predicate, and object, we start with three English statements:

```
Buddy Belden owns a business.
The business has a Web site accessible at http://www.c2i2.com/~budstv.
Buddy is the father of Lynne.
```

In your business, you could imagine extracting sentences like these from daily routines and processes in your business. There are even products that can scan email and documents for common nouns and verbs. In other words, capturing statements in a formal way allows the slow aggregation of a corporate knowledge base in which you capture processes and best practices, as well as spot trends. This is knowledge management via a bottom-up approach instead of a top-down approach. Now let's examine how we capture the preceding sentences in N3 notation:

```
<#Buddy> <#owns> <#business>.
<#business> <#has-website> <http://www.c2i2.com/~budstv>.
<#Buddy> <#father-of> <#Lynne>.
```

From each sentence we have extracted the relevant subject, predicate, and object. The # sign means the URI of the concepts would be the current document. This is a shortcut done for brevity; it is more accurate to replace the # sign with an absolute URI like "http://www.c2i2.com/buddy/ontology" as a formal namespace. In N3 you can do that with a prefix tag like this:

```
@prefix bt:   <http://www.c2i2.com/buddy/ontology/>.
```

Using the prefix, our resources would be as follows:

```
<bt:Buddy> <bt:owns> <bt:business>.
```

Of course, we could also add other prefixes from other vocabularies like the Dublin Core:

```
@prefix dc:   <http://purl.org/dc/elements/1.1/>.
```

This would allow us to add a statement like "The business title is Buddy's TV and VCR Service" in this way:

```
<bt:business> <dc:title> "Buddy's TV and VCR Service".
```

Tools are available to automatically convert the N3 notation into RDF/XML format. One popular tool is the Jena Semantic Web toolkit from Hewlett-Packard, available at http://www.hpl.hp.com/semweb/. Listing 5.2 is the generated RDF/XML syntax.

```
<rdf:RDF
    xmlns:RDFNsId1='#'
    xmlns:rdf='http://www.w3.org/1999/02/22-rdf-syntax-ns#'>
    <rdf:Description rdf:about='#Buddy'>
        <RDFNsId1:owns>
            <rdf:Description rdf:about='#business'>
                <RDFNsId1:has-website
rdf:resource='http://www.c2i2.com/~budstv' />
            </rdf:Description>
        </RDFNsId1:owns>
        <RDFNsId1:father-of rdf:resource='#Lynne'/>
    </rdf:Description>
</rdf:RDF>
```

Listing 5.2 RDF/XML generated from N3.

The first thing you should notice is that in the RDF/XML syntax, one RDF statement is nested within the other. It is this sometimes nonintuitive translation of a list of statements into a hierarchical XML syntax that makes the direct authoring of RDF/XML syntax difficult; however, since there are tools to generate correct syntax for you, you can just focus on the knowledge engineering and not author the RDF/XML syntax. Second, note how predicates are represented by custom elements (like RDFNsId1:owns or RDFNsId1:father-of). The objects are represented by either the rdf:resource attribute or a literal value.

WARNING

The RDF/XML serialization of predicates and objects can use either elements or attributes. Therefore, it is better to use a conforming RDF parser that understands how to translate either format into a triple instead of a custom parser that may not understand such subtlety.

Figure 5.4 displays an IsaViz graph of the three RDF statements.

While the triple is the centerpiece of RDF, other elements of RDF offer additional facilities in composing these knowledge graphs. The other RDF facilities are discussed in the next section.

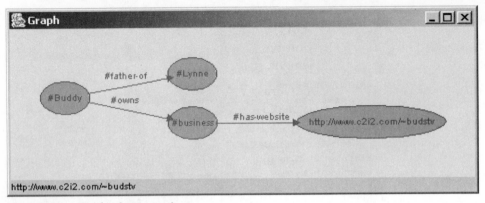

Figure 5.4 Graph of N3 notation.
IsaViz is copyrighted by the W3C. All Rights Reserved.
http://www.w3.org/Consortium/Legal/.

Other RDF Features

The rest of the features of RDF assist in increasing the composeability of statements. Two main categories of features do this: a simple container model and reification (making statements about statements). The container model allows groups of resources or values. Reification allows higher-level statements to capture knowledge about other statements. Both of these features add some complexity to RDF, so we will demonstrate them with basic examples.

We need a container to model the sentence "The people at the meeting were Joe, Bob, Susan, and Ralph." To do this in RDF, we create a container, called a bag, for the objects in the statement, as shown in Listing 5.3.

```
<rdf:RDF
    xmlns:ex='http://www.example.org/sample#'
    xmlns:rdf='http://www.w3.org/1999/02/22-rdf-syntax-ns#'>
    <rdf:Description rdf:about='ex:meeting'>
        <ex:attendees>
        <rdf:Bag rdf:ID="people">
            <rdf:li rdf:resource='ex:Joe'/>
            <rdf:li rdf:resource='ex:Bob'/>
            <rdf:li rdf:resource='ex:Susan'/>
            <rdf:li rdf:resource='ex:Ralph'/>
        </rdf:Bag>
        </ex:attendees>
    </rdf:Description>
</rdf:RDF>
```

Listing 5.3 An RDF bag container.

In Listing 5.3 we see one rdf:Description element (one subject), one predicate (attendees), and an object, which is a bag (or collection) of resources. A bag is an unordered collection where each element of the bag is referred to by an rdf:li or "list item" element. Figure 5.5 graphs the RDF in Listing 5.3.

Figure 5.5 nicely demonstrates that the "meeting" is "attended" by "people" and that people is a type of bag. The members of the bag are specially labeled as a member with an rdf:_# predicate. RDF containers are different than XML containers in that they are explicit. This is the same case as relations between elements, which are also implicit in XML, whereas such relations (synonymous with predicates) are explicit in RDF. This explicit modeling of containers and relations is an effort to remove ambiguity from our models so that computers can act reliably in our behalf. On the downside, such explicit modeling is harder than the implicit modeling in XML documents. This has had an effect on adoption, as discussed in the next section.

Three types of RDF containers are available to group resources or literals:

Bag.   An rdf:bag element is used to denote an unordered collection. Duplicates are allowed in the collection. An example of when to use a bag would be when all members of the collection are processed the same without concern for order.

Sequence.   An rdf:seq element is used to denote an ordered collection (a "sequence" of elements). Duplicates are allowed in the collection. One reason to use a sequence would be to preserve the alphabetical order of elements. Another example would be to process items in the order in which items were added to the document.

Alternate.   An rdf:alt element is used to denote a choice of multiple values or resources. This is referred to as a choice in XML. Some examples would be a choice of image formats (JPEG, GIF, BMP) or a choice of makes and models, or any time you wish to constrain a value to a limited set of legal values.

Now that we have added the idea of collections to our statements, we need a way to make statements either about the collection or about individual members of the collection. You can make statements about the collection by attaching an rdf:ID attribute to the container. Making statements about the individual members is the same as making any other statement by simply referring to the resource in the collection as the object of your statement.

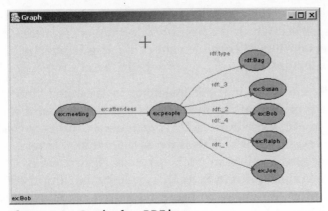

Figure 5.5 Graph of an RDF bag.

IsaViz is copyrighted by the W3C. All Rights Reserved.
http://www.w3.org/Consortium/Legal/.

While containers affect the modeling of a single statement (for example, an object becoming a collection of values), reification allows you to treat a statement as the object of another statement. This is often referred to as "making statements about statements" and is called *reification*. Listing 5.4 shows a simple example of reification.

```
@prefix : <http://example.org/onto#>.
@prefix earl: <http://www.w3.org/2001/03/earl/0.95#>.
@prefix rdf: <http://www.w3.org/1999/02/22-rdf-syntax-ns#>.
@prefix dc: <http://purl.org/dc/elements/1.1/>.

:Jane earl:asserts
    [ rdf:subject :MyPage;
      rdf:predicate earl:passes;
      rdf:object "Accessibility Tests" ];
  earl:email <mailto:Jane@example.org>;
  earl:name "Jane Jones".

:MyPage
  a earl:WebContent;
  dc:creator <http://example.org/onto/person/Mary/>.
```

Listing 5.4 N3 example of reification.

Listing 5.4 demonstrates (in N3 notation) that Jane has tested Mary's Web page and asserts that it passes the accessibility tests. The key part relating to reification is the statement with explicit subject, predicate, and object parts that are the object of "asserts." Listing 5.5 shows the same example in RDF:

```
<rdf:RDF
    xmlns:dc='http://purl.org/dc/elements/1.1/'
    xmlns:rdf='http://www.w3.org/1999/02/22-rdf-syntax-ns#'
    xmlns:earl='http://www.w3.org/2001/03/earl/0.95#'>
    <rdf:Description rdf:about='http://example.org/onto#Jane'>
        <earl:asserts rdf:parseType='Resource'>
            <rdf:subject>
                <earl:WebContent
                    rdf:about='http://example.org/onto#MyPage'>
                    <dc:creator
                    rdf:resource='http://example.org/onto/person/Mary/'/>
                </earl:WebContent>
            </rdf:subject>
            <rdf:predicate>
             rdf:resource='http://www.w3.org/2001/03/earl/0.95#passes'/>
            <rdf:object>Accessibility Tests</rdf:object>
        </earl:asserts>
        <earl:email rdf:resource='mailto:Jane@example.org'/>
        <earl:name>Jane Jones</earl:name>
    </rdf:Description>
</rdf:RDF>
```

Listing 5.5 Generated RDF example of reification.

The method for reifying statements in RDF is to model the statement as a resource via explicitly specifying the subject, predicate, object, and type of the statement. Once the statement is modeled, you can make statements about the modeled statement. The reification is akin to statements as argument instead of statements as fact, which is useful in cases where the trustworthiness of the source is carefully tracked (for example, human intelligence collection). This is important to understand, as reification is not applicable to all data modeling tasks. It is easier to treat statements as facts.

Figure 5.6 displays a graph of the reified statement. Note that the statement is treated as a single entity via an anonymous node. The anonymous node is akin to a Description element without an rdf:about attribute. The rdf:parseType attribute in Listing 5.5 means that the content of the element is parsed similar to a new Description element.

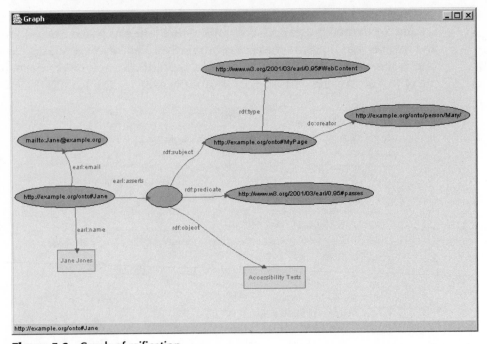

Figure 5.6 Graph of reification.

IsaViz is copyrighted by the W3C. All Rights Reserved. http://www.w3.org/Consortium/Legal/.

Admittedly, reification is not simple. Many people come to RDF understanding the basics of the triple but missing the utility of reification. Most databases treat data as facts, so it is a stretch to think about data as assertions. One commonsense application of reification is annotations of other people's work. Annotations, by nature, are statements about someone else's statements. So, clearly, reification fits there. At the same time, it will take training for developers and modelers to understand where to use reification and what rules apply to reified statements. In fact, some current Semantic Web applications explicitly eliminate reification from their knowledge bases to reduce the complexity. Complexity hurts adoption, and the adoption of RDF by mainstream developers has been significantly slower than other W3C technologies. The next section examines the reasons why.

Why Is RDF Not in the Mainstream?

The Resource Description Framework has been a W3C Recommendation (synonymous with standard) since February 22, 1999, only slightly more than a year after the XML 1.0 Recommendation. When giving briefings on the future of XML, we are thus surprised to learn that many people have never heard of RDF. Outside of the digital library and artificial intelligence communities, RDF has not achieved mindshare with developers or corporate management. A demonstration of this mindshare gap is to compare the adoption of XML to the adoption of RDF. One simple measure is to compare, at this writing, the number of technical books on RDF versus XML and the number of commercial products supporting RDF versus XML as shown in Figure 5.7.

Figure 5.7 is based on simple Web queries of online retailers, and though not scientific, the disparity is so stark that you can easily confirm the results yourself. The Books column is a count of technical books available on Amazon.com, Software Products is a count of software available from Programmer's Paradise (www.programmersparadise.com), and Vendor Site Hits is a count of Web results returned by a search of Microsoft.com. Similar ratios were found when examining other sites or even the Web at large via a Google.com search.

Why has RDF adoption been so weak? There are multiple reasons:

RDF doesn't yet play well with XML documents.   At this writing, you cannot validate RDF embedded in other XML or XHTML documents because of RDF's open grammar. In other words, RDF allows you to mix in any namespace-qualified elements you want (as demonstrated in the preceding examples). Additionally, there is a fairly esoteric issue regarding a difference between how XML Schema and RDF process namespaces. This has led many people to view RDF and XML documents as two separate paths for meta data. Therefore, the businesses traveling along the XML/XHTML path assume that their direction is incompatible with the RDF path. This is not true. The fact that RDF is serialized as XML means that both XML Schema and RDF share a common syntax. In the debates on this subject, it is clear that the intent of the W3C RDF Working Group is to resolve these differences so that RDF can be successfully embedded in XHTML and XML documents. Additionally, several tools mix RDF and HTML (including SMORE, demonstrated in the next section), so it is clear that bridges are being built to resolve this issue. Lastly, several solutions to this issue were proposed by Sean Palmer in the document "RDF in HTML: Approaches," available at http://infomesh.net/2002/rdfinhtml/.

Parts of RDF are complex.   Several factors combined make RDF significantly more complex than XML documents. The three chief culprits in this equation are mixing metaphors, the serialization syntax, and reification. First, the model mixes metaphors by using terms from different data representation communities to include linguistic, object-oriented, and relational data, as shown in Table 5.1. This type of flexibility is a double-edged sword: Good because it unifies modeling concepts from different domains, yet bad in that it causes confusion. This attempt to meld viewpoints is stated in the RDF Recommendation: "As a result of many communities coming together and agreeing on basic principles of meta data representation and transport, RDF has drawn influence from several different sources. The main influences have come from the Web standardization community itself in the form of HTML meta data and PICS, the library community, the structured document community in the form of SGML and more importantly XML, and also the knowledge representation (KR) community."[1] One other potential problem with such metaphor unification is frustration by inexact or poor mapping to the original concepts specified by each community.

Second, RDF syntax allows the RDF graph to be serialized via attributes or elements. In other words, you can express one RDF model in two different ways. This can be yet another problem for validation due to too much flexibility.

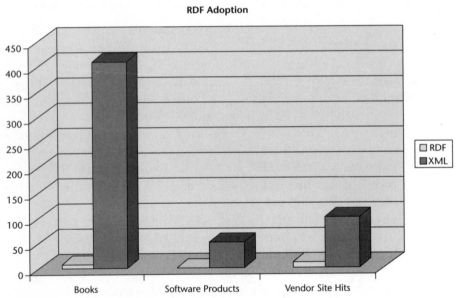

Figure 5.7 RDF adoption.

Table 5.1 RDF Metaphors for Its Modeling Primitives

METAPHOR	PART1	PART2	PART3
Language	Subject	Predicate	Object
Object-oriented	Class	Property	Value
Graph	Node	Edge	Node
Web link	Source	Link	Destination
Database	Entity	Relation	Entity

[1] Resource Description Framework (RDF) Model and Syntax Specification, W3C Recommendation, February 22, 1999.

Third, the hierarchical RDF/XML syntax (called the "striped" syntax) is difficult to author by hand and is better left to tools. In general, it is confusing to represent lists of statements as a hierarchical tree. The current method used in the RDF/XML syntax makes differentiating between objects and properties very difficult. Lastly, reification has not yet proven itself and adds another level of abstraction to the RDF model. For XML developers first trying to move from the simple name/value pairs of XML to the triple, statements about statements are too complex. While reification matches natural language, it is a foreign concept to all of the other data communities. In other words, if you deem a triple to be a fact, you don't want assertions saying it is not a fact. Most applications treat data as facts and implement data integrity procedures to ensure that axiom holds true. With reification, nothing is bedrock; everything is just an assertion, and you must follow a potentially infinite chain of assertions about assertions where one may contradict another at any time. Several RDF implementations and knowledge bases disallow the use of reification. Reification is a feature of RDF that is not for every application and can be safely avoided. The authors believe that the complexity of RDF will be resolved by the emerging set of tools, training and familiarity with the concepts, and the willingness to accept some additional complexity for the additional benefits of higher-fidelity meta data.

Early RDF examples are weak.   RDF applications like Dublin Core (DC) and RDF Site Summary (RSS) are weak in that they do not highlight the unique characteristics of RDF. It is important to note that both of these examples are highlighted in the RDF Primer (available at http://www .w3.org/RDF). While the Dublin Core elements are useful standard definitions for resource description, they are not exclusive to RDF and can be used in HTML or XML documents. Table 5.2 demonstrates a Dublin Core description in RDF and HTML.

In Table 5.2, it is evident that the Dublin Core elements are a vocabulary that means the same thing in either representation format. In RDF, they are represented as an element (like dc:title), and in HTML, they are represented as attributes of the meta element. Therefore, the Dublin Core elements are not strictly an RDF application but a small vocabulary that can be used in RDF as well as in other markup languages. The RDF Site Summary (RSS) is an XML syntax that has flip-flopped between an RDF syntax and an XML Schema syntax. The acronym RSS originally stood for Rich Site Summary as an XML document, then changed to RDF Site Summary with the 1.0 version and recently has been reintroduced by Dave Winer of UserLand Software as the Real Simple Syndication format as RSS 2.0. The purpose of RSS is to provide syndication of a set of story headlines called channels. The developers in favor of an XML Schema version of RSS point to its simpler syntax and easy validation. In Table 5.3 we see the differences between the implementations of RSS. The XML syntax is simple and straightforward, but it does not make use of namespaces. The RDF syntax has four significant differences:

- The root element must be rdf:RDF.
- Namespaces must be used.
- The rdf:Seq container is used to list the resources described in the channel.
- RDF has required attributes like rdf:about and rdf:resource.

An important element of the XML RSS version (on the left) is the declaration of a Document Type Definition (DTD) to validate the contents of the document. This switching back and forth between a DTD and RDF demonstrates the fact that these applications do not highlight RDF's main strength: predicates.

Table 5.2 Dublin Core in RDF and HTML

RDF VERSION	HTML VERSION

`<?xml version="1.0" ?>`
`<!DOCTYPE rdf:RDF PUBLIC "-//DUBLIN CORE//DCMES DTD 2002/07/31//EN"`
`"http://dublincore.org/documents/2002/07/31/dcmes-xml/dcmes-xml-dtd.dtd">`
`<rdf:RDF`
`xmlns:rdf =`
`"http://www.w3.org/1999/02/22-rdf-syntax-ns#"`
`xmlns:dc =`
`"http://purl.org/dc/elements/1.1/" >`
`<rdf:Description`
`about="http://c2i2.com/~budstv" />`
`     `**`<dc:title> Buddys TV Service`**
`Web Site </dc:title>`
`     <dc:creator>Michael`
`Daconta</dc:creator>`
`     <dc:format>text/html</dc:format>`
`     <dc:language>en</dc:language>`
`  </rdf:Description>`
`</rdf:RDF>`
	`<HTML>`
	`<HEAD>`
	` <TITLE> Buddy's TV Service </TITLE>`
	` <link rel = "schema.DC"`
	`    href  =`
	`"http://purl.org/DC/elements/1.0/">`
	` `**`<meta name    = "DC.Title"`**
	`    `**`content = "Buddys TV Services`**
	`Web Site">`
	` <meta name    = "DC.Creator"`
	`    content = "Michael Daconta">`
	` <meta name    = "DC.Format"`
	`    content = "text/html">`
	` <meta name    = "DC.Language"`
	`    content = "en">`
	`</HEAD>`
	`<BODY>`
	`<H1> <CENTER> Buddy's TV Service`
	`</CENTER> </H1>`
	`<HR>`
	`<CENTER> <IMG SRC=`
	`"stripmap.jpg" /> </CENTER>`
	`<UL>`
	`<! — omitted for brevity —>`
	`</BODY>`
	`</HTML>`

Table 5.3 RSS in XML and in RDF

RSS IN XML	RSS IN RDF

```<?xml version="1.0" ?>```
```<!DOCTYPE rss PUBLIC```
```"-//Netscape Communications//DTD RSS 0.91//EN"```
```"http://my.netscape.com/publish/formats/rss-0.91.dtd">```
```<rss version="0.91">```
```<channel>```
```<title>Super News Site</title>```
```<link>http://snn.com</link>```
```<description>News for Insomniacs</description>```
```<language>en-us</language>```
```<copyright>Copyright 2003 SuperNews</copyright>```
```<managingEditor> editor@snn.com</managingEditor>```
```<webMaster>```
``` webmaster@snn.com```
```</webMaster>```
```<image>```
```<title>WriteTheWeb</title>```
```<url>http://snn.com/logo.gif</url>```
```<link>http://snn.com</link>```
```<width>88</width>```
```<height>31</height>```
```<description>News for insomniacs</description>```
```</image>```
```<item>```
```<title>The Next Web</title>```
```<link>http://snn.com/article1</link>```
```<description>This article explores how the semantic web will change business.</description>```
```</item>```
```<item>```
```<title>Syndication controversy</title>```
```<link>http://snn.com/article2</link>```
```<description>How the RSS format flip-flops have caused strife and confusion among developers.</description>```
```</item>```
```</channel>```
```</rss>```
	```<?xml version="1.0" ?>```
	```<rdf:RDF xmlns:rdf=```
	```"http://www.w3.org/1999/02/22-rdf-syntax-ns#"```
	```xmlns:dc="http://purl.org/dc/elements/1.1/"```
	```xmlns:sy=```
	```"http://purl.org/rss/1.0/modules/syndication/"```
	```xmlns:co="http://purl.org/rss/1.0/modules/company/"```
	```xmlns="http://purl.org/rss/1.0/" >```
	```<channel rdf:about=```
	```"http://snn.com">```
	```<title>News for Insomniacs</title>```
	```<link>http://snn.com</link>```
	```<description>News for Insomniacs</description>```
	```<dc:publisher>Super News Network</dc:publisher>```
	```<dc:creator>Michael Daconta</dc:creator>```
	```<sy:updatePeriod>hourly</sy:updatePeriod>```
	```<sy:updateFrequency>2</sy:updateFrequency>```
	```<image rdf:resource=```
	```"http://snn.com/logo.gif" />```
	```<items>```
	```<rdf:Seq>```
	```<rdf:li resource=```
	```"http://snn.com/article1" />```
	```<rdf:li resource=```
	```"http://snn.com/article2" />```
	```</rdf:Seq>```
	```</items>```
	```</channel>```
	```<image rdf:about="http://snn.com/logo.gif">```
	```<title>News for Insomniacs</title>```
	```<url>http://snn.com/logo.gif</url>```
	```<link>http://snn.com</link>```
	```</image>```
	```<item rdf:about=```
	```"http://snn.com/article1">```
	```<title>The Next Web</title>```

(continued)

Table 5.3   *(continued)*

RSS IN XML	RSS IN RDF

	`<link>http://snn.com/article1</link>`
	`<dc:description>`
	This article explores how the semantic web will change business.
	`</dc:description>`
	`<dc:publisher>Super News Network</dc:publisher>`
	`<co:name>XML.com</co:name>`
	`<co:market>NASDAQ</co:market>`
	`<co:symbol>SNN</co:symbol>`
	`</item>`
	`<item rdf:about="http://snn.com/article2">`
	`<title>Syndication Controversy</title>`
	`<dc:description>` How the RSS format flip-flops have caused strife and confusion among developers.`</dc:description>`
	`<link>http://snn.com/article2"/</link>`
	`</item>`
	`</rdf:RDF>`

The explicit expression of associations between entities is not available in XML documents and is therefore a major benefit of RDF. Two applications of RDF that stress association between entities are the Publishing Requirements for Industry Standard Metadata (PRISM), available at http://www.prismstandard.org, and the Friend Of A Friend (FOAF) vocabulary, available at http://xmlns.com/foaf/0.1/. While we will not go into the details of these formats, it is encouraging that the proficiency with RDF is growing to the point where compelling vocabularies are being developed.

We will close this section on a positive note, because we believe that RDF adoption will pick up. Like the proverbial Chinese bamboo tree, RDF is a technology that has a long lead time. The Chinese bamboo tree must be cultivated and nourished for four years with no visible signs of growth; however, in the first three months of the fifth year, the Chinese bamboo tree will grow 90 feet. The authors believe that RDF's watering and fertilizing has been in the form of mainstream adoption of XML and namespaces and that we are now entering that growth phase of RDF. Here are the five primary reasons that RDF's adoption will grow:

- Improved tutorials
- Improved tool support
- Improved XML Schema integration
- Ontologies
- Noncontextual modeling

Improved tutorials like this book, the W3C's RDF Primer, and resources on the Web fix the complexity issue. Improved tool support for RDF editing, visualizing, translation, and storage (like Jena and IsaViz, which we have seen, and Protégé, which we will see in the next section) fix the syntax problem by abstracting your applications away from the syntax. This not only isolates the awkward parts of the syntax but also future-proofs your applications via a tool to mediate the changes.

TIP

━━━━━ **Most RDF authors write their RDF assertions in N3 format and then convert the N3 to RDF/XML syntax via a conversion tool (like Jena's n3 program).**

Improved integration with XML documents is being pushed both inside and outside of the W3C, and many bridges are being built between these technology families. The RDF Core Working Group recently added the ability for RDF literals to be typed via XML Schema data types. Another example of RDF/XML document integration is an RDF schema available to validate the RDF in simple Dublin Core documents. This schema is available at http://www.dublincore.org/documents/dcmes-xml/. Another way to solve the validation problem is to have the namespace URI point to a document, which describes it as proposed by the Resource Directory Description Language (RDDL), available at http://www.rddl.org/. There is work under way to allow RDF assertions in RDDL. So, the momentum and benefits to combining XML and RDF are increasing, as highlighted in the article "Make Your XML RDF-Friendly" by Bob DuCharme and John Cowan, available at http://www.xml.com/pub/a/2002/10/30/rdf-friendly.html. Ontologies and ontology languages like the Web Ontology Language (OWL), discussed in Chapter 8, are layered on top of RDF.

Many see ontologies as the killer application for the Semantic Web and thus believe they will drive the adoption of RDF. In the next section, we examine RDF Schema, which is a lightweight ontology vocabulary layered on RDF. Lastly, ontologies are not the only killer application for RDF; noncontextual modeling makes RDF the perfect glue between systems and fixed data models. Noncontextual modeling is discussed in detail later in this chapter.

What Is RDF Schema?

RDF Schema is language layered on top of RDF. This layered approach to creating the Semantic Web has been presented by the W3C and Tim Berners-Lee as the "Semantic Web Stack," as displayed in Figure 5.8. The base of the stack is the concepts of universal identification (URI) and a universal character set (Unicode). Above those concepts, we layer the XML Syntax (elements, attributes, and angle brackets) and namespaces to avoid vocabulary conflicts. On top of XML are the triple-based assertions of the RDF model and syntax we discussed in the previous section. If we use the triple to denote a class, class property, and value, we can create class hierarchies for the classification and description of objects. This is the goal of RDF Schema, as discussed in this section.

Above RDF Schema we have ontologies (a taxonomy is a lightweight ontology, as described in Chapter 7, and robust ontology languages like OWL, described in Chapter 8). Above ontologies, we can add logic rules about the things in our ontologies. A rule language allows us to infer new knowledge and make decisions. Additionally, the rules layer provides a standard way to query and filter RDF. The rules layer is sort of an "introductory logic" capability, while the logic framework will be "advanced logic." The logic framework allows formal logic proofs to be shared. Lastly, with such robust proofs, a trust layer can be established for levels of application-to-application trust. This "web of trust" forms the third and final web in Tim Berners-Lee's three-part vision (collaborative web, Semantic Web, web of trust). Supporting this web of trust across the layers are XML Signature and XML Encryption, which are discussed in Chapter 6.

In this section, we focus on examining the RDF Schema layer in the Semantic Web stack. RDF Schema is a simple set of standard RDF resources and properties to enable people to create their own RDF vocabularies. The data model expressed by RDF Schema is the same data model used by object-oriented programming languages like Java. The data model for RDF Schema allows you to create classes of data. A *class* is defined as a group of things with common characteristics. In object-oriented programming (OOP), a class is defined as a template or blueprint for an object composed of characteristics (also called data members) and behaviors (also called methods). An object is one instance of a class. OO languages also allow classes to inherit characteristics and behaviors from a parent class (also called a super class). The software industry has recently standardized a single notation called the Unified Modeling Language (UML) to model class hierarchies. Figure 5.9 displays a UML diagram modeling two types of employees and their associations to the artifacts they write and the topics they know.

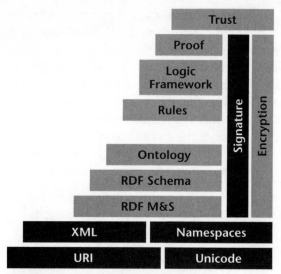

Figure 5.8 The Semantic Web Stack.

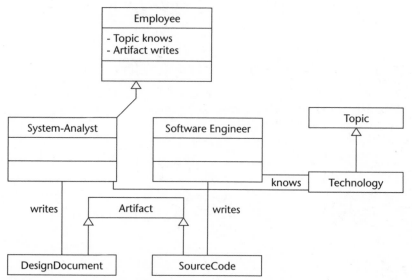

Figure 5.9 UML class diagram of employee expertise.

Figure 5.9 uses several UML symbols to denote the concepts of class, inheritance, and association. The rectangle with three sections is the symbol for a class. The three sections are for the class name, the class attributes (middle section), and the class behaviors or methods (bottom section). RDF Schema only uses the first two parts of a class, since it is for data modeling and not programming behaviors. Also, to reduce the size of the diagram, we eliminated the bottom two sections of the class for Topic, Technology, Artifact, and so on. Inheritance is when a subclass inherits the characteristics of a superclass. The arrow from the subclass to the superclass denotes this. The inheritance relation is often called "isa," as in "a software engineer *is a*(n) employee."

Lastly, a labeled line between two classes denotes an association (like knows or writes). The key point of Figure 5.9 is that we are modeling two types of employees: software engineer and system-analyst. The key difference between the employees that we want to capture is the different types of artifacts that they create. Whereas both employees may know about a technology, the key differentiator of developing source code to implement a technology is important enough to be formally captured in RDF. This is precisely the type of key determining factor that is often lost in a jumble of plaintext. So, let's see how we would model this in RDF Schema.

Figure 5.10 displays the Protégé open source ontology editor developed by Stanford University with the same class hierarchy. Protégé is available at http://protege.stanford.edu/. Protégé allows you to easily describe classes and class hierarchies.

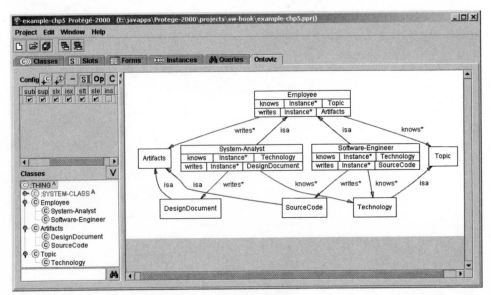

Figure 5.10 Improved expertise modeling via RDFS.

Notice in Figure 5.10 the right pane is a visualization of the ontology, while the left pane allows you to choose what class or classes to visualize from the class list (bottom left pane). The Protégé class structure is identical to the UML model except for the lack of behaviors. RDFS classes only have a name and properties. After modeling the classes, Protégé allows you to generate both the RDF schema and an RDF document if you create instances of the Schema (Figure 5.10 has one tab labeled "Instances"). Remember, a class is the blueprint from which you can create many instances. So, if the class describes the properties of an address like street, city, state, and zip code, you can create an number of instances of addresses like "3723 Saint Andrews Drive," "Sierra Vista," "Arizona," and "85650." Listing 5.6 is the RDF Schema for the class model in Figure 5.10. Listing 5.7 is an RDF document with instances of the classes in Listing 5.6.

```
<?xml version='1.0' encoding='ISO-8859-1'?>
<!DOCTYPE rdf:RDF [
    <!ENTITY rdf 'http://www.w3.org/1999/02/22-rdf-syntax-ns#'>
    <!ENTITY example_chp5
'http://protege.stanford.edu/example-chp5#'>
    <!ENTITY rdfs 'http://www.w3.org/TR/1999/PR-rdf-schema-19990303#'>
]>
<rdf:RDF xmlns:rdf="&rdf;"
    xmlns:example_chp5="&example_chp5;"
    xmlns:rdfs="&rdfs;">
<rdfs:Class rdf:about="&example_chp5;Artifacts"
    rdfs:label="Artifacts">
  <rdfs:subClassOf rdf:resource="&rdfs;Resource"/>
</rdfs:Class>
<rdfs:Class rdf:about="&example_chp5;DesignDocument"
    rdfs:label="DesignDocument">
  <rdfs:subClassOf rdf:resource="&example_chp5;Artifacts"/>
</rdfs:Class>
<rdfs:Class rdf:about="&example_chp5;Employee"
    rdfs:label="Employee">
  <rdfs:subClassOf rdf:resource="&rdfs;Resource"/>
</rdfs:Class>
<rdfs:Class rdf:about="&example_chp5;Software-Engineer"
    rdfs:label="Software-Engineer">
  <rdfs:subClassOf rdf:resource="&example_chp5;Employee"/>
</rdfs:Class>

<!-- Classes SourceCode, System-Analyst, Technology, and Topic omitted
     for brevity.  They are similar to the above Classes. -->
```

Listing 5.6 RDF schema for Figure 5.9. *(continued)*

```
<rdf:Property rdf:about="&example_chp5;knows"
    rdfs:label="knows">
  <rdfs:domain rdf:resource="&example_chp5;Employee"/>
  <rdfs:range rdf:resource="&example_chp5;Topic"/>
</rdf:Property>
<rdf:Property rdf:about="&example_chp5;writes"
    rdfs:label="writes">
  <rdfs:range rdf:resource="&example_chp5;Artifacts"/>
  <rdfs:domain rdf:resource="&example_chp5;Employee"/>
</rdf:Property>
</rdf:RDF>
```

Listing 5.6   *(continued)*

Listing 5.6 uses the following key components of RDF Schema:

rdfs:Class.   An element that defines a group of related things that share a set of properties. This is synonymous with the concept of type or category. Works in conjunction with rdf:Property, rdfs:range, and rdfs:domain to assign properties to the class. Requires a URI as an identifier in the rdf:about attribute. In Listing 5.6 we see the following classes defined: "Artifacts," "DesignDocument," "Employee," and "Software-Engineer."

rdfs:label.   An attribute that defines a human-readable label for the class. This is important for applications to display the class name in applications even though the official unique identifier for the class is the URI in the rdf:about attribute.

rdfs:subclassOf.   An element that specifies that a class is a specialization of an existing class. This follows the same model as biological inheritance, where a child class can inherit the properties of a parent class. The idea of specialization is that a subclass adds some unique characteristics to a general concept. Therefore, going down the class hierarchy is referred to as *specialization*, while going up the class hierarchy is referred to as *generalization*. In Listing 5.6, the class "Software-Engineer" is defined as a subclass of "Employee." Therefore, Software-Engineer is a specialization of Employee.

rdf:Property.   An element that defines a property of a class and the range of values it can represent. This is used in conjunction with rdfs:domain and rdfs:range properties. It is important to understand a key difference between modeling classes in RDFS versus modeling classes in object-oriented programming, in that RDFS takes a bottom-up approach to class modeling, whereas OOP takes a top-down approach. In OOP, you define a class and everything it contains. In RDFS, you define properties and state what class they belong to. So, in OOP we are going down from the class to the properties. In RDFS, we are going up from the properties to the class.

rdfs:domain.   This property defines which class a property belongs to (formally, its sphere of activity). The value of the property must be a previously defined class. In Listing 5.6, we see that the domain of the property "knows" is the "Employee" class.

rdfs:range.   This property defines the legal set of values for a property. The value of this attribute must be a previously defined class. In Listing 5.6, the range of the "knows" property is the "Topic" class.

Some other important RDFS definitions not used in Listing 5.6 are as follows:

rdf:type.   A standard property to define that an RDF subject is of a type defined in an RDF schema. For example, you could say that a person with Staff ID of 865 is a type of employee like this:

```
<rdf:Description rdf:about= "http://www.mybiz.com/staff/ID/865">
  <rdf:type rdf:resource ="&example_chp5;Employee">
```

rdfs:subPropertyof.   A property that declares that the property that is the subject of the statement is a subproperty of another existing property. This feature actually goes beyond common OOP languages like Java and C# that only offer class inheritance. An example of this would be to declare a property called "weekend," which would be a subPropertyof "week."

rdfs:seeAlso.   A utility property that allows you to refer to a resource that can provide additional RDF information about the current resource.

rdfs:isDefinedBy.   A property to define the namespace of a subject. This is a subPropertyOf rdfs:seeAlso. In practice, the namespace can point to the RDF Schema document.

rdfs:comment.   A utility property to add additional descriptive information to explain the classes and properties to other users of the schema. As in programming, good comments are essential to fostering understanding and adoption.

rdfs:Literal.   A property that represents a constant value represented as a character string. In Listing 5.7, the value of the example_chp5:name attribute is a literal (like "Jane Jones"). RDF/XML syntax revision has recently added *typed literals* to RDF so that you can specify any of the types in the XML Schema specification (like integer or float).

rdfs:XMLLiteral.   A property that represents a constant value that is well-formed XML. This allows XML to be easily embedded in RDF.

In addition to the classes and properties described in the preceding lists, RDF Schema describes classes and properties for the RDF concepts of containers and reification. For containers, RDF Schema defines rdfs:Container, rdf:Bag, rdf:Seq, rdf:Alt, rdfs:member, and rdfs:ContainerMembershipProperty. The purpose for defining these is to allow you to subclass these classes or properties. For reification, RDF Schema defines rdf:Statement, rdf:subject, rdf:predicate, and rdf:object. These can be used to explicitly model a statement to assert additional statements about it. Additionally, as with the Container classes and properties, you can extend these via subclasses or subproperties.

Listing 5.7 displays an RDF instance document generated by Protégé conforming to the RDF schema in Listing 5.6.

```
<?xml version='1.0' encoding='ISO-8859-1'?>
<!DOCTYPE rdf:RDF [
    <!ENTITY rdf 'http://www.w3.org/1999/02/22-rdf-syntax-ns#'>
    <!ENTITY example_chp5 'http://protege.stanford.edu/example-chp5#'>
    <!ENTITY rdfs 'http://www.w3.org/TR/1999/PR-rdf-schema-19990303#'>
]>
<rdf:RDF xmlns:rdf="&rdf;"
    xmlns:example_chp5="&example_chp5;"
    xmlns:rdfs="&rdfs;">
<example_chp5:SourceCode rdf:about="&example_chp5;example-chp5_00015"
    example_chp5:name="stuff.java"
    rdfs:label="example-chp5_00015"/>
<example_chp5:System-Analyst rdf:about="&example_chp5;example-
chp5_00016"
    example_chp5:name="Jane Jones"
    rdfs:label="example-chp5_00016">
  <example_chp5:writes rdf:resource="&example_chp5;example-chp5_00017"/>
</example_chp5:System-Analyst>
<example_chp5:DesignDocument rdf:about="&example_chp5;example-
chp5_00017"
    example_chp5:name="system.sdd"
    rdfs:label="example-chp5_00017"/>
<example_chp5:Software-Engineer rdf:about="&example_chp5;example-
chp5_00018"
    example_chp5:name="John Doe"
    rdfs:label="example-chp5_00018">
  <example_chp5:writes rdf:resource="&example_chp5;example-chp5_00015"/>
</example_chp5:Software-Engineer>
</rdf:RDF>
```

Listing 5.7 RDF instance document.

In Listing 5.7, notice that the classes of the RDF schema in Listing 5.6 are not defined using rdf:type or rdf:about; instead, they use an abbreviation called using a "typed node element." For example, instead of <rdf:Description>, Listing 5.7 has <example_chp5:System-Analyst, which is an rdfs:Class in Listing 5.6. In terms of knowledge capture, Listing 5.7 captures the fact that the System-Analyst, Jane Jones wrote the DesignDocument named "system.sdd," and that the Software-Engineer, John Doe, wrote SourceCode called "stuff.java."

In this section, we saw how RDF is the foundation layer for RDF Schema that enables you to create new RDF classes and properties. Another key benefit of RDF is that it allows you to do noncontextual modeling, described in the following section.

What Is Noncontextual Modeling?

Over the years, businesses have used standard document types to easily convey the context of a specific business transaction. For example, a purchase order is a common document shared between companies with little difficulty even if there is some variation in specific fields or the order of fields. The shared understanding is facilitated because the context is conveyed or fixed by the document type. In that same vein, XML documents have a fixed context provided by their root element and governing schema (formerly called the Document Type Definition, or DTD). For example, in the XML.org schema registry, there are many specific document types for each vertical industry. If we examine the Human Resources-XML Consortium Schema for a Resume (http://www.hr-xml.org), we could probably guess most of the fields even without looking at the sample in Listing 5.8.

```
<?xml version="1.0" encoding="UTF-8"?>
<Resume xmlns="http://ns.hr-xml.org/RecruitingAndStaffing/SEP-2_0"
xmlns:xsi="http://www.w3.org/2001/XMLSchema-instance"
xsi:schemaLocation="http://ns.hr-xml.org/RecruitingAndStaffing/SEP-2_0
Resume-2_0.xsd">
  <StructuredXMLResume>
    <ContactInfo>
     <PersonName>
        <FormattedName>John Doe</FormattedName>
     </PersonName>
    <ContactMethod>
      <Telephone>
         <FormattedNumber>123-456-7890</FormattedNumber>
      </Telephone>
      <InternetEmailAddress>jdoe@fakeaddress.com</InternetEmailAddress>
      <PostalAddress>
         <CountryCode>US</CountryCode>
         <Region>MA</Region>
         <Municipality>Brooklyn</Municipality>
         <DeliveryAddress>
            <AddressLine>27 </AddressLine>
            <StreetName>Pine Street</StreetName>
         </DeliveryAddress>
      </PostalAddress>
```

Listing 5.8 Example of contextual modeling (a resume). *(continued)*

```
        </ContactMethod>
      </ContactInfo>
<Objective> To obtain a leadership position in the field of Electronic
Commerce</Objective>
<EmploymentHistory>
    <EmployerOrg employerOrgType="soleEmployer">
    <EmployerOrgName>General Electric</EmployerOrgName>
    <PositionHistory positionType="directHire">
        <Title> E-Business Program Manager - Business to Business integra-
tion (B2Bi) Program</Title>
        <OrgName>
            <OrganizationName>Aircraft Engines (GEAE)</OrganizationName>
        </OrgName>
        <Description>Key Player in the GE growth initiative bringing IT
leadership into our acquisition/ JV strategy.
Ensured fundamental IT capabilities were present in acquisition targets
in order to maintain a competitive advantage and ensure future growth.
Led cross-functional team on due diligence, and negotiations activity
for $100M+ acquisitions.
Led several new market opportunity assessments and Instrumental in
acquisition strategy development including negotiation of partnership
structures and negotiating potential new market opportunities.
        </Description>
<!-- remainder omitted for brevity. -->
</Resume>
```

Listing 5.8 *(continued)*

Before continuing our discussion, it is very important to understand that this section is not making a value judgment on contextual versus noncontextual modeling, as both are useful. It is not a question of better or worse, but a question of whether your specific application is better served by fixing the context or not fixing the context. In some ways this is the classic trade-off between flexibility in the face of change versus reliable execution via static processes. For many applications, fixing the context at the document level is the best method. One example of this would be high-volume static transactions between well-known trading partners. When the environment is stable and the volume is high, it is both easier and more efficient to strictly fix the context of documents and messages to reduce errors and increase throughput. Of course, the opposite situation, where neither the environment is stable nor the volume is high, is the classic example where flexibility and noncontextual modeling are the best choice. We will examine more situations where noncontextual modeling is applicable in the following paragraphs.

Noncontextual modeling is a continuum and not a single point. In fact, markup languages have been following the trend toward noncontextual modeling over the last several years via namespaces and modularization. Namespaces divide a set of terms (used as elements or attributes) into domain-specific vocabularies with fixed definitions. Modularization allows namespaces to be mixed and matched to assemble a document (sometimes on the fly) that conveys the desired meaning. Two examples of such modularization are XHTML and XBRL. XHTML is described in detail in the next chapter. XHTML modularization allows you to mix and match vocabularies inside of HTML documents. The extensible business reporting language (XBRL) uses both modularization and taxonomies (discussed in Chapter 7) for the description of financial statements for public and private companies. The XBRL specifications are available at http://www.xbrl.org.

RDF takes this trend toward composeable context to its logical conclusion. How does RDF implement noncontextual modeling? RDF creates a collection of statements and not a document. Therefore, the context of a set of RDF statements cannot be determined beforehand; instead, it is wholly dependent on the statements themselves and the relationships between the sentences. In a sense, this disconnect between a list of statements and a hierarchical tree is the root cause of the difficulty in encoding RDF in RDF/XML syntax, because it attempts to marry a list of statements with a hierarchical tree structure. Following are two key aspects of this noncontextual modeling:

Non-contextual modeling uses explicit versus implicit relationships.
XML documents create a hierarchy of name/value pairs. As demonstrated in Chapter 3, both elements and attributes revolve around a name and a typed value. However, XML does not state the relationship between the name and the value. The relationship between them is implicit. On the contrary, RDF uses an explicit relationship between the name and the value with the triple structure: subject, predicate, and object.

A graph is less brittle than a tree. A collection of RDF statements can be added to dynamically without regard to order or even previous statements. In fact, a previous statement can be reified and deprecated by another statement. This allows the RDF graph to be robust in the face of change and suffer less from the brittle data problem and need for versioning and compatibility issues that can plague XML documents. Why is this? Part of the reason is the basic difference between a document and a collection of RDF statements. Tim Berners-Lee highlighted several of these differences in his document entitled "Why RDF Model is Different from the XML Model," available at http://www.w3.org/DesignIssues/RDF-XML.html. He stresses several differences between the XML document model and an RDF graph. First is that there are many possible XML documents that can express a set of semantic assertions. Therefore, RDF simplifies this via a semantic model also known as the triple model. In other words, RDF makes you explicitly define the semantics of your data and thus avoid confusion and alternate syntaxes.

Another obvious difference he highlights is that order is often very important in a document but not important to an RDF graph. Many times the order reflects implicit context not expressed in the name/value pairs. By forcing explicit relationships between subjects and objects, RDF avoids this. Of course, if order is important and it changes, you have an incompatible change to the document structure; hence, this is another example where an RDF list of statements is less affected by change and therefore less brittle.

One application (among many) that is bridging the gap between contextual and noncontextual modeling is called SMORE, developed by Aditya Kalyanpur of the University of Maryland, College Park. SMORE stands for Semantic Markup, Ontology, and RDF Editor. It allows you to embed RDF markup inside of HTML documents during the HTML authoring process. Figure 5.11 displays embedding an RDF triple in a simple HTML document by highlighting some text in the HTML editor.

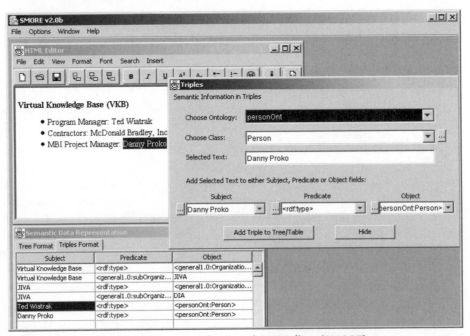

Figure 5.11 Semantic Markup, Ontology, and RDF Editor (SMORE).

Figure 5.11 is a simplified view of the SMORE desktop, which starts out with four windows: an HTML editor (shown), semantic data representation (shown), Web browser (not shown), and an ontology manager (not shown). SMORE allows you to select an ontology and easily add triples about the information in your Web pages to your HTML document. Listing 5.9 displays the generated document with the RDF embedded in the head of the HTML document.

```
<html>
  <head>
  <script type="application/rdf+xml">
   <?xml version="1.0"?>
   <rdf:RDF
   xmlns:rdf="http://www.w3.org/1999/02/22-rdf-syntax-ns#"
   xmlns:general1.0="http://www.cs.umd.edu/projects/plus/DAML/onts/gen-
eral1.0.daml#"
    xmlns:personOnt="http://www.wam.umd.edu/~mhgrove/personOnt.rdf#">
     <general1.0:Organization rdf:ID="Virtual_Knowledge_Base_">
         <general1.0:subOrganizationOf>JIVA</general1.0:subOrganiza-
tionOf>
     </general1.0:Organization>
     <general1.0:Organization rdf:ID="JIVA">
         <general1.0:subOrganizationOf>DIA</general1.0:subOrganiza-
tionOf>
     </general1.0:Organization>
     <personOnt:Person rdf:ID="Ted_Wiatrak"></personOnt:Person>
     <personOnt:Person rdf:ID="Danny_Proko"></personOnt:Person>
   </rdf:RDF>
  </script>
  </head>
  <body>
    <p>
      <b>Virtual Knowledge Base (VKB) </b>
    </p>
    <!-- omitted for brevity. -->
  </body>
</html>
```

Listing 5.9   RDF embedded in HTML (via SMORE).

Listing 5.9 demonstrates the embedding of RDF in HTML using a script element. The script specifies that its contents are an RDF document using the RDF MIME type "application/rdf+xml". The RDF captures statements about the organizations, suborganizations, and people discussed in the HTML page.

A project from IBM's Knowledge Management Group and Stanford's Knowledge Systems Laboratory that enables the distributed processing of chunks of RDF knowledge is the TAPache subproject of the TAP project at http://tap.stanford.edu. TAPache is a module for the Apache HTTP server that enables you to publish RDF data via a standard Web service called getData(). This allows easy integration of distributed RDF data. This further highlights the ability to assemble context even from disparate servers across the network.

This section demonstrated several concepts and ideas that leverage RDF's strength in noncontextual modeling. The idea that context can be assembled in a bottom-up fashion is a powerful one. This is especially useful in applications where corporate offices span countries and continents. In the end, it is the end user that is demanding the power to assemble information as he or she sees fit. This building-block analogy in information processing is akin to the "do-it-yourself" trend of retail stores like Home Depot and Lowe's. The end user gets the power to construct larger structures from predefined definitions and a simple connection model among statements. In the end, it is that flexibility and power that will drive the adoption of RDF and provide a strong foundation layer for the Semantic Web.

Summary

In this chapter, we learned about the foundation layer of the Semantic Web called the Resource Description Framework (RDF). The sections built upon each other, demonstrating numerous applications of RDF, highlighting the strengths and weaknesses of the language, and offering ideas and concepts for leveraging it in your organization.

The first section answered the question "What is RDF?" It began by highlighting its most obvious use in describing opaque resources like images, audio, and video. We then began dissecting the technology into its core model, syntax, and additional features. The core model revolves around denoting concepts with Universal Resource Identifiers (URIs) and structured knowledge as a collection of statements. An RDF statement has three parts: a subject, a predicate, and an object. The RDF/XML syntax uses a striped syntax and a set of elements like rdf:Description and attributes like rdf:about, and rdf:resource. The other features discussed in the section were RDF containers and reification. RDF containers allow an object to contain multiple values or resources. RDF reification allows you to make statements about statements.

The second section cast a skeptic's eye on the slow adoption of RDF. We first noted this phenomenon by comparing RDF's adoption to XML's adoption via simple Web queries. We then listed several possible reasons for the slow adoption: the difficulties in combining RDF and XML documents, the complexity of RDF concepts and syntax, and the weakness of current examples like RSS and Dublin core that do not highlight the unique characteristics of RDF. However, we are confident that RDF's strengths outweigh its weaknesses and forecast strong adoption in the coming year. Its two main engines of growth will be ontologies (like RDF Schema) and noncontextual modeling.

The third section covered the layer above RDF called RDF Schema. RDF Schema provides simple RDF subjects (classes) and predicates (properties) for defining new RDF vocabularies. This section demonstrated the power of RDF via the Protégé ontology editor and an example of how a good ontology models the key determinants of decision making that often get muddled or lost in free text descriptions. Thus, RDF strengthens the basic proposition of the Web: Adding meta data and structure to information improves the effectiveness of our processing and in turn our processes.

The final section of the chapter explored a powerful new trend called noncontextual modeling. To define the concept, we began with its antonym, contextual modeling. We stressed the continuum between these two extremes and how neither is good or bad, just less or more appropriate to solving the particular business problem. Whereas document types provide context and implicit relationships supporting the document divisions and fields, noncontextual modeling builds its context by connecting its statements. In other words, either the context is fed onto the information or the context is derived from the information. We believe that noncontextual modeling and the merging of contextual and noncontextual modeling will rise exponentially in the next five years. This loosely coupled, slowly accrued knowledge that is supported by well-defined concepts and relationships specified in ontologies and knitted together from within and outside your organization will enable huge productivity gains through better data mining, knowledge management, and software agents.

CHAPTER 6

Understanding the Rest of the Alphabet Soup

"In reality, XML just clears away some of the syntactical distractions so that we can get down to the big problem: how we arrive at common understandings about knowledge representation."

—Jon Bosak

The world of XML has brought us great things, but it has brought us so many new acronyms and terms that it is hard to keep up. Some are more important to your understanding the big picture than others are. This chapter aims to provide you with an understanding of some of the key standards that are not covered in the other chapters. In our discussion of these specifications, we give you a high-level overview. Although it is not our intention to get into a lot of the technical details, we show examples of each standard and explain why it is important. We have included sections on the following XML technologies: XPath, XSL, XSLT, XSLFO, XQuery, XLink, XPointer, XInclude, XML Base, XHTML, XForms, and SVG. After reading this chapter, you should be familiar with the goals and practical uses of each.

XPath

XPath is the XML Path Language, and it plays an important role in the XML family of standards. It provides an expression language for specifically addressing parts of an XML document. XPath is important because it provides key semantics, syntax, and functionality for a variety of standards, such as XSLT, XPointer, and XQuery. By using XPath expressions with certain software frameworks and APIs, you can easily reference and find the values of individual components of an XML document. Before we get into an XPath overview, Figure 6.1 shows examples of XPath expressions, their meaning, and their result.

A W3C Recommendation written in 1999, XPath 1.0 was the joint work of the W3C XSL Working Group and XML Linking Working Group, and it is part of the W3C Style Activity and W3C XML Activity. In addition to the functionality of addressing areas of an XML document, it provides basic facilities for manipulation of strings, numbers, and booleans. XPath uses a compact syntax to facilitate its use within URIs and XML attribute values. XPath gets its name from its use of a path notation as in URLs for navigating through the hierarchical structure of an XML document. By using XPath, you can unambiguously define where components of an XML document live. Because we can use XPath to specifically address where components can be defined, it provides an important mechanism that is used by other XML standards and larger XML frameworks and APIs.

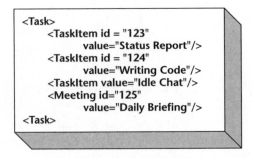

```
<Task>
    <TaskItem id = "123"
            value="Status Report"/>
    <TaskItem id = "124"
            value="Writing Code"/>
    <TaskItem value="Idle Chat"/>
    <Meeting id="125"
            value="Daily Briefing"/>
<Task>
```

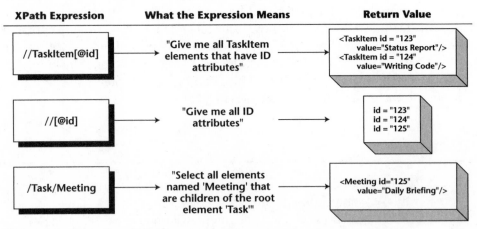

XPath Expression	What the Expression Means	Return Value
//TaskItem[@id]	"Give me all TaskItem elements that have ID attributes"	`<TaskItem id = "123" value="Status Report"/> <TaskItem id = "124" value="Writing Code"/>`
//[@id]	"Give me all ID attributes"	id = "123" id = "124" id = "125"
/Task/Meeting	"Select all elements named 'Meeting' that are children of the root element 'Task'"	`<Meeting id="125" value="Daily Briefing"/>`

Figure 6.1 Examples of XPath expressions.

Although the original XPath specification (1.0) is an addressing language, the XPath 2.0 specification is a product of the XML Query and XML Style Working Groups and thus shares common features with the next generation of XQuery, the XML query language. XQuery Version 1.0 is, in fact, an extension of XPath Version 2.0, so the two will be very closely related. The XPath 2.0 Working Draft, released in August 2002, states that "it is intended that XPath should be embedded in a host language, such as XQuery and XSLT."

What role does XPath play in other standards? With XSLT, you can define a template in advance using XPath expressions that allow you to specify how to style a document. XQuery is a superset of XPath and uses XPath expressions to query XML native databases and multiple XML files. XPointer uses XPath expressions to "point" to specific nodes in XML documents. XML Signature, XML Encryption, and many other standards can use XPath expressions to reference certain areas of an XML document. In a Semantic Web ontology, groups of XPath expressions can be used to specify how to find data and the relationships between data. The DOM Level 3 XPath specification, a Working Draft from the W3C, also provides interfaces for accessing nodes of a DOM tree using XPath expressions.

XPath has been incredibly successful. Its adoption has been widespread in both practical technology applications and within other XML standards. XPath alone is a strong addressing mechanism, but it is often difficult to comprehend its power without looking at how other specifications use them. As we discuss some of the other standards in this chapter, you will see more references to this specification.

The Style Sheet Family: XSL, XSLT, and XSLFO

Style sheets allow us to specify how an XML document can be transformed into new documents, and how that XML document could be presented in different media formats. The languages associated with style sheets are XSL (Extensible Stylesheet Language), XSLT (Extensible Stylesheet Language: Transformations), and XSLFO (Extensible Stylesheet Language: Formatting Objects). A style sheet processor takes an XML document and a style sheet and produces a result. XSL consists of two parts: It provides a mechanism for transforming XML documents into new XML documents (XSLT), and it provides a vocabulary for formatting objects (XSLFO). XSLT is a markup language that uses template rules to specify how a style sheet processor transforms a document and is a Recommendation by the W3C (http://www.w3.org/TR/xslt). XSLFO is a pagination markup language and is simply the formatting vocabulary defined in the XSL W3C Recommendation (http://www.w3.org/TR/xsl/).

It is important to understand the importance of styling. Using style sheets adds presentation to XML data. In separating content (the XML data) from the presentation (the style sheet), you take advantage of the success of what is called the Model-View-Controller (MVC) paradigm. The act of separating the data (the model), how the data is displayed (the view), and the framework used between them (the controller) provides maximum reuse of your resources. When you use this technology, XML data can simply be data. Your style sheets can transform your data into different formats, eliminating the maintenance nightmare of trying to keep track of multiple presentation formats for the same data. Embracing this model allows you to separate your concerns about maintaining data and presentation. Because browsers such as Microsoft Internet Explorer have style sheet processors embedded in them, presentation can dynamically be added to XML data at download time.

Figure 6.2 shows a simple example of the transformation and formatting process. A style sheet engine (sometimes called an XSLT engine) takes an original XML document, loads it into a DOM source tree, and transforms that document with the instructions given in the style sheet. In specifying those instructions, style sheets use XPath expressions to reference portions of the source tree and capture information to place into the result tree. The result tree is then formatted, and the resulting XML document is returned. Although the original document must be a well-formed XML document, the resulting document may be any format. Many times, the resulting document may be post-processed. In the case of formatting an XML document with XSLFO styling, a post-processor is usually used to transform the result document into a different format (such as PDF or RTF—just to name a few).

At this point, we will show a brief example of using style sheets to add presentation to content. Listing 6.1 shows a simple XML file that lists a project, its description, and its schedule of workdays. Because our example will show a browser dynamically styling this XML, we put the processing directive (the styling instructions) on the second line.

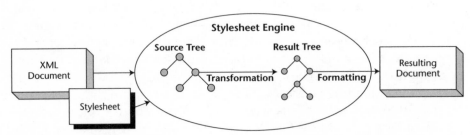

Figure 6.2 Styling a document.

```
<?xml version="1.0" encoding="UTF-8"?>
<?xml-stylesheet href="simplestyle.xsl" type="text/xsl"?>
<project name="Trumantruck.com">
   <description>Rebuilding a 1967 Chevy Pickup Truck</description>
   <schedule>
        <workday>
            <date>20000205</date>
            <description>Taking Truck Body Apart</description>
        </workday>
        <workday>
            <date>20000225</date>
            <description>Sandblasting, Dismantling Cab</description>
        </workday>
        <workday>
            <date>20000311</date>
            <description>Sanding, Priming Hood and Fender</
description>
        </workday>
   </schedule>
</project>
```

Listing 6.1   A simple XML file.

To create an HTML page with the information from our XML file, we need to
write a style sheet. Listing 6.2 shows a simple style sheet that creates an HTML
file with the workdays listed in an HTML table. Note that all pattern matching
is done with XPath expressions. The <xsl:value-of> element returns the value
of items selected from an XPath expression, and each template is called by the
XSLT processor if the current node matches the XPath expression in the match
attribute.

```
<xsl:stylesheet xmlns:xsl="http://www.w3.org/TR/WD-xsl">
    <xsl:template match="/">
        <html>
            <TITLE>Schedule For
            <xsl:value-of select="/project/@name"/>
- <xsl:value-of select="/project/description"/>
            </TITLE>
            <CENTER>
                <TABLE border="1">
                    <TR>
                        <TD><B>Date</B></TD>
                        <TD><B>Description</B></TD>
                    </TR>
                    <xsl:apply-templates/>
                </TABLE>
```

Listing 6.2   A simple style sheet. *(continued)*

```
            </CENTER>
        </html>
    </xsl:template>
    <xsl:template match="project">
        <H1>Project:
        <xsl:value-of select="@name"/>
        </H1>
        <HR/>
        <xsl:apply-templates/>
    </xsl:template>
    <xsl:template match="schedule">
        <H2>Work Schedule</H2>

        <xsl:apply-templates/>
    </xsl:template>
    <xsl:template match="workday">
        <TR>
            <TD>
                <xsl:value-of select="date"/>
            </TD>
            <TD>
                <xsl:value-of select="description"/>
            </TD>
        </TR>
    </xsl:template>
</xsl:stylesheet>
```

Listing 6.2 *(continued)*

The resulting document is rendered dynamically in the Internet Explorer browser, shown in Figure 6.3.

Why are style sheets important? In an environment where interoperability is crucial, and where data is stored in different formats for different enterprises, styling is used to translate one enterprise format to another enterprise format. In a scenario where we must support different user interfaces for many devices, style sheets are used to add presentation to content, providing us with a rich mechanism for supporting the presentation of the same data on multiple platforms. A wireless client, a Web client, a Java application client, a .NET application client, or the application of your choice can have different style sheets to present a customized view. In a portal environment, style sheets can be used to provide a personalized view of the data that has been retrieved from a Web service. Because there is such a loose coupling between data content and presentation, style sheets allow us to develop solutions faster and easier. Because we can use style sheet processors to manipulate the format of XML documents, we can support interoperability between enterprise applications supporting different XML formats.

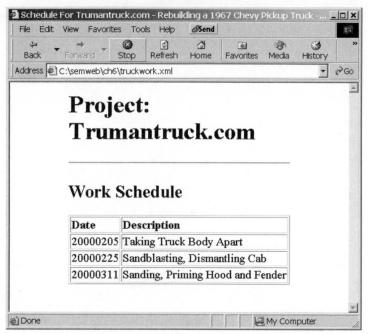

Figure 6.3 A browser, using style sheets to render our example.

Figure 6.4 shows a diagram of many practical examples of style sheets in use. In this diagram, different style sheets are applied to an XML document to achieve different goals of presentation, interoperation, communication, and execution. At the top of the diagram, you see how different style sheets can be used to add presentation to the original XML content. In the case of XSLFO, sometimes a post-processor is used to transform the XSLFO vocabulary into another format, such as RTF and PDF. In the "interoperation" portion of Figure 6.4, a style sheet is used to transform the document into another format read by another application. In the "communication" portion of Figure 6.4, a style sheet is used to transform the XML document into a SOAP message, which is sent to a Web service. Finally, in the "execution" section, there are two examples of how XML documents can be transformed into code that can be executed at run time. These examples should give you good ideas of the power of style sheets.

Hopefully, this section has given you the big picture on the importance of style sheets and their uses. As you can see, the sky is the limit for the uses of style sheets.

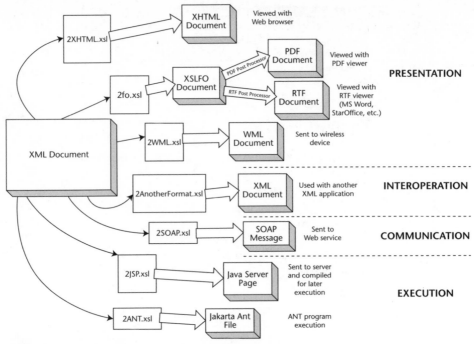

Figure 6.4 Practical examples of style sheets in use.

XQuery

XQuery is a language designed for processing XML data, and it is intended to make querying XML-based data sources as easy as querying databases. Although there have been attempts at XML query languages before—such as XQL, XML-QL, and Quilt—XQuery, a product of the W3C, is the first to receive industry-wide attention. The Query Working Group of the W3C has made it clear that there is a need for a human-readable query syntax, and there is also a requirement for an XML-based query syntax. XQuery was designed to meet the human-readable syntax requirement. It is an expression language that is an extension of XPath. With few exceptions, every XPath expression is also an XQuery expression. What XQuery provides, however, is a human-readable language that makes it easy to query XML sources and combine that with programming language logic.

Similar to using style sheet transformations, the XQuery process uses XPath expressions and its own functions to query and manipulate XML data. It is a strongly typed language, and its syntax is very similar to a high-level programming language, such as Perl. To demonstrate how XQuery works, we will use the example XML file shown in Listing 6.1. The following is a valid

XQuery expression that returns the workdays from the file, sorted alphabetically by the description of each workday:

```
let $project := document("trumanproject.xml")/project
let $day := $project/schedule/workday
return $day sortby (description)
```

The first line loads the XML document and assigns a variable to the <project> element. The second line assigns the collection of <workday> elements to the $day variable by using an XPath expression. Finally, the last line sorts the elements alphabetically based on the value of the <description> element. The result of that XQuery expression is as follows:

```
<workday>
  <date>20000225</date>
  <description>Sandblasting, Dismantling Cab</description>
</workday>
<workday>
  <date>20000311</date>
  <description>Sanding, Priming Hood and Fender</description>
</workday>
<workday>
  <date>20000205</date>
  <description>Taking Truck Body Apart</description>
</workday>
```

As you can see by the result of the XQuery expression, the <workday> elements have now been sorted alphabetically based on their <description> child element.

XQuery is important because it will provide a standard query interface to XML databases and data stores. XQuery is currently in Working Draft status at the W3C (http://www.w3.org/TR/xquery/), and it is continuing to evolve. Its syntax has received some criticism for not being in XML, but its syntax was developed for human readability. An XML version of the XQuery syntax, XQueryX, is also a Working Draft of the W3C (http://www.w3.org/TR/xqueryx), and because it is XML, it has potential for success as an alternative syntax. There are several early adopters of XQuery including Lucent (http://db.bell-labs.com/galax/), Software AG (http://www.softwareag.com), Microsoft (http://xqueryservices.com), and Oracle (http://otn.oracle.com/sample_code/tech/xml/xmldb/jxqi.html). As XQuery evolves and is adopted in industry, its future looks promising.

XLink

XLink is the XML Linking Language from the W3C. It allows elements to be inserted into XML documents in order to create and describe links between resources, associate meta data, and link external documents. Part of the specification is similar to hyperlinks in HTML, but XLink goes far beyond the linking capabilities in HTML in offering advanced behavior features that make hyperlinking more flexible. XLink allows you to link multiple targets, roles, resources, and responses to elements.

A *link* is defined by the XLink W3C recommendation as "an explicit relationship between resources or portions of resources."[1] It is made explicit by an XLink-conforming XML element. With XLink, not only can XML authors link external documents, but also elements can be linked to other elements, and the relationships between them can be linked. XLink-compliant links can be simple and complex. Listing 6.3 shows a simple example of XLink in use. As you can see, the example is quite similar to the <A> linking element in HTML.

```xml
<?xml version="1.0" encoding="UTF-8"?>
<doc>
 <name xlink:type='simple'
 xlink:href='instructors/busdriver.xml'>Clay Richardson</name>
 is an employee at
   <company xlink:type='simple' xlink:href='#mcbrad'>
       McDonald Bradley, Inc.
   </company>, and teaches
   <course xlink:type='simple' xlink:href='#CS593'>
       Computer Science 593
   </course>.
 <employers>
   <company id='mcbrad'>McDonald Bradley</company>
   <company id='btg'>BTG</company>
   <company id='grumman'>Northrup Grumman</company>
   <company id='orionsci'>Orion Scientific</company>
 </employers>
 <courselist>
   <course id='CS141'>CS 141 - Intro to Comp Sci</course>
   <course id='CS444'>CS 444 - Operating Systems</course>
   <course id='CS593'>CS 593 - Object-Oriented Design</course>
   <course id='CS669'>CS 669 - Keeping it Real</course>
 </courselist>
</doc>
```

Listing 6.3 Simple XLink example.

In Listing 6.3, we have an example that discusses employers and courses in a document. Throughout the XML file, the xlink:type attribute of the element is set to 'simple', and the xlink:href attribute is set to link to external documents and to elements within the document. This is the simplest example of linking.

[1] http://www.w3.org/TR/xlink/-"XML Linking Language (XLink) Version 1.0," W3C Recommendation, June 27, 2001.

XLink can also connect relationships together. If, for example, we wanted to link descriptions with our courses and employers, we could use the XLink 'extended' link type to connect our descriptions with our elements. A bit more complicated than the simple links shown in Listing 6.3, extended links allow arcs to describe relationships between elements and remote resources. Listing 6.4 shows an example of our simple XLink example from Listing 6.3 modified to incorporate relationships between some of the elements.

```xml
<?xml version="1.0" encoding="UTF-8"?>
<doc>
 <extendedlink xlink:type='extended'>
    <loc xlink:type='locator' xlink:label='mcbrad' xlink:href='#mcbrad'>
    </loc>
    <loc xlink:type='locator' xlink:label='cs593'xlink:href='#CS593'>
    </loc>
    <loc xlink:type='locator' xlink:label='cs593description'
        xlink:href='courses/cs593.xml'>
    </loc>
    <loc xlink:type='locator' xlink:label='mcbraddescription'
        xlink:href='employers/mcbrad.xml'>
    </loc>
    <arc xlink:type='arc' xlink:from='cs593' xlink:to='cs593description'>
    </arc>
    <arc xlink:type='arc' xlink:from='mcbrad' xlink:to='
mcbraddescription'>
    </arc>
 </extendedlink>
 <name xlink:type='simple'
      xlink:href='instructors/busdriver.xml'>Clay Richardson</name>
                  is an employee at
 <company xlink:type='simple' xlink:href='#mcbrad'>
        McDonald Bradley, Inc.
 </company>, and teaches
 <course xlink:type='simple' xlink:href='#CS593'>
        Computer Science 593
 </course>
 <employers>
    <company id='mcbrad'>McDonald Bradley</company>
    <company id='btg'>BTG</company>
 </employers>
 <courselist>
    <course id='CS141'>CS 141 - Intro to Comp Sci</course>
    <course id='CS444'>CS 444 - Operating Systems</course>
    <course id='CS593'>CS 593 - Object-Oriented Design</course>
    <course id='CS669'>CS 669 - Keeping it Real</course>
 </courselist>
</doc>
```

Listing 6.4 An XLink example with element relationships.

As you can see from the code in Listing 6.4, adding the <extendedlink> element with the xlink:type attribute of 'extended' allows us to make relationships between the elements. In the example, an 'arc' xlink:type attributes allow us to connect a course with its description, an employer, and a description.

What is XLink's importance? It is the W3C's recommendation for generic linking, and it is intended for use in hypertext systems. Languages such as Scalable Vector Graphics (SVG) and MathML use XLink for hypertext references. At this point, the Resource Directory Description Language (RDDL) uses XLink syntax to specify the relationship between URLs and other resources. It is the intention of the W3C that XLink be used for generic linking mechanisms in XML languages.

The future of XLink is still debatable. Although the final W3C recommendation for XLink was released in 2001, product adoption has been slow, and attention has been focused elsewhere.[2] Because specifications like RDF and XTM also provide the concept of mapping associations between resources, it seems that more focus has been placed on those technologies than on XLink for describing associations. Last September, the XHTML community seemingly rejected XLink in XHTML 2.0, by developing another linking Working Draft called HLink. HLink "extends XLink use to a wider class of languages than those restricted to the syntactic style allowed by XLink."[3] After HLink was developed, the W3C Technical Architecture Group (TAG) released an opinion, saying that XLink, not HLink, should be used for hypertext references in XHTML 2.0.[4] Debates such as these have arisen within the XML community about the future of XLink. Regardless, there are some notable products, such as the DocZilla and Mozilla browsers, that use partial functionality of XLink.

XPointer

XPointer is the XML Pointer Language from the W3C, which is used as a fragment identifier for any URI reference that locates an XML-based resource. A powerful language, XPointer can "point" to fragments of remote documents using XPath expressions and can point to ranges of data and points of data in documents.

[2] Bob DuCharme, "XLink: Who Cares?" March 13, 2002, http://www.xml.com/pub/a/2002/03/13/xlink.html.

[3] http://www.w3.org/TR/hlink-HLink: Link Recognition for the XHTML Family, W3C Working Draft, September 13, 2002.

[4] Kendall Clark, "TAG Rejects HLink," October 2, 2002, http://www.xml.com/lpt/a/2002/10/02/deviant.html.

An example of using XPointer is shown in Listing 6.5, where we can rewrite the data contained in the <extendedlink> element of Listing 6.4. As you can see, XPointer expressions are used in the xlink:href attributes of the <loc> element in order to point directly to the elements. The links address the <company> element with an ID "mcbrad" and a <course> element with the ID attribute of "CS593".

```
<extendedlink xlink:type='extended'>
  <loc xlink:type='locator' xlink:label='mcbrad'
      xlink:href='#xpointer(//company[@id='mcbrad'])'></loc>
  <loc xlink:type='locator' xlink:label='cs593'
      xlink:href='#xpointer(//course[@id='CS593'])'></loc>
  <loc xlink:type='locator' xlink:label='cs593description'
      xlink:href='courses/cs593.xml'></loc>
  <loc xlink:type='locator' xlink:label='mcbraddescription'
      xlink:href='employers/mcbrad.xml'></loc>
  <arc xlink:type='arc' xlink:from='cs593'
      xlink:to='cs593description'></arc>
  <arc xlink:type='arc' xlink:from='mcbrad'
      xlink:to='mcbraddescription'></arc>
</extendedlink>
```

Listing 6.5 A simple XPointer example.

As is seen in Listing 6.5, XPointer relies on XPath expressions to point to resources. In addition, XPointer includes functions that make it able to do some things that XPath cannot do, such as specifying ranges of elements and specifying points within a document. For example, the following XPointer expression points to objects within our document that was shown in Listing 6.1:

```
xpointer(string-range(//*,'Truck'))
```

That expression points to every 'Truck' string in the document. Looking at our earlier Listing 6.1, that expression would point to the 'Truck' string in the text node 'Rebuilding a 1967 Pickup Truck' in the <description> element, as well as the 'Truck' string in the 'Taking Truck Body Apart' node, shown later in the document.

XPointer is a powerful specification, and it offers a rich mechanism for addressing pieces of XML documents. In the summer of 2002, the XML Linking Group of the W3C broke the XPointer specification into four Working Draft pieces: an XPointer core framework, The XPointer element() scheme for addressing XML elements, the XPointer xmlns() scheme to allow correct interpretation of namespace prefixes in pointers, and the XPointer xpointer() scheme for full XPointer addressing flexibility. Both XLink and XInclude can use XPointer expressions, and it is likely that there will be more adoption into products and other specifications.

XInclude

XML Inclusions (XInclude) is a W3C Candidate Recommendation used for the purpose of including documents, elements, or other information in an XML document. With it, you can build large XML documents from multiple fragmentary XML documents, well-formed XML documents, or non-XML text documents. It also has a "fallback" feature in case the external document is not available or the server is down. The simplest example of this is shown in the following, where the beginning of this chapter could be separated in multiple files:

```
<?xml version="1.0"?>
<chapter xmlns:xi="http://www.w3.org/2001/XInclude">
  <title>Understanding the Rest of the Alphabet Soup</title>
  <xi:include href="http://www.wiley.com/SemWeb/ch6/xpath.xml"/>
  <xi:include href="http://www.wiley.com/SemWeb/ch6/stylesheets.xml"/>
  <xi:include href="http://www.wiley.com/SemWeb/ch6/xquery.xml"/>
  <xi:include href="http://www.wiley.com/SemWeb/ch6/xlink.xml"/>
</chapter>
```

This code is very basic. External XML files for each chapter section are included in one document with XInclude. The rendered version would look like a large document. XInclude is a bit more powerful than that, however. Listing 6.6 gives a more complex example where non-XML content and portions of documents can be brought into an XML document, and where the XInclude "fallback" mechanism is used.

```
<?xml version='1.0'?>
<document xmlns:xi="http://www.w3.org/2001/XInclude">
  <p>The relevant excerpt is:</p>
  <quotation>
    <xi:include
        href="source.xml#xpointer(string-range(chapter/p[1],
'Sentence 2')/
              range-to(string-range(chapter/p[2]/i,'3.',1,2)))">
      <xi:fallback>
          <xi:include href="error.xml"/>
      </xi:fallback>
    </xi:include>
  </quotation>
  <p>Code that was used to write the cool program was:</p>
  <code>
    <xi:include parse="text" href="code/Datamover.java">
      <xi:fallback>
        Sorry - The code is unavailable at this time!
```

Listing 6.6 A more complex example of XInclude.

```
        </xi:fallback>
      </xi:include>
    </code>
  </document>
```

Listing 6.6   (continued)

In Listing 6.6, the first <include> element uses an XPointer expression to bring in a portion of another document. The second <include> element within the <code> tag brings in the text code of a Java document into the main document. Both <include> elements use a contained <fallback> tag that presents alternative text in the case that the server is down or if the referenced document is unavailable.

Support for XInclude is limited, but it is growing. Many in the XML community are looking at security implications of browser-based XInclude, because there could be potential misuses.[5] As we have discussed in this section, however, XInclude offers a powerful capability, and we assume that the XML community and vendor adopters will work out some of the security issues that have been discussed. There are several adopters of this specification, including Apache Cocoon and GNU JAXP.

XML Base

XML Base is a W3C Recommendation that allows authors to explicitly specify a document's base URI for the purpose of resolving relative URIs. Very similar to HTML's base element, it makes resolving relative paths in links to external images, applets, form-processing programs, style sheets, and other resources. Using XML Base, an earlier example in the last section could be written the following way:

```
<?xml version="1.0"?>
<chapter xmlns:xi="http://www.w3.org/2001/XInclude"
         xml:base="http://www.wiley.com/SemWeb/ch6">
  <title>Understanding the Rest of the Alphabet Soup</title>
  <xi:include href="xpath.xml"/>
  <xi:include href="stylesheets.xml"/>
  <xi:include href="xquery.xml"/>
  <xi:include href="xlink.xml"/>
</chapter>
```

[5] Kendall Grant Clark, "Community and Specifications," XML Deviant column at XML.com, October 30, 2002 http://www.xml.com/pub/a/2002/10/30/deviant.html.

The xml:base attribute in the <chapter> element makes all the referenced documents that follow relative to the URL "http://www.wiley.com/SemWeb/ch6." In the href attributes in the <include> elements in the preceding example, the following documents are referenced:

- http://www.wiley.com/SemWeb/ch6/xpath.xml
- http://www.wiley.com/SemWeb/ch6/stylesheets.xml
- http://www.wiley.com/SemWeb/ch6/xlink.xml

Using XML Base makes it easier to resolve relative paths. Developed by a part of the W3C XML Linking Working Group, it is a simple recommendation that makes XML development easier.

XHTML

XHTML, the Extensible Hypertext Markup Language, is the reformulation of HTML into XML. The specification was created for the purpose of enhancing our current Web to provide more structure for machine processing. Why is this important? Although HTML is easy for people to write, its loose structure has become a stumbling block on our way to a Semantic Web. It is well suited for presentation for browsers; however, it is difficult for machines to understand the meaning of documents formatted in HTML. Because HTML is not well formed and is only a presentation language, it is not a good language for describing data, and it is not extremely useful for information gathering in a Semantic Web environment. Because XHTML is XML, it provides structure and extensibility by allowing the inclusion of other XML-based languages with namespaces. By augmenting our current Web infrastructure with a few changes, XHTML can make intermachine exchanges of information easier. Because the transition from HTML to XHTML is not rocket science, XHTML promises to be successful.

XHTML 1.0, a W3C Recommendation released in January 2000, was a reformulation of HTML 4.0 into XML. The transition from HTML to XHTML is quite simple. Some of the highlights include the following:

- An XHTML 1.0 document should be declared as an XML document using an XML declaration.
- An XHTML 1.0 document is both valid and well formed. It must contain a DOCTYPE that denotes that it is an XHTML 1.0 document, and that also denotes the DTD being used by that document. Every tag must have an end tag.

- The root element of an XHTML 1.0 document is <html> and should contain a namespace identifying it as XHTML.

- Because XML is case-sensitive, elements and attributes in XHTML must be lowercase.

Let's look at a simple example of making the transition from HTML to XHTML 1.0. The HTML in Listing 6.7 shows a Web document with a morning to-do list.

```
<HTML>
   <HEAD>
      <TITLE>Morning to-do list</TITLE>
   </HEAD>
   <BODY>
      <LI>Wake up
      <LI>Make bed
      <LI>Drink coffee
      <LI>Go to work
   </BODY>
</HTML>
```

Listing 6.7 An HTML example.

Going from the HTML in Listing 6.7 to XHTML 1.0 is quite easy. Listing 6.8 shows how we can do it. The first change is the XML declaration on the first line. The second change is the DOCTYPE declaration using a DTD, and the root tag <html> now uses the XHTML namespace. All elements and attributes have also been changed to lowercase. Finally, we make it a well-formed document by adding end tags to the <li> tags. Otherwise, nothing has changed.

```
<?xml version="1.0"?>
<!DOCTYPE html
     PUBLIC "-//W3C//DTD XHTML 1.0 Strict//EN"
    "http://www.w3.org/TR/xhtml1/DTD/xhtml1-strict.dtd">
<html xmlns="http://www.w3.org/1999/xhtml" xml:lang="en" lang="en">
  <head>
    <title>Morning to-do list</title>
  </head>
  <body>
     <li>Wake up</li>
     <li>Make bed</li>
     <li>Drink coffee</li>
     <li>Go to work</li>
  </body>
</html>
```

Listing 6.8 Simple XHTML 1.0 file.

The difference between Listings 6.7 and 6.8 shows that this transition between HTML and XHTML is quite smooth. Because XHTML 1.0 is well formed and valid, it can be processed easier by user agents, can incorporate stronger markup, and can reap the benefits of being an XML-based technology.

There are obviously a few more additions to the XHTML specification than what we've covered so far, and one that is worth mentioning is the extensibility of XHTML. In XML, it is easy to introduce new elements or add to a schema. XHTML is designed to accommodate these extensions through the use of XHTML modules. XHTML 2.0, a W3C Working Draft released in August 2002, is made up of a set of these modules that describe the elements and attributes of the language. XHTML 2.0 is an evolution of XHTML 1.0, as it is not intended to be backward-compatible. New element tags and features (such as the XForms module and XML Events discussed later in this chapter) are in this Working Draft. The learning curve is minimal for authors who understand XHTML 1.0. XHTML 2.0 is still in its early stages, and it continues to evolve.

XHTML shows promise because it builds on the success of HTML but adds XML structure that makes machine-based processing easier. As more organizations recognize its value, and as browsers begin showing the newer features of XHTML (especially those in XHTML 2.0), more XHTML content will be added to the Web.

XForms

XForms is a W3C Candidate Recommendation that adds new functionality, flexibility, and scalability to what we expect to existing Web-based forms. Dubbed "the next generation of forms for the Web," XForms separates presentation from content, allows reuse, and reduces the number of round-trips to the server, offers device independence, and reduces the need for scripting in Web-based forms.[6] It separates the model, the instance data, and the user interface into three parts, separating presentation from content. XHTML 2.0 includes the XForms module, and XForms will undoubtedly bring much interest to the XHTML community.

Web forms are everywhere. They are commonplace in search engines and e-commerce Web sites, and they exist in essentially every Web application. HTML has made forms successful, but they have limited features. They mix purpose and presentation, they run only on Web browsers, and even the simplest form-based tasks are dependent on scripting. XForms was designed to fix these shortcomings and shows much promise.

---

[6] "XForms 1.0 Working Draft," http://www.w3.org/TR/xforms/.

Separating the purpose, presentation, and data is key to understanding the importance of XForms. Every form has a purpose, which is usually to collect data. The purpose is realized by creating a user interface (presentation) that allows the user to provide the required information. The data is the result of completing the form. With XForms, forms are separated into two separate components: the XForms model, which describes the purpose, and the XForms user interface, which describes how the form is presented. A conceptual view of an XForms interaction is shown in Figure 6.5, where the model and the presentation are stored separately. In an XForms scenario, the model and presentation are parsed into memory as XML "instance data." The instance data is kept in memory during user interaction. Because XML Forms uses XML Events, a general-purpose event framework described in XML, many triggered events can be script-free during this user interaction. Using an XML-based syntax, XForms developers can display messages to users, perform calculations and screen refreshes, or submit a portion (or all) of the instance data. After the user interaction is finished, the instance data is serialized as XML and sent to the server. Separating the data, the model, and the presentation allows you to maximize reusability and can help you build powerful user interfaces quickly.

The simplest example of XForms in XHTML 2.0 is in Listing 6.9. As you can see, the XForms model (with element <model>) belongs in the <head> section of the XHTML document. Form controls and user interface components belong in the <body> of the XHTML document. Every form control element has a required <label> child element, which contains the associated label. Each input has a ref attribute, which uniquely identifies that as an XForms input.

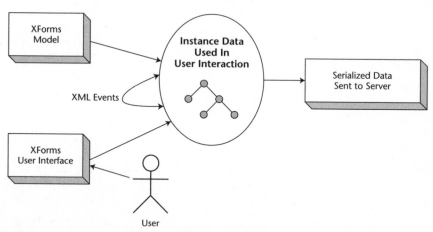

Figure 6.5   Conceptual view of XForms interaction.

```
<?xml version="1.0"?>
<!DOCTYPE html PUBLIC "-//W3C//DTD XHTML 2.0//EN"
    "http://www.w3.org/TR/xhtml2/DTD/xhtml2.dtd">
<html xmlns="http://www.w3.org/2002/06/xhtml2"
  xmlns:xforms="http://www.w3.org/2002/08/xforms/cr">
    <head>
        <title>Simple example</title>
        <xforms:model id="simpleform">
            <xforms:submission
                action="https://www.wiley.com/simpleXFormsExample/
submit"/>
        </xforms:model>
    </head>
    <body>
        <p>Enter your credit card number below</p>
        <xforms:input ref="username">
            <xforms:label>Name:</xforms:label>
         </xforms:input>
        <xforms:input ref="creditcard">
            <xforms:label>Credit Card:</xforms:label>
        </xforms:input>
        <xforms:input ref="expires">
            <xforms:label>Expires:</xforms:label>
        </xforms:input>
        <xforms:submit>
            <xforms:label>Submit</xforms:label>
        </xforms:submit>
    </body>
</html>
```

Listing 6.9   A simple XHTML 2.0 XForms example.

If the code from Listing 6.9 were submitted, the instance data similar to the following would be produced:

```
<instanceData>
    <username>Kenneth Kyle Stockman</username>
    <creditcard>55555555555555</creditcard>
    <expires>5/92</expires>
</instanceData>
```

Of course, this was a simple example. XForms also can take advantage of model item constraints by placing declarative validation information in forms from XML Schemas and XForms-specific constraints. In the preceding example, we could bind the <creditcard> and <expires> values to be valid to match certain schema types. We could also describe our data in our <model>, like the example shown in Listing 6.10, with validation constraints. In that example, you see that the instance is defined in the model. The <xforms:bind> element uses the isValid attribute to validate the form. In this case, if someone attempts to submit the information without typing in anything, it will throw an invalid XForm event. Also notice that in the body of the document, individual components of the model are referenced by XPath expressions (in the ref attribute of the input elements).

```xml
<?xml version="1.0" encoding="ISO-8859-1"?>
<!--<!DOCTYPE html PUBLIC "-//W3C//DTD XHTML Basic 1.0//EN"
"http://www.w3.org/TR/xhtml-basic/xhtml-basic10.dtd">-->
<html xmlns="http://www.w3.org/1999/xhtml"
        xmlns:ev="http://www.w3.org/2001/xml-events"
        xmlns:testcase="testcase"
        xmlns:xforms="http://www.w3.org/2002/01/xforms">
    <head>
        <link href="controls.css" rel="stylesheet" type="text/css"/>
        <xforms:model id="form1">
            <xforms:submitInfo id="submit1"
                    localfile="temp2.xml" method2="postxml"
                    target2="http://www.trumantruck.com/"/>
            <xforms:instance id="instance1" xmlns="">
                <testcase>
                    <username/>
                    <secret/>
                </testcase>
            </xforms:instance>
            <xforms:bind
                isValid="string-length(.)&gt;0" ref="testcase/secret"/>
            <xforms:bind
                isValid="string-length(.)&gt;0" ref="testcase/username"/>
        </xforms:model>
    </head>
    <body>
        <b>User Name:</b>
        <xforms:input ref="testcase/testcase:input" xmlns:my="test">
            <xforms:caption>Enter your name</xforms:caption>
        </xforms:input>
        <b>Password:</b>
        <xforms:secret ref="testcase/secret">
            <xforms:caption>Password</xforms:caption>
        </xforms:secret>
        <b>submit</b>
        <xforms:submit>
            <xforms:caption>Submit Me</xforms:caption>
        </xforms:submit>
    </body>
</html>
```

Listing 6.10   An XForms example with validation.

Figure 6.6 shows the result rendered in the XSmiles browser, a Java-based XForms-capable browser available at http://www.xsmiles.org/. In this example, the username was entered, but the password was not. Because our XForm specified that it would not be valid, an error was thrown.

XForms is one of the most exciting tools that will be included in the XHTML 2.0 specification. It is still a Working Draft, which means that it is continuing to evolve. Because of its power and simplicity, and because instance data is serialized as XML, XForms has the potential to be a critical link between user interfaces and Web services. Commercial support for XForms continues to grow.

Figure 6.6 Example rendering of an XForm-based program.

SVG

Scalable Vector Graphics (SVG) is a language for describing two-dimensional graphics in XML. A W3C Recommendation since September 2001, there are many tools and applications that take advantage of this exciting technology. With SVG, vector graphics, images, and text can be grouped, styled, and transformed. Features such as alpha masks, filter effects, and nested transformations are in this XML-based language, and animations can be defined and triggered. Many authors use scripting languages that access the SVG's Document Object Model to perform advanced animations and dynamic graphics.

The potential for SVG is quite exciting. Because it is an XML language, data content can be transformed into SVG to create graphically intense programs and animations. Online maps can easily convey the plotting of data, roads, and buildings with SVG.

What does an SVG file look like? Listing 6.11 gives a brief example.

```
<?xml version="1.0" standalone="no"?>
<!DOCTYPE svg PUBLIC "-//W3C//DTD SVG 20010904//EN"
  "http://www.w3.org/TR/2001/REC-SVG-20010904/DTD/svg10.dtd">
    <svg width="5cm" height="3cm" viewBox="0 0 5 3"
        xmlns="http://www.w3.org/2000/svg"
        xmlns:xlink="http://www.w3.org/1999/xlink">
  <desc>Example link01 - a link on an ellipse</desc>
  <rect x=".01" y=".01" width="4.98" height="2.98"
        fill="none" stroke="blue"  stroke-width=".03"/>
  <a xlink:href="http://www.w3.org">
    <ellipse cx="2.5" cy="1.5" rx="2" ry="1" fill="red" />
</a>
</svg>
```

Listing 6.11 Simple SVG example.

Listing 6.11, an example taken from the SVG Recommendation of the W3C, creates an image of a red ellipse, shown in Figure 6.7. When a user clicks on the ellipse, the user is taken to the W3C Web site. Of course, this is one of the simplest examples. SVG takes advantage of XLink for linking.

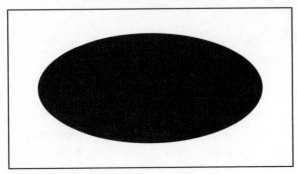

Figure 6.7 Rendering a simple SVG file.

If product adoption is any indicator, the SVG specification is quite successful. In a very short time, vendors have jumped on the SVG bandwagon. The Adobe SVG Viewer, the Apache Batik project, the SVG-enabled Mozilla browser, the W3C's Amaya editor/browser, and Jasc's WebDraw application support SVG, to name a few. Some are SVG renderers, and some projects generate SVG content on the server side. Because it is natively XML, Web services can generate rich graphical content. SVG is an important technology that can be a part of a service-oriented Web.

Summary

This chapter has provided a very brief tour of some very important XML technologies. Because the purpose of this chapter was to provide a big picture of some of the key technologies, Table 6.1 presents a reference of some of the key issues.

Table 6.1 Summary of Technologies in This Chapter

STANDARD	DESCRIPTION	W3C STATUS	KEY RELATED TECHNOLOGIES
XPath	Standard addressing mechanism for XML nodes	XPath 1.0— Recommendation; XPath 2.0—Working Draft	Almost every XML technology uses it, notably XSLT, XPointer, XLink, XInclude, XQuery.
The Stylesheet Languages (XSLT/XSL/ XSLFO)	Used for transforming and formatting XML documents	XSL 1.0— Recommendation; XSLT 1.0— Recommendation; XSLT 2.0—Working Draft	XPath provides an addressing basis for XSLT.
XQuery	Querying mechanism for XML data stores ("The SQL for XML")	XQuery 1.0— Working Draft	XQuery and XPath share the same data model.
XLink	General, all-purpose linking specification	XLink 1.0— Recommendation	SVG uses it; XLink can use XPointer.
XPointer	Used to address nodes, ranges, and points in local and remote XML documents	XPointer framework, xpointer() scheme, xmlns() scheme, and element() scheme — All Working Drafts	XPath provides an addressing basis. Can be used in XLink, XInclude.
XInclude	Used to include several external documents into a large document	XInclude 1.0— Candidate Recommendation	N/A
XML Base	Mechanism for easily resolving relative URIs	W3C Recommendation	N/A
XHTML	A valid and well-formed version of HTML, with noted improvements	XHTML 1.0— Recommendation; XHTML 2.0— Working Draft	HTML
XForms	A powerful XML-based form-processing mechanism for the next-generation Web	XForms 1.0— Candidate Recommendation	Uses XPath for addressing
SVG	XML-based rich-content graphic rendering	SVG 1.0— Recommendation	Uses XLink

All the technologies in Table 6.1 have a future. However, they are all evolving. Of the standards we've discussed, XPath, XSLT/XSL, XHTML, and SVG seem to have the most support and adoption. However, they all achieve important goals, and as the influence of XML grows, so will support. For more information on these standards, visit the W3C's Technical Reports page at http://www.w3.org/TR/.

CHAPTER 7

Understanding Taxonomies

"The Semantic Web is an extension of the current web in which information is given well-defined meaning, better enabling computers and people to work in cooperation."

—Tim Berners-Lee, James Hendler, Ora Lassila, "The Semantic Web," *Scientific American,* **May 2001**

The first step toward a Semantic Web and using Web services is expressing a taxonomy in machine-usable form. But what's a taxonomy? Is it related to a schema? Is a taxonomy something like a thesaurus? Is it a controlled vocabulary? Is it different from an ontology? What do these concepts have to do with the Semantic Web and Web services? What should you know about these concepts?

This chapter attempts to answer these questions by discussing what a taxonomy is and isn't. Some example taxonomies are depicted and described. Taxonomies are also compared to some of the preceding concepts using the framework of the Ontology Spectrum as a way of relating the various information models in terms of increasing semantic richness. Because a language for representing taxonomies is necessary, especially if the taxonomy is to be used on the Web, for Web services, or other content, this chapter will also introduce a Web language standard that enables you to define machine-usable taxonomies. Topic Maps is then compared with RDF (introduced in Chapter 5). This chapter concludes with a look ahead to Chapter 8 and ontologies.

Overview of Taxonomies

This section defines *taxonomy*, describes what kind of information a taxonomy tries to structure, and shows how it structures this information. The business world has many taxonomies, as does the nonbusiness world. In fact, the world cannot do without taxonomies, since it is in our nature as human beings to classify. That is what a taxonomy is: a way of classifying or categorizing a set of things—specifically, a classification in the form of a hierarchy. A *hierarchy* is simply a treelike structure. Like a tree, it has a root and branches. Each branching point is called a *node*.

If you look up the definition of *taxonomy* in the dictionary, the definition will read something like the following (from Merriam-Webster OnLine: http://www.m-w.com/):

> *The study of the general principles of scientific classification: SYSTEMATICS CLASSIFICATION; especially: orderly classification of plants and animals according to their presumed natural relationships*

So, the two key ideas for a *taxonomy* are that it is a *classification* and it is a *tree*. But now let's be a bit more precise as to the information technology notion of a taxonomy. The rapid evolution of information technology has spawned terminology that's rooted in the dictionary definitions but defined slightly differently. The concepts behind the terminology (and that thus constitute the definitions) are slightly different, because these concepts describe *engineering products* and are not just abstract or ordinary human natural language constructs. Here is the information technology definition for a taxonomy:

> *The classification of information entities in the form of a hierarchy, according to the presumed relationships of the real-world entities that they represent*

A taxonomy is usually depicted with the root of the taxonomy on top, as in Figure 7.1. Each node of the taxonomy—including the root—is an information entity that stands for a real-world entity. Each link between nodes represents a special relation called the *is subclassification of* relation (if the link's arrow is pointing up toward the parent node) or *is superclassification of* (if the link's arrow is pointing down at the child node). Sometimes this special relation is defined more strictly to be *is subclass of* or *is superclass of*, where it is understood to mean that the information entities (which, remember, stand for the real-world entities) are classes of objects. This is probably terminology you are familiar with, as it is used in object-oriented programming. A *class* is a generic entity. In Figure 7.1, examples include the class Person, its subclasses of Employee and Manager, and its superclass of Agent (a legal entity, which can also include an Organization, as shown in the figure).

As you go up the taxonomy toward the root at the top, the entities become more general. As you go down the taxonomy toward the leaves at the bottom, the entities become more specialized. Agent, for example, is more general than Person, which in turn is more general than Employee. This kind of classification system is sometimes called a *generalization/specialization* taxonomy.

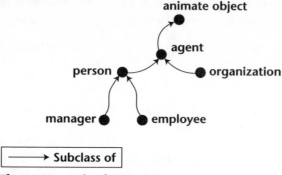

Figure 7.1 A simple taxonomy.

Taxonomies are good for classifying information entities semantically; that is, they help establish a simple semantics (semantics here just means "meaning" or a kind of meta data) for an information space. As such, they are related to other information technology *knowledge* products that you've probably heard about: meta data, schemas, thesauri, conceptual models, and ontologies. Whereas the next chapter discusses ontologies in some detail, this chapter helps you make the distinction among the preceding concepts.

A taxonomy is a semantic hierarchy in which information entities are related by either the *subclassification of* relation or the *subclass of* relation. The former is semantically weaker than the latter, so we make a distinction between semantically weaker and semantically stronger taxonomies. Although taxonomies are fairly weak semantically to begin with—they don't have the complexity to express rich meaning—the stronger taxonomies try to use this notion of a distinguishing property. Each information entity is distinguished by a *distinguishing property* that makes it unique as a subclass of its parent entity (a synonym for *property* is *attribute* or *quality*). If you consider the Linnaeus-like biological taxonomy shown in Figure 7.2, which has been simplified to show where humans fit in the taxonomy. In Figure 7.1, the property that distinguishes a specific subclass at the *higher* level (closer to the root) is probably actually a large set of properties.

Consider the distinction between mammal and reptile under their parent subphylum *Vertebrata* (in Figure 7.2, a dotted line between *Mammalia* and *Diapsida* shows that they are at the same level of representation, both being subclassifications of *Vertebrata*). Although both mammals and reptiles have four legs (common properties), mammals are warm-blooded and reptiles are cold-blooded. So *warm-bloodedness* can be considered at least one of the properties that distinguishes mammals and reptiles; there could be others. One other distinguishing property between mammals and reptiles is the property of *egg-laying*. Although there are exceptions (the Australian platypus, for example), mammals in general do not lay eggs, whereas reptiles do. (Reptiles also share this property with birds, fish, and most amphibians, but we will not elaborate that distinction here.)

Again, if you consider the Linnaeus biological taxonomy, the property that distinguishes a specific subclass at the *lower* level (closer to the leaves) is probably one specific property.

Similarly, what are the distinguishing properties between the three hammers shown in Figure 7.3? We know we can talk about their different functions, and so functional properties distinguish them. But we can also see that there are physical differences, which may distinguish them too. Actually, the functional properties necessarily influence the physical properties; the physical properties depend on the functional properties (i.e., pounding or retracting nails, or pounding a stake into the ground). We know that the leftmost hammer is the common claw hammer (but related to the longer and heavier framing hammer) and that it is used to drive and pull nails. The middle hammer is the ball peen hammer, which is generally used for shaping or working with metal. Finally, the rightmost hammer is the sledge hammer, which is used to pound stakes, work concrete, hit wedges to split wood, and so on. In general, we might say that in many cases, "form follows function" or "purpose proposes property"—at least for human-designed artifacts.

Kingdom: Animalia
  Phylum: Chordata
    Subphylum: Vertebrata
      Class: Mammalia
        Subclass: Theria
          Infraclass: Eutheria
            Order: Primates
              Suborder: Anthropoidea
                Superfamily: Hominoidea
                  Family: Hominidae
                    Genus: Homo
                      Species: Sapiens
      Class: Diapsida (Reptiles, Dinosaurs, Birds)

Figure 7.2 Linnaean classification of humans.

Figure 7.3 Different hammers: claw versus ball peen versus sledge.

What's important to remember from this discussion is that there usually is (and should be, especially if the taxonomy is trying to be a semantically rich and well-defined structure, a semantically stronger taxonomy) a specific distinguishing property for each subclass of a taxonomy. Furthermore, the specificity—that is, the degree of fineness or granularity—of the property increases as you go down the taxonomy.

But enough with the insects and hand tools. What does this notion of distinguished property mean to you? Well, consider: Is a manager an employee? Should a manager and an employee really be distinguished at the same level in the taxonomy, as subclasses of person, as is displayed in Figure 7.1? Isn't a manager an employee too? So, shouldn't manager and some other information entity (call it X for now) be considered as subclasses of employee? Maybe the distinction should be between manager and nonmanager. But then perhaps these distinctions are somehow incorrect. Maybe person is a legitimate class of information entity, but manager and employee are not really subclasses of person; instead, they are different roles (a different relation) that any given person may have. This latter view complicates the picture, of course, but it may be more accurate if your intent is to model the real world as semantically accurately as possible. After all, a manager is an employee too, no? He or she is an employee of an organization that also has employees who are not managers.

This concept is similar to a subdirectory in a file directory: A subdirectory is a file (at least, when you look at how it's actually implemented) that contains files. Of course, in this latter case, the subdirectory is more like an *aggregation* or *collection* of files. Files are *part of* a subdirectory. And yes, the *part of* relation itself, quite like the *subclass of* relation, can constitute a taxonomy. A taxonomy based on the *part of* relation would be an *aggregation* taxonomy (as opposed to a generalization/specialization taxonomy, the first kind of taxonomy we looked at). As business folks, we know all about parts trees, bills of materials, and related notions, don't we? Well, now we also know these are taxonomies.

Table 7.1 displays a portion of the better-known taxonomy used in electronic commerce, the Universal Standard Products and Services Classification (UNSPSC, http://www.eccma.org). Although this taxonomy is displayed in tabular format, we can display it in tree format, as in Figure 7.4, with the Segment node being the root (of the subtree of Live Plant and Animal Segment 10) and the Family nodes being the first branch level (beneath which would be the Class and then the Commodity branches).

Taxonomies are good for classifying your information entities. They express at least the bare minimum of the semantics necessary to distinguish among the objects in your information space. As such, they are a simple *model* of the distinguishable items you are interested in. They are a way of structuring and characterizing your *content meta data*. Because taxonomies are trees, sometimes there is redundant information in a taxonomy. Why? Because there is only one parent node for each child node, you may sometimes have to have duplicate children nodes under different parents. For example, if you had the subclasses of Manager and Employee situated under Person, as in the example discussed previously, all managers would be placed under both nodes, since they are both managers and employees, resulting in duplication. Much therefore depends on how the taxonomy is structured. As we will see in the next section, ontologies use taxonomies as their backbones. The basic taxonomic *subclass of* hierarchies act as the skeleton of ontologies, but ontologies add additional muscle and organs—in the form of additional relations, properties/attributes, property values. So, taxonomies provide the basic structure for the information space, and ontologies flesh it out.

Table 7.1 A Portion of the UNSPSC Electronic Commerce Taxonomy

SEGMENT	FAMILY	CLASS	COMMODITY	TITLE
10	00	00	00	Live Plant and Animal Material and Accessories and Supplies
10	10	00	00	Live Animals
10	10	15	00	Livestock
10	10	15	01	Cats
10	10	15	02	Dogs

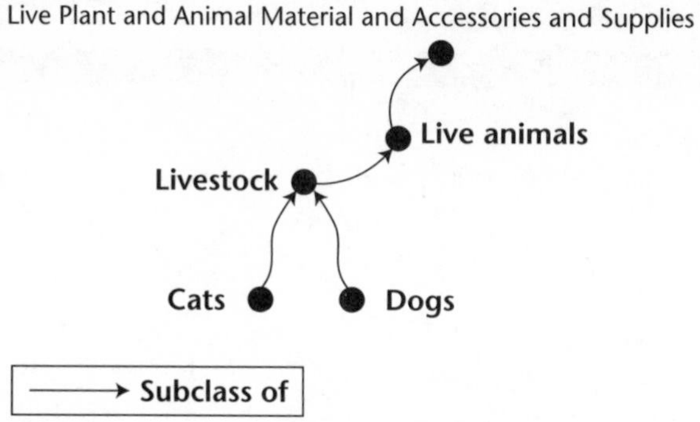
Live Plant and Animal Material and Accessories and Supplies
Live animals
Livestock
Cats
Dogs
Subclass of

Figure 7.4 Tree representation of Table 7.1.

Why Use Taxonomies?

Why should you be interested in classifying your information entities, in giving some semantics and structure to them as you would by defining a taxonomy? Consider a search on the Internet. You use a search engine to try to find the topics you are interested in, by using keywords or keywords strung together by *ands* and *ors* in a boolean keyword search. Sometimes you search to find products and services you would like to purchase. Other times you would like people and other companies to find the products and services that you or your company provides. In either case, if you or they can't find a product or service, it can't be considered and then purchased. You can't find what you need. They can't find what they need. If they can't find your valuable product or service, they will make a purchase somewhere else. Your product or service may actually be the best value to them of any on the entire Internet, but because they can't find it, it's of no value to them.

The most common use of taxonomies (really, the primary rationale for using taxonomies rather than other, more complicated knowledge structures) is thus to browse or navigate for information, especially when you only have a general idea of what you are looking for. Consider the Dewey Decimal System, the taxonomy encountered and used by nearly everyone who has ever visited a public library. The top categories (the roots of the tree) of the system (http://www.loc.gov/cds/lcsh.html) are 10 very general *buckets* of possible book topics, in other words, 10 ways of partitioning the subject matter of the world, as Table 7.2 shows.

Table 7.2 The Dewey Decimal System: A Taxonomy

CODE	DESCRIPTION
000	Generalities
100	Philosophy and psychology
200	Religion
300	Social sciences
400	Language
500	Natural sciences and mathematics
600	Technology (Applied sciences)
700	The arts
800	Literature and rhetoric
900	Geography and history

Much like the Linnaeus and the United Nations Standard Products and Services Code (UNSPSC) taxonomies, each of these root categories has much finer elaboration of subject matter beneath them. Table 7.3 shows one example: Category 500, Natural Sciences and Mathematics.

Table 7.3 The Dewey Decimal System: 500 Natural Sciences and Mathematics

CODE	DESCRIPTION	CODE	DESCRIPTION
500	Natural sciences and mathematics	550	Earth sciences
501	Philosophy and theory	551	Geology, hydrology, meteorology
502	Miscellany	552	Petrology
503	Dictionaries and encyclopedias	553	Economic geology
504	Not assigned or no longer used	554	Earth sciences of Europe
505	Serial publications	555	Earth sciences of Asia
506	Organizations and management	556	Earth sciences of Africa
507	Education, research, related topics	557	Earth sciences of North America
508	Natural history	558	Earth sciences of South America
509	Historical, areas, persons treatment	559	Earth sciences of other areas

Table 7.3 *(continued)*

CODE	DESCRIPTION	CODE	DESCRIPTION
510	Mathematics	560	Paleontology Paleozoology
511	General principles	561	Paleobotany
512	Algebra and number theory	562	Fossil invertebrates
513	Arithmetic	563	Fossil primitive phyla
514	Topology	564	Fossil Mollusca and Molluscoidea
515	Analysis	565	Other fossil invertebrates
516	Geometry	566	Fossil Vertebrata (Fossil Craniata)
517	Not assigned or no longer used	567	Fossil cold-blooded vertebrates
518	Not assigned or no longer used	568	Fossil Aves (Fossil birds)
519	Probabilities and applied mathematics	569	Fossil Mammalia
520	Astronomy and allied sciences	570	Life sciences
521	Celestial mechanics	571	Not assigned or no longer used
522	Techniques, equipment, materials	572	Human races
523	Specific celestial bodies and phenomena	573	Physical anthropology
524	Not assigned or no longer used	574	Biology
525	Earth (Astronomical geography)	575	Evolution and genetics
526	Mathematical geography	576	Microbiology
527	Celestial navigation	577	General nature of life
528	Ephemerides	578	Microscopy in biology
529	Chronology	579	Collection and preservation
530	Physics	580	Botanical sciences
531	Classical mechanics Solid mechanics	581	Botany

(continued)

Table 7.3 *(continued)*

CODE	DESCRIPTION	CODE	DESCRIPTION
532	Fluid mechanics Liquid mechanics	582	Spermatophyta (Seed-bearing plants)
533	Gas mechanics	583	Dicotyledones
534	Sound and related vibrations	584	Monocotyledones
535	Light and paraphotic phenomena	585	Gymnospermae (Pinophyta)
536	Heat	586	Cryptogamia (Seedless plants)
537	Electricity and electronics	587	Pteridophyta (Vascular cryptograms)
538	Magnetism	588	Bryophyta
539	Modern physics	589	Thallobionta and Prokaryotae
540	Chemistry and allied sciences	590	Zoological sciences
541	Physical and theoretical chemistry	591	Zoology
542	Techniques, equipment, materials	592	Invertebrates
543	Analytical chemistry	593	Protozoa, Echinodermata, related phyla
544	Qualitative analysis	594	Mollusca and Molluscoidea
545	Quantitative analysis	595	Other invertebrates
546	Inorganic chemistry	596	Vertebrata (Craniata, Vertebrates)
547	Organic chemistry	597	Cold-blooded vertebrates: Fishes
548	Crystallography	598	Aves (Birds)
549	Mineralogy	599	Mammalia (Mammals)

If you were looking for a book on dinosaurs, you would probably look under Category 567 ("Fossil cold-blooded vertebrates") if you thought dinosaurs were reptiles ("cold-blooded"), or possibly under Category 568 ("Fossil Aves: Fossil Birds") if you thought dinosaurs were birds, or possibly under the more general Category 566 ("Fossil Vertebra: Fossil Craniata") if all you knew is that dinosaurs had backbones or if you knew that *Fossil Craniata* meant "animals having skulls." And if you knew that, then you probably knew that animals having skulls have backbones.

This discussion also demonstrates a difficulty: How do you map taxonomies to each other? Perhaps you want to map the Dewey Decimal categorization for *dinosaur* to the Linnaeus categorization (*Class Diaspida* or something below that?) and to the UNSPSC categorization (maybe "dinosaur bones" are a product that you can buy or sell; where would you classify it?). We look at the general problem of *semantic mapping* in the next chapter. Semantic mapping is a critical issue for information technologists considering using multiple knowledge sources. But let's return to what a taxonomy is.

A taxonomy, like a thesaurus or an ontology, is a way of structuring your data, your information entities, and of giving them at least a simple semantics. On the Web, taxonomies can be used to help your customers find your products and services. Taxonomies can also help you get a handle on your own information needs, by classifying your interests (whether they include products and services or not). Because taxonomies are focused on classifying *content* (semantics or meaning), they enable search engines and other applications that utilize taxonomies directly to find information entities much faster and with much greater accuracy. Back in 2000, Forrester Research published a report entitled "Must Search Stink?" (Hagen, 2000) In this study, Forrester Research answered its own question: If you really address search issues (read: content categorization) and use emerging best practices, search does not have to stink. In fact, taxonomies and other content representations will definitely improve search efficiency.

In Chapter 4, UDDI was introduced. In a real sense, UDDI requires taxonomies and ontologies. A directory or registry of Web products and services absolutely needs some way of classifying those products and services; otherwise, how can anything be found? UDDI has proposed the tModel (http://www/uddi.org) as the placeholder for taxonomies such as UNSPSC and the North American Industry Classification System (NAICS)[1] that can be used to classify Web products and services. When you look in the Yellow Pages of a phone book, you see that under the Automobile heading are many other subheadings or categories: Automobile Accessories, Automobile Body Repairing and Painting, Automobile Dealers (New or Used), Automobile Parts and Supplies, Automobile Renting, Automobile Repair, and so on. This is a simple taxonomy. The entire Yellow Pages is a huge taxonomy. It is ordered alphabetically to be of additional assistance to a person looking for products or services, but its primary function is as a taxonomy classifying the available content. The Yahoo and Google taxonomies act in much the same way: They assist a user looking for content by categorizing that content as naturally (as semantically realistically) as possible.

---

[1] The North American Industry Classification System (NAICS): http://www.census.gove/epod/www/naics.html. See also its ongoing related effort at classifying products, the North American Product Classification System (NAPCS).

The next section will help you differentiate among the concepts related to taxonomies: schemas, thesauri, conceptual models, and ontologies. All of these expand on the simple classification semantics and structure expressed by taxonomies. In the next section, the Ontology Spectrum is introduced. This is a framework for comparing these concepts.

Defining the Ontology Spectrum

We discuss the notion of *ontology* and ontologies in greater detail in the next chapter, but this section introduces some crucial distinctions that we make in the general ontological/classificational space we call the Ontology Spectrum. We have discussed taxonomies up to this point. The subsequent sections of this chapter talk about Topic Maps and RDF, and their similarities and differences. But can Topic Maps and RDF enable you to represent taxonomies or ontologies? Or both or neither or something in between? Before we can make sense of the question and its possible answers, we need to make sure we understand what we are talking about—at least to a certain extent. Do we need to know everything about taxonomies and ontologies? No. But we need to know the basic distinctive properties of each and place each concept within some relative context of use. Taxonomies were defined in the previous section. Ontologies are defined in the next chapter. How do you distinguish them? We'll answer this question here.

The following concepts all attempt to address issues in representing, classifying, and disambiguating semantic content (meaning): taxonomies, thesauri, conceptual models, and logical theories. This section will help you distinguish these concepts. The Ontology Spectrum (see Figure 7.5) tries to depict these concepts in a general classification or ontology space, and displays the relationships among concepts such as "classification system," "taxonomy," "thesaurus," "ontology," "conceptual model," and "logical theory." The following common languages and technologies are displayed in the diagram:

- Database models: the relational language (R), the Entity-Relational language and model (ER), and the Extended Entity-Relational model (EER)
- Object-oriented models: Unified Modeling Language (UML)

This framework was developed for comparing the semantic richness of classification and knowledge-based models, most of which have been employed or discussed by various groups in multiple conceptual paradigms and used for the representation, classification, and disambiguation of semantics in or across particular subject matter domains. As you go up the spectrum from lower left to upper right, the semantic richness increases. We characterize the poles of the spectrum as "weak semantics" and "strong semantics." What we mean is that the richness of the expressible or characterizable semantics increases from weak to strong. At the "weaker" side, you can express only very simple meaning; at the "stronger" side, you can express arbitrarily complex meaning.

Figure 7.5 includes terms you may not yet know much about (though we touched on a few of these in earlier chapters): DAML+OIL, OWL, description logic, first-order logic, and modal logic. Don't worry yet about what the acronyms stand for; we will describe them in detail either in this chapter or the next.

What is normally known as an *ontology* can thus range from the simple notion of a *taxonomy* (knowledge with minimal hierarchic or parent/child structure), to a *thesaurus* (words and synonyms), to a *conceptual model* (with more complex knowledge), to a *logical theory* (with very rich, complex, consistent, meaningful knowledge).

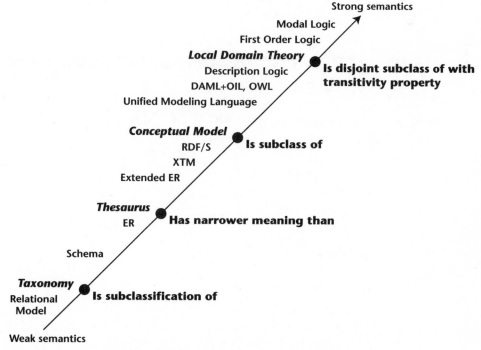

Figure 7.5 The ontology spectrum: Weak to strong semantics.

Taxonomy

The lower-left endpoint of Figure 7.5 designates a *taxonomy*. In a taxonomy, as we've seen, the semantics of the relationship between a parent and a child node is relatively underspecified or ill defined. In some cases, the relationship is the *subclass of* relation; in others, it is the *part of* relation. In still others, it is simply undefined. If you consider your computer's directory structure, the relationship between any given directory and one of its specific subdirectories is arbitrary. Say, for example that in one case, you create a subdirectory to hold a special subset (a subclass) of the directory documents; in another, you create a subdirectory to place documents representing conferences and workshops addressing the general subject matter of the parent directory.

Figure 7.6 displays a subset of a directory structure (Microsoft Windows 2000). Note that under the highlighted Logic Programming subdirectory are the logic programming systems subdirectories (Prolog and Eclipse, which might be considered subclasses of logic programming), as well as subdirectories, Logic Programming Conferences and Logic Programming Research Projects, which are just things that are related somehow (and the relationship is not really spelled out) to the parent directory.

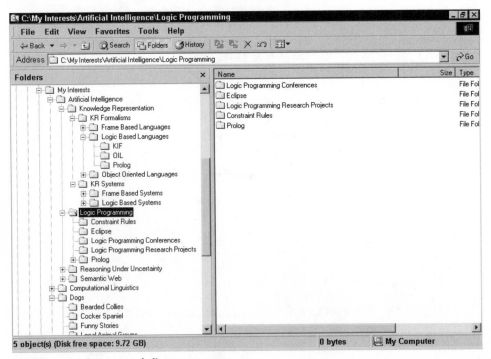

Figure 7.6 Directory-subdirectory taxonomy.

In general, all you can say about the relationship between a parent and a child in a semantically weaker taxonomy is that it means *is subclassification of*: a fairly ill-defined semantics. But as we've seen in the semantically stronger taxonomies, the relationship can be the stronger *subclass of* relation. It is a semantically stronger taxonomy (using the *subclass of* relation) that is the backbone of conceptual models and ontologies.

The next point up toward the right designates a *thesaurus*. A thesaurus concerns the relationships between *terms* (words or phrases) structured in a (semantically weak) taxonomy. So a thesaurus is a taxonomy plus some term semantic relations.

Thesaurus

The ANSI/NISO Monolingual Thesaurus Standard defines a thesaurus as "a controlled vocabulary arranged in a known order and structured so that equivalence, homographic, hierarchical, and associative relationships among terms are displayed clearly and identified by standardized relationship indicators . . .. The primary purposes of a thesaurus are to facilitate retrieval of documents and to achieve consistency in the indexing of written or otherwise recorded documents and other items."[2] These relationships can be categorized four ways:

- Equivalence
- Homographic
- Hierarchical
- Associative

Table 7.4 shows these relationships and synonyms for the relations, and it provides definitions and examples.

A thesaurus is typically used to associate the rough meaning of a term to the rough meaning of another term. In Figure 7.7 (Center for Army Lessons Learned [CALL] Thesaurus, 2002), "radar imagery" is narrower than "aerial imagery," which in turn is narrower than "imagery" and related to "imaging systems."

[2] ANSI/NISO Z39.19-1993 (R1998), p. 1.

Table 7.4 Semantic Relations of a Thesaurus

SEMANTIC RELATION	DEFINITION	EXAMPLE
Synonym Similar to Equivalent Used for	A term X has nearly the same meaning as a term Y.	"Report" is a synonym for "document."
Homonym Spelled the same Homographic	A term X is spelled the same way as a term Y, which has a different meaning.	The "tank," which is a military vehicle, is a homonym for the "tank," which is a receptacle for holding liquids.
Broader Than (Hierarchic: parent of)	A term X is broader in meaning than a term Y.	"Organization" has a broader meaning than "financial institution."
Narrower Than (Hierarchic: child of)	A term X is narrower in meaning than a term Y.	"Financial institution" has a narrower meaning than "organization."
Associated Associative Related	A term X is associated with a term Y, i.e., there is some unspecified relationship between the two.	A "nail" is associated with a "hammer."

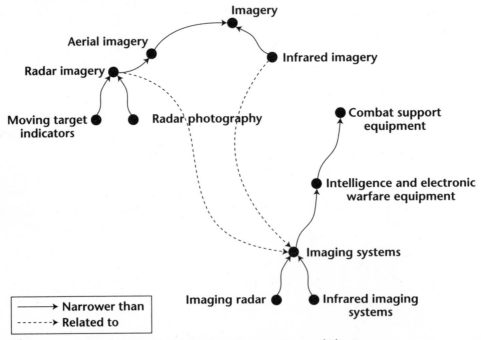

Figure 7.7 Example from Center for Army Lessons Learned Thesaurus.

Thus, a thesaurus is controlled vocabulary designed to support information retrieval by guiding both the person assigning meta data and the searcher to choose the same terms for the same concept. For example, a thesaurus conforming to ISO 2788 supports navigation and term selection by showing relationships between terms that are close in meaning.

A thesaurus ensures that:

- Concepts are described in a consistent manner.

- Experienced users are able to easily refine their searches to locate the information they need.

- Users do not need to be familiar with technical or local terminology.

Although most people are familiar with *Roget's Thesaurus*[3], (it's probably sitting on the shelf above your desk right next to the dictionary), a common resource available to technologists is the WordNet thesaurus (WordNet: http://www.cogsci.princeton.edu/~wn/).[4] WordNet was designed according to psycholinguistic theories of human lexical memory. WordNet can be searched interactively online or downloaded and used by software developers who wish to incorporate thesaural knowledge into their applications.

In WordNet, a word is given a definition or definitions (distinct definitions for an individual word are usually called *word senses* for that word; the notion that a given word such as *bank* has multiple meanings or word senses is called *polysemy* ("multiple senses") in linguistics. A word (or common phrase) in WordNet also has the information typically associated with it according to the ISO 2788 standard.

- *Synonyms*—Those nodes in the taxonomy that are in the *mean the same as* relation; in neo-Latinate, "same name."

- *Hypernyms*—Those nodes that are in the *parent of* or *broader than* relation in the taxonomy; in neo-Latinate "above name"; if the taxonomy is a tree, there is only one parent node.

- *Hyponyms*—Those nodes that are in the *children of* or *narrower than* relation; in neo-Latinate, "below name."

---

[3] Roget's Thesaurus has multiple versions. The free version (because the copyright has expired, i.e., the 1911 edition) is available at many sites, including http://www.cix.co.uk/~andie/cogito/roget.shtml or http://promo.net/cgi-promo/pg/t9.cgi?entry=22&full=yes&ftpsite= ftp://ibiblio.org/pub/docs/books/gutenberg/. Both are the result of the Project Gutenberg project: http://www.gutenberg.net/.

[4] Also see Fellbaum (1998), Miller et al. (1993).

In WordNet 1.7.1, for example, the word *bank* has the following definitional (word sense) and hypernymic (*parent of* or *broader than*) information associated with it:

1. depository financial institution, bank, banking concern, banking company—(a financial institution that accepts deposits and channels the money into lending activities; "he cashed a check at the bank"; "that bank holds the mortgage on my home")

2. bank—(sloping land (especially the slope beside a body of water); "they pulled the canoe up on the bank"; "he sat on the bank of the river and watched the currents")

3. bank—(a supply or stock held in reserve for future use (especially in emergencies)

4. bank, bank building—(a building in which commercial banking is transacted; "the bank is on the corner of Nassau and Witherspoon")

5. bank—(an arrangement of similar objects in a row or in tiers; "he operated a bank of switches")

6. savings bank, coin bank, money box, bank—(a container (usually with a slot in the top) for keeping money at home; "the coin bank was empty")

7. bank—(a long ridge or pile; "a huge bank of earth")

8. bank—(the funds held by a gambling house or the dealer in some gambling games; "he tried to break the bank at Monte Carlo")

9. bank, cant, camber—(a slope in the turn of a road or track; the outside is higher than the inside in order to reduce the effects of centrifugal force)

10. bank—(a flight maneuver; aircraft tips laterally about its longitudinal axis (especially in turning); "the plane went into a steep bank")

In WordNet, the various relations are really between synonym sets, or *synsets*. This means that the distinct words or phrases, called *terms*, that are synonymous at roughly the same level of abstraction (i.e., they are not at either the parent or child level, with respect to each other) are grouped together as a set. The *synset* therefore acts as a *concept*—a mental construct in the human being (or the information system or knowledge representation) that stands behind the *term* and represents the mental signification of the term. The concept, in turn, as we shall see, "stands in" for the real- or possible-world object. So, we distinguish *term* from *concept* in knowledge or semantic representations, though we cannot elaborate the distinction until the next chapter. A *term* is the label or string representation for the underlying meaning indexed by that term; the underlying meaning is the *concept* and the *attributes, attribute values,* and *relationships* to other concepts that that concept participates in. Figure 7.8 displays the taxonomic structure for the first *word sense* for *bank*.

Group, Grouping

   ⇐ Social Group

     ⇐ Organization

       ⇐ Institution

         ⇐ Financial Institution

           ⇐ Depository Financial Institution

Figure 7.8 WordNet word sense 1 for *bank*: Hypernymic taxonomy from root down.

In Figure 7.9, the first 3 of 10 total word senses for the word *bank* are displayed, along with each sense's *hypernymic* (*parent of*, or *broader term than* relation). Each => indicates the immediate parent of the preceding term (an increase in indentation is also used to indicate stepping up a level in the taxonomic structure). For example, consider *word sense 1* of this: the sense of bank as a *depository financial institution* has immediately as parent *financial institution*, which in turn has as parent *institution*, and so on. Another way to look at this taxonomic structure is with the "root" of the taxonomic tree at the top, and note that we have reversed the arrow to <= to show that the parent is above the child.

The next step toward increasing semantic richness is the conceptual model. As we move from taxonomies and thesauri to conceptual models and logical theories, we are increasingly in the realm of ontologies. Although our framework is entitled the Ontology Spectrum, to show that the whole ontological or semantic space includes a range of possibilities in a progressive order, the upper right half more appropriately represents the common notion of *ontology*.

What is a conceptual model? A *conceptual model* is a model of a subject area or area of knowledge, sometimes called a domain, that represents the primary entities (the things of the domain), the relationships among entities, the attributes and attribute values (sometimes called properties and property values) of the entities and the relationships, and sometimes rules that associate entities, relationships, and attributes (or all three) in more complicated ways. A rule is simply something along the lines of the following examples:

- If *X* is true, then *Y* must also be true.
- If (*W* and *X*) or (*Y* and not *Z*) are true, then (*U* and *V*) must also be true.

where *U*, *V*, *W*, *X*, *Y*, and *Z* are simple or complex assertions about the entities, relations, or attributes.

Word Sense and Hypernimic Taxomic Representation

Sense 1: depository financial institution, bank, banking concern, banking company—(a financial institution that accepts deposits and channels the money into lending activities; "he cashed a check at the bank"; "that bank holds the mortgage on my home")

> ⇒ financial institution, financial organization, financial organisation—(an institution (public or private) that collects funds (from the public or other institutions) and invests them in financial assets)
>> ⇒ institution, establishment—(an organization founded and united for a specific purpose)
>>> ⇒ organization, organisation—(a group of people who work together)
>>>> ⇒ social group—(people sharing some social relation)
>>>>> ⇒ group, grouping—(any number of entities (members) considered as a unit)

Sense 2: bank—(sloping land (especially the slope beside a body of water); "they pulled the canoe up on the bank"; "he sat on the bank of the river and watched the currents")

> ⇒ slope, incline, side—(an elevated geological formation; "he climbed the steep slope"; "the house was built on the side of the mountain")
>> ⇒ geological formation, geology, formation—(the geological features of the earth)
>>> ⇒ natural object—(an object occurring naturally; not made by man)
>>>> ⇒ object, physical object—(a tangible and visible entity; an entity that can cast a shadow; "it was full of rackets, balls, and other objects")
>>>>> ⇒ entity, physical thing—(that which is perceived or known or inferred to have its own physical existence (living or nonliving))

Sense 3: bank—(a supply or stock held in reserve for future use (especially in emergencies))

Figure 7.9 WordNet entry for *bank*: First three word senses and their hypernymic taxonomies conceptual model.

The *if* part of the rule is sometimes called the *antecedent*; the *then* part is called the *consequent*. Rules are like axioms or constraints. Although we briefly talk about axioms in the next section, most of the discussion will have to wait until Chapter 8. These logical rules are related to rules you may be more familiar with: the production rules of expert systems. Production rules are condition-action rules of the form:

■ If condition X is true, then perform action Y.

where X again is an arbitrarily complex set of conditions that hold (or are true) in the current state of the environment, and Y is an arbitrarily complex set of actions.

Actions here include setting specific values to variables, asserting variables (conditions) to be true, or executing other production rules, in a rule-chaining style sometimes called *forward-chaining* (or top-down or right-to-left inference, the prototypical reasoning method employed by expert systems). In other words, if the antecedent of the production rule is true, then the actions of the consequent are executed, thereby changing the state of the environment, and so possibly enabling the conditions of other rules in the entire rule set to become true, thus causing them to fire (become activated). Other common synonyms for production rules are *demon* and *trigger*, the latter sometimes used as a mechanism in database technology for changing the state of a database.

The opposite type of rule execution in expert systems is called *backward-chaining* (bottom-up, right-to-left, goal-directed reasoning), where the consequent's goal states are considered true, and so its conditions would generate new goals, with the new goals matching the consequents of other rules.[5] In general, the production rules of expert systems are essentially nonlogical implementations of inference—that is, they simulate inference. Although production rules are still in use today, in practice, more modern knowledge technologies (such as ontological engineering, which we discuss in Chapter 8) employ logical rules in true logical inference.

In a conceptual model, it truly is possible to define and express the subclass of relation between a parent class and a child class. Object-oriented programming modeling languages such as UML (and tools such as Rational Rose that use UML) are rich enough to express the semantics of the subclass of relation between two given classes.[6] What is also important is that the definitions of a class, superclass, and subclass be semantically well specified at the meta-model level so that the object-model level classes such as Person and its subclass Employee can be well specified semantically. The object-model level is the level that we are interested in. It is the level at which we construct our domain and system models. The meta-model level is the level that defines the constructs such as class, relation, and attribute that we will use at the object-model level to define our content models. The meta-model level is often the level where the conceptual modeling language (such as UML) itself is defined. What is defined at the modeling language level enables us to express things in that language (i.e., construct our own models using the language) at the object level. This notion of meta level and object level can be confusing, so it is a topic that we will return to in the next chapter when we look at ontologies.

---

[5] For a more detailed description of expert systems and their problems, see Obrst and Liu (2003), pp. 113 to 116.

[6] For readers unfamiliar with the object-oriented programming paradigm, we suggest Graham (2000) and Rumbaugh et al. (1991). For general information on and specifications of UML, see http://www.uml.org/. For information on Rational Rose and UML, see http://www.rational.com/uml/index.jsp.

The Entity-Relational (ER) model or language (and the Enhanced or Extended ER or EER model)[7] that is used to define a conceptual schema for a database is also considered a conceptual modeling language. When one designs a database, one first creates a conceptual schema (which is where the initial conception of the domain of the eventual database is modeled), reduces that to a logical schema, and finally reduces that in turn to a physical schema. These schemas represent levels of abstraction: from the human conceptual level to the database table/column level to the actual implemented tables, columns, and keys.

Logical Theory

The upper-right endpoint designates a *logical theory*. Ontologies represented as logical theories are directly semantically interpretable by our software. This is the high-end notion of an ontology: a logical theory. Much of current ontological engineering and knowledge representation (we will talk about these disciplines in more detail later) aspires to building ontologies as logical theories. We investigate ontologies and Semantic Web languages used to express ontologies more in Chapter 8. For now, all we need to say about logical theories is that they are built on axioms (a range of primitive to complex statements asserted to be true) and inference rules (rules that, given premises/assumptions, provide valid conclusions), which together are used to prove theorems about the domain represented by the ontology-as-logical-theory. The whole set of axioms, inference rules, and theorems together constitute the logical theory.

In a logical theory, we can express the semantics of a model to the highest degree possible. The *subclass of* relation can become a richer relation, perhaps defined as the *disjoint subclass of* relation with the *property of transitivity*. A class's superclass relation to its subclasses can also be defined as *exhaustive*—that is, the subclasses exhaustively partition the superclass. Similar fine semantic distinctions can be made of relations and attributes, and other modeling constructs such as *facets*, which represent meta data associated with relations (or assertions on assertions).

Ontology

Now that we have looked at the Ontology Spectrum, ranging from taxonomies to logical theories, can we define what an ontology is? Let's look at a preliminary definition and save the elaboration until next chapter. An *ontology* defines the common words and *concepts* (meanings) used to describe and represent an area of knowledge, and so standardizes the meanings. Ontologies are used by

---

[7] For the distinction between ER and EER and the kinds of schemas built for databases, refer to nearly any standard database text. We like Halpin (1995) and Ullman (1989).

people, databases, and applications that need to share domain information (a *domain* is just a specific subject area or area of knowledge, like medicine, counterterrorism, imagery, automobile repair, etc.). Ontologies include computer-usable definitions of basic concepts in the domain and the relationships among them. They encode knowledge in a domain and also knowledge that spans domains. So, they make that knowledge reusable.

An ontology includes the following:

- Classes (general things) in the many domains of interest
- Instances (particular things)
- Relationships among those things
- Properties (and property values) of those things
- Functions of and processes involving those things
- Constraints on and rules involving those things

Having completed our discussion of the Ontology Spectrum, let's now turn to describing a language (actually a language and an entire modeling paradigm) that is often used to model Web objects and the things that can be said of Web objects, and that can structure that model into a taxonomy or a set of taxonomies.

Topic Maps

This section briefly describes Topic Maps (sometimes abbreviated TM). Topic Maps is a technology that has arisen in recent years to address the issue of semantically characterizing and categorizing documents and sections of documents on the Web with respect to their *content*—in other words, what *topics* or subject areas those documents actually address. As such, they are closely related to other efforts in general characterized as the Semantic Web. Topic Maps provides a content-oriented *index* into a set of documents, much like the index of a book but with this qualification: an index of a book does not typically characterize the contents of that book as a set of linked topics, but rather as a set of mostly isolated subject references with occasional cross-references to other subjects.

A Topic Map, however, does act as a set of linked topics that index a document collection. In addition, in the Topic Maps paradigm, one can have multiple topic maps indexing the same Web document collections (much as a book may have multiple indexes, such as a subject index, a name index, and so forth; the important point here is that one can have multiple topic maps indexing the subjects in different ways). Topic maps can be viewed as information overlays on documents or arbitrary information resources. They enable content-based navigation over these resources irrespective of the latter's form. Topic maps thus act as taxonomies—ways of describing, classifying, and indexing an information space consisting of Web and, as we'll see, non-Web objects. Whether or not Topic Maps can constitute full-fledged *ontologies* is subject to some dispute, and we will hold off on that discussion until the next chapter.

Topic Maps Standards

The development of Topic Maps began in the pre-XML and pre-WWW era when SGML (Standard Generalized Markup Language, a document composition language, of which a simpler subset became XML) reigned supreme. SGML was based on DTDs that later became the driving structural definition of early XML, now largely being superseded by XML Schema. So, the early Topic Maps standard was in fact based on SGML and used a non-XML syntax. The problem, then as now, is this: How do you characterize the semantics of your documents? How do you represent what your content means—in a way that a machine can use?

Topic Maps today, as defined by the International Standards Organization (ISO) 13250 standard (hereafter referred to as ISO 13250),[8] are specified in terms of two different interchange syntaxes: a more recent one based on XML and an older one based on an SGML DTD that used the ISO 19744 HyTime standard (a standard for specifying hypertext that includes resource addressing and linking). To simplify the exposition, this chapter focuses only on the XML TM syntax, referred to as *XTM*.[9]

Figure 7.10 shows the components of the Topic Maps standard and their relationship to each other. The ISO 13250 components are on the left, and the OASIS Published Subject Indicator Technical Committees are on the right. Note that items marked with a * have yet to be fully defined—though versions do exist. The Standard Application Model (SAM) defines the formal data model of Topic Maps and its semantics in natural language.[10] The Reference Model is intended to be a more abstract model of Topic Maps than SAM and to enable Topic Maps to semantically interoperate with other knowledge representation formalisms and Semantic Web ontology languages.[11] The Topic Map Query Language (TMQL) will be an SQL-like language for querying topic map information. The Topic Map Constraint Language (TMCL) will give a database schemalike capability to Topic Maps enabling constraints on the meaning to be defined for Topic Maps. Both TMQL and TMCL are dependent on the final elaboration of SAM, which is itself dependent on RM.[12]

---

[8] For additional information on the various Topic Maps standards, see Biezunski et al., 2002.

[9] Garshol and Moore (2002a).

[10] Garshol and Moore (2002b).

[11] See Newcomb and Biezunski (2002) for a view of what the RM might look like.

[12] Biezunski et al. (2002) makes these relationships clear.

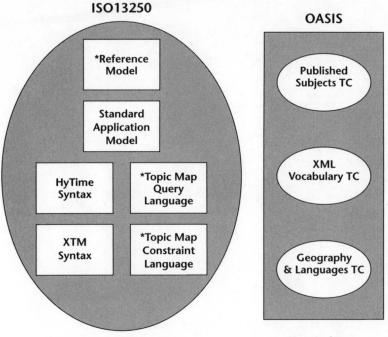

Figure 7.10 Components of the Topic Maps Standard.

The products of the OASIS technical committees are intended to be layered onto the ISO 13250 standard's products.[13] The Published Subjects Technical Committee will define and manage *published subjects* (which will be discussed shortly), and establish usage requirements for these. The XML Vocabulary Technical Committee will define the vocabulary to enable Topic Maps to interact with existing and emerging XML standards and technologies; the vocabulary will be defined as *published subjects* according to the standards defined by the Published Subjects TC. Finally, the Geography and Languages Technical Committee will define geographical country, region, and language-based *published subjects* to ensure interoperability across geographical and linguistic boundaries. All of the OASIS technical committees are currently actively pursuing their objectives.

Listing 7.1 depicts a simple XTM topic map. We will refer to this example in the subsequent discussion of the important concepts of Topic Maps.[14]

---

[13] See OASIS Topic Maps technical committees.

[14] The left-hand side of Figure 7.10 is adapted from Biezunski et al. (2002).

```
<topic id="Front Royal">
    <instanceOf><topicRef xlink:href="#city"/></instanceOf>
    <baseName>
      <baseNameString>Front Royal</baseNameString>
      <variant>
          <parameters><topicRef xlink:href="#display"/></parameters>
              <variantName>
                  <resourceData>Gateway to Skyline Drive</resourceData>
              </variantName>
          </variant>
    </baseName>
    <occurrence>
      <instanceOf><topicRef xlink:href="#portal"/></instanceOf>
      <resourceRef
xlink:href="http://www.ci.front-royal.va.us/"/>
    </occurrence>
  </topic>

<topic id="Winchester">
    <instanceOf><topicRef xlink:href="#city"/></instanceOf>
    <baseName>
      <baseNameString>Winchester</baseNameString>
    </baseName>
    <occurrence>
      <instanceOf><topicRef xlink:href="#portal"/></instanceOf>
      <resourceRef xlink:href="http://www.ci.winchester.va.us/"/>
    </occurrence>
  </topic>
```

Listing 7.1   A Simple XTM topic map: Topics, occurrences.

Topic Maps Concepts

The XTM standard[15] identifies the key concepts of Topic Maps. The key concepts are *topic, association, occurrence, subject descriptor*, and *scope*. We describe these concepts in the following text.

Topic

Anything can be a topic—that is, any distinct subject of interest for which assertions can be made. Nearly everything in Topic Maps can become a topic, including many of the other XTM constructs we talk about in this section. A topic is a representation of the subject; according to the XTM standard, it acts as a resource that is a proxy for the subject.

[15] See Pepper and Moore (2001) for the online XTM V1.0 standard.

The notion of subject in Topic Maps deserves some discussion. A *subject* is the *what*—for instance, "Front Royal, Virginia" or "the Mars Lander" or "inventory control" or "agriculture"; a *topic* is an information representation of the *what*. So a topic represents the subject that is referred to. If the subject is "Front Royal," then the topic would be Front Royal. Because subjects can be anything, topics can be anything. A topic is just a construct in Topic Maps, one of the essential building blocks. The way the subject of a topic is referred to is by having the topic point to a *resource* that expresses the subject. The resource either *constitutes* the subject (and so addresses the subject) or *indicates* the subject.[16] In either case, the subject of the topic is represented by an *occurrence* of a resource, and it is the nature of that resource that determines the addressability of the subject. If the resource uses the *resourceRef* XTM construct, then it *constitutes* the subject and is addressable. If the resource uses the *subjectIndicatorRef* construct, then it *indicates* the subject and is not directly addressable. Web objects are addressable; non-Web objects are not directly addressable and so must be indicated (for example, all occurrences of the same topic are about the same subject, though they are distinct resources). A resource *occurrence* can also have a data value that is directly specified inline.

In Listing 7.1, the topic map is enclosed by the *<topic>* and *</topic>* delimiters. The topic is identified by the *id="Front Royal"*. The topic is an *instance* of another topic, identified by the *<topicRef>* markup.

```
<instanceOf><topicRef xlink:href="#city"/></instanceOf>
```

In this case, Front Royal is a city, so the topic *Front Royal* is itself an instance of the topic reference *city*. Because the *resourceRef* construct is used, this example illustrates a topic that *constitutes* the subject, and the resource is addressable:

```
<occurrence>
       ...
       <resourceRef xlink:href="http://www.ci.front-royal.va.us/"/>
   </occurrence>
```

A topic is identified by a *name*. The primary way of identifying a topic map is to use the required *base name*. In the example, the base name of the topic is represented as:

```
<baseName>
           <baseNameString>Front Royal</baseNameString>
       ...
</baseName>
```

[16] See Biezunski (2003), p. 19.

The *<basename>* and *</basename>* delimiters enclose this base name. The base name is meant to uniquely identify the topic (within a particular *scope*, which we will discuss later). In addition to the base name, however, a variant name, specifically, a *display name* and/or a *sort name,* can be used. In the example, a *display name* is represented, within the base name markup:

```
<variant>
        <parameters><topicRef xlink:href="#display"/></parameters>
           <variantName>
              <resourceData>Gateway to Skyline Drive</resourceData>
           </variantName>
</variant>
```

Each topic is implicitly an instance of a *topic type*—that is, the class of the topic, though the type may not be explicitly marked in any given topic map. If the topic type is not explicitly marked, then the topic is considered implicitly of type http://www.topicmaps.org/xtm/1.0/core.xtm#topic. A similar circumstance holds for typing *associations* and *occurrences*: If no type is specified, then an *association* or an *occurrence* is defined to be, respectively, of type http://www.topicmaps.org/xtm/1.0/core.xtm#association or http://www.topicmaps.org/xtm/1.0/core.xtm#occurrence.

Occurrence

As noted in the preceding text, an *occurrence* is a resource specifying some information about a topic. The resource is either addressable (using a URI) or has a data value specified inline. For the former, *resourceRef* is used. The example in Listing 7.1 illustrates this usage:

```
<occurrence>
      ...
        <resourceRef xlink:href="http://www.ci.front-royal.va.us/"/>
      </occurrence>
```

For the latter, the inline value, *resourceData,* is used (this is not part of Listing 7.1) for arbitrary character data:

```
<occurrence       ...
   <resourceData>Front Royal is on the Shenandoah River
   </resourceData>
</occurrence>
```

Note, however, that in Listing 7.1, the alternative use of *resourceData* is exemplified—not to specify an *occurrence,* but to specify a variant name:

```
<variantName>
        <resourceData>Gateway to Skyline Drive</resourceData>
</variantName>
```

Like topics, occurrences can also be of different types, specified by the *topicRef* markup. *Occurrences* are ways to characterize a topic. Because they can represent any information to be associated with a topic, they can also act as *attributes* of a topic, though XTM does not really distinguish attributes from other information, a distinction that is sometimes made in other schema or knowledge representation languages.

Association

An *association* is the relationship between (one or more) topics. Associations are delimited by *<association>* and *</association>*. In Listing 7.2, the association *located-in* is asserted to hold between two topic references: Front Royal (indicated by the URI that is the value of one *topicRef*) and Virginia (indicated by the URI that is the value of the other *topicRef*). The specification of the semantics of *located-in* is not explicitly represented but is assumed to be defined by or known to the creator of the topic map (and could remain implicit).

```
<association>
    <instanceOf><topicRef xlink:href="#located-in"/></instanceOf>
    <member>
      <roleSpec><topicRef xlink:href="#city"/></roleSpec>
      <topicRef xlink:href="#Front-Royal"/>
    </member>
    <member>
      <roleSpec><topicRef xlink:href="#state"/></roleSpec>
      <topicRef xlink:href="#Virginia"/>
    </member>
  </association>
```

Listing 7.2 Topic map associations.

As depicted in the preceding example, the association *located-in* is specified to be a (undirected) relationship between two members. A *member* is just a set of topics, in this case two topics identified as the URIs *#Front-Royal* and *#Virginia*, and demarcated by the *topicRef* constructs. This example also shows an important aspect of associations: The topics that are related by the association assume different *roles* in that association. The topic referenced as *#Front-Royal* is in the *#city* role, and the topic *#Virginia* is in the *#state* role of the *#located-in* association. An association is similar to the database notion of a relation or, as we shall see in the next section comparing Topic Maps to RDF/S and in the next chapter on ontologies, to the ontology notion of a predicate (sometimes also called relation or property). An association *role* specifies how a particular topic acts as a member of an association, its manner of playing in that association. If there were a *uses* association between Sammy Sosa and a Rawlings 34-inch Pro

Model baseball bat, then Sammy would be in the *batter* role and the Rawlings would be in the *bat* role, as the following hypothetical portion of a topic map makes clear:

```
<association>
            <instanceOf><topicRef xlink:href="#uses"/></instanceOf>
            <member>
               <roleSpec><topicRef xlink:href="#batter"/></roleSpec>
               <topicRef xlink:href="#Sammy-Sosa"/>
            </member>
            <member>
               <roleSpec><topicRef xlink:href="#bat"/></roleSpec>
               <topicRef xlink:href="#Rawlings-34-inch-Pro-Model-
Baseball-Bat "/>
            </member>
        </association>
```

Subject Descriptor

We've looked at subjects in our discussion of topics. A *subject indicator* is just a way of indicating subjects. And topics are really the information representation of subjects. Typically (as we've seen), a subject is *indicated* by defining a *resource*. If two given topics in fact use the same resource, then their subjects (identified or indicated by those resources) are identical. For example, see Listing 7.3.

```
<topic id="Front Royal">
    <instanceOf><topicRef xlink:href="#city"/></instanceOf>
    <baseName>
      <baseNameString>Front Royal</baseNameString>
      <variant>
         <parameters><topicRef xlink:href="#display"/></parameters>
            <variantName>
               <resourceData>Gateway to Skyline Drive</resourceData>
            </variantName>
      </variant>
    </baseName>
    <occurrence>
      <instanceOf><topicRef xlink:href="#portal"/></instanceOf>
      <resourceRef
    xlink:href="http://www.ci.front-royal.va.us/"/>
    </occurrence>
</topic>

<topic id="Front Royal, Virginia">
    <instanceOf><topicRef xlink:href="#city"/></instanceOf>
```

Listing 7.3 Topic map subject indicators.

```
<baseName>
  <baseNameString>Front Royal, Virginia</baseNameString>
</baseName>
<occurrence>
  <instanceOf><topicRef xlink:href="#portal"/></instanceOf>
  <resourceRef
xlink:href="http://www.ci.front-royal.va.us/"/>
</occurrence>
</topic>
```

Listing 7.3 *(continued)*

In the listing, we'd like to say that both topics (*Front Royal* and *Front Royal, Virginia*) are really about the same subject. This judgment is confirmed, not by the near identity of the strings "Front Royal" and "Front Royal, Virginia" (whose string and concept similarity is apparent to a human being), but by the fact that both topics have the same resource or *subject indicator*, as represented by the common *occurrence* specification:

```
<occurrence>
  <instanceOf><topicRef xlink:href="#portal"/></instanceOf>
  <resourceRef
xlink:href="http://www.ci.front-royal.va.us/"/>
</occurrence>
```

The XTM standard also allows for a *published subject indicator* or, more simply, a published subject. A *published subject* is simply a subject that has general definition and usage and is identified by a specific published reference. In fact, the XTM standard states that there are default, mandatory published subjects, made mandatory by the requirements of the XTM standard itself. They include *topic, association, occurrence, class-instance relationship, class, instance, superclass-subclass relationship, superclass, subclass, suitability for sorting,* and *suitability for display.*[17]

Scope

Scope in Topic Maps is similar to the notion of namespace in other markup languages. *Scope* specifies the applicability or context of the topic, its occurrences and resources, and its associations. Subjects have a scope. The names of topics are unique within a scope. Resources specified within a particular topic have

[17] See Pepper and Moore (2001), Section 2.3.2, "XTM Mandatory Published Subject Indicators," for the specification of these.

the same scope as that topic. That is why topic maps should be merged if they have the same *base name*; they indicate the same subject having the same scope.

We note that the notion of scope is not explicitly called out by a Topic Maps markup construct but is defined with respect to the naming conventions of topics: Any topic map utilizing or specifying a topic that has the same *base name* is in the same *scope* defined by that unique name.

Topic Maps versus RDF

We are now able to compare Topic Maps to RDF.[18] We will discuss RDF Schema (abbreviated RDFS) and its constructs as needed to provide context for comparing RDF/S (which is how we will abbreviate the combination of RDF and RDFS) and Topic Maps. In general, however, we will postpone a more detailed description of RDFS to the next chapter.[19] We will see that RDF and Topic Maps are fairly aligned; their respective concepts can be reasonably mapped to each other. On the one hand, it will seem as though they provide redundant functionality. On the other hand, we will try to demonstrate that they actually complement each other.

The crucial distinction is this: RDF expresses *instance*-level semantic relations phrased in terms of a triple. RDFS expresses *class*-level relations describing acceptable instance-level relations phrased in terms of a *triple*, which will be described in more detail shortly.

All of the following are equivalent notions of a triple:

```
<subject, verb, object>
<object1, relation1, object2>
<resource, property, property-value>
```

RDF Revisited

In Chapter 5, we examined RDF and RDF Schema. We saw that RDF has the following important concepts: resource, property (and property value), and statement. Let's take a brief look at each of these.

RDF was developed primarily to represent meta data resources about Web objects and to support the meaning-preserving exchange of information about those objects. A *resource* is anything being described by an RDF expression.

---

[18] For an extended comparison, see Freese (2003).

[19] For the RDF specification, see Lassila and Swick (1999). For the most recent revision of the RDF/XML Syntax Specification, see Beckett (2001). For the RDFS specification, see Brickley and Guha (2002).

A resource can be a Web page (an HTML or XML document) in whole or part, a collection of Web pages, and even objects that do not exist on the Web. This is similar to the notion of *addressability* in XTM; some objects exist in the real world and can only be indicated and not directly accessed. Resources are named by using a URI and can also include an optional anchor identifier.

A *property* is a specific piece of information used to describe a resource. It can be an aspect, characteristic, attribute, or relation. These can mean different things to different people, so we won't try to distinguish these concepts here but will discuss them in the next chapter. A property of a resource will have a defined meaning and can have a defined range of acceptable *property values* (either simple enumerated types or more complex values), or they will simply "relate" to other resources and will typically have relationships with other properties. A property value can thus be another resource (again, identified by a URI) or a literal (a primitive XML data type or a simple string).

A *statement* in RDF pulls resources, properties, and property values together. Statements are typically called *triples*—though, as we shall see, they can also be viewed as *graphs*—because they include a subject (the resource), a predicate/verb (the property), and an object (the property value or another resource). For example, the following is an RDF statement in XML serialization syntax:

```
<?xml version="1.0"?>
    <rdf:RDF
            xmlns:rdf="http://www.w3.org/1999/02/22-rdf-syntax-ns#"
            xmlns:j="http://www.johnshome.org/schema/">
            <rdf:Description
about="http://www.johnshome.org/Home/JohnAL">
                    <j:Creator>John Author Livingston</j:Creator>
            </rdf:Description>
</rdf:RDF>
```

In this example, the entire statement is delimited by *<rdf:RDF>* and *</rdf:RDF>*. The subject here is the resource specified by "http://www.john shome.org/Home/JohnAL". The predicate is property Creator. The object is the resource (literal) John Author Livingston. The statement is equivalent to the English statement:

```
"The creator of page http://www.johnshome.org/Home/JohnAL is John Author
Livingston"
```

RDF statements can also be depicted as directed graphs. The graph form equivalent to the preceding triple representation is shown in Figure 7.11. Note that the figure is simplified slightly. For example, namespace information has been removed. Actually, the property *creator* is defined in the namespace prefixed by *j:*.

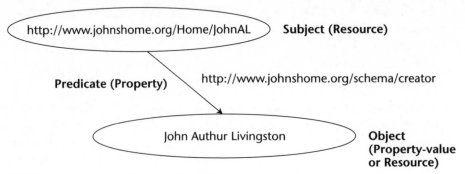

Figure 7.11   RDF statement as a graph.

Comparing Topic Maps and RDF

Both Topic Maps and RDF attempt to describe the information content of Web objects in terms of resources. Both standards exist in order to establish content meta data (data being about *other* data) about Web objects, to make those objects and their content more easily accessible. In Topic Maps, a topic is a Web object having occurrences (defined as resources—i.e., arbitrary information about the topic). The subject of the topic itself is represented by an occurrence of a resource, which can be addressable or not. Recall that an addressable subject is a Web object; a nonaddressable, indicated subject is not a Web object. Topics are linked by associations, and each topic in an association has a particular role that it plays in that association. But RDF was explicitly developed to enable the description (and linkage) of meta data to Web objects, whereas Topic Maps was meant to enable multiple content-based indexing of documents. If that distinction is kept in mind, then Topic Maps and RDF can be seen to be complementary paradigms. If indexing (or overlays of topic structure) represent the linking of subjects, then in fact it might be the case that RDF could represent the set of assertions that attempt to constitute the meaning of those subjects. In that case, Topic Maps and RDF can equitably coexist, each borrowing on the other's strengths and purposes.

In RDF, a resource (subject) has a property (predicate, relation), which has a property-value (object), which in turn can be a resource. This complicates the picture somewhat, at least with respect to Topic Maps, insofar as Topic Maps doesn't have this same notion of a resource's property itself being a resource, which by definition can have its own properties. And so on. This kind of linking means that RDF is a bit more complicated than Topic Maps. Whether Topic Maps evolves to have comparable machinery remains an open question. Currently, it is probably easier to represent a given complicated topic map in RDF than it is to represent a complicated RDF set of assertions in Topic Maps.

Table 7.5 shows the closest comparable constructs between Topic Maps and RDF.

The table cannot do real justice to the mappings between the constructs in these two paradigms, since, in general, so many qualifications would have to be made about the *comparable equivalence* between a topic and a resource (Is a topic really a resource? Is a resource about a subject as a topic is? Isn't the mapping of these constructs more along the lines of a mapping between comparable *triples*?) that the ultimate comparison is more suggestive than real.

Topic Maps does not yet have a defined Reference Model (RM), whereas RDF currently has RDF Schema, which is another distinction between the two paradigms. RDF Schema is a *meta* level or more abstract model that describes the *object* level of RDF. When the RM is defined (possibly with assistance from the Topic Map Constraint Language, itself under development), it may then be that the two paradigms have more comparable, formal power in defining assertions about topics and associations or resources and properties in terms of the semantics of those assertions. This is a topic (pun slightly intended) that we address in more detail in the next chapter.

Table 7.5   Comparing Topic Maps to RDF

TOPIC MAPS CONSTRUCTS	RDF CONSTRUCTS
Topic	Resource
Occurrence[20]	Property
Property value	
Association[21]	Property
Scope	Namespace
Subject[22]	Resource

[20] Occurrence in the Topic Maps paradigm is, strictly speaking, more like an instance in the object-oriented or ontology paradigms. With respect to RDF, a TM *occurrence*, because it is something that is relevant to a topic, can really be either a *resource* or *property*, simply because an *instance* in RDF is a triple specifying a specific object having a specific property/relation to another specific object—that is, a *resource* having a *property* and a *value* for that property (all of which can technically be *resources*).

[21] An *association* is a relation between *subjects* (i.e., *topics*). As such, perhaps a better understanding is that is it is a *type* of *property* under the RDF perspective.

[22] Although a *subject* is technically not a first-class construct in Topic Maps, because it crucially stands behind the notion of *topic*, which is the first-class notion, we include it in the comparison.

Summary

A taxonomy is a hierarchic classification (typically in a tree structure) of real-world objects. In information technology, a taxonomy is used to classify the information correlates of those objects. Because taxonomies are so closely related to other classification, vocabulary description, and information model representations, this chapter also described a framework called the Ontology Spectrum. The Ontology Spectrum distinguishes taxonomies from other representations in this space: thesauri, conceptual models, and logical theories. Taxonomies are important because they help structure and provide at least a simple semantics for an information space.

This chapter also introduced Topic Maps and the various TM standards. Any given topic map is at least a taxonomy in the sense that it tries to say something about how subjects are structured and related, using the notions of topics and associations. One can have multiple topic maps covering the same collection of Web and non-Web objects, just as one can have multiple indexes of the same document or documents.

If Topic Maps is a way of describing and structuring an information space in terms of *topics* and *associations*, then, in contrast, RDF is a Web language for describing and structuring an information space in terms of *resources* and *properties*. But after revisiting what RDF is—and to a limited extent, introducing some aspects of RDF Schema, which we look at more closely in the next chapter—we saw that Topic Maps and RDF actually have many similarities. The primary differences between the two paradigms are (1) they were developed by different communities for slightly different classification tasks and (2) RDF has a schema level (RDF Schema) that enables you to describe a set of properties and the relationships between these properties and other resources—in other words, a *meta* model to the RDF *object* model—whereas Topic Maps currently does not have such a level. With the eventual development of the Reference Model and a Topic Map Constraint Language, however, this latter distinction may be weakened.

As we shall see in the next chapter, RDF and Topic Maps pave the way for increasing the representational capabilities of an information model over that of a taxonomy. Both paradigms provide some of the essential building blocks for constructing the semantically richer notion of ontologies.

CHAPTER 8

Understanding Ontologies

"Ontology is the very first science. Ontology involves discovering categories and fitting objects into them in ways that make sense . . . . When we make a list of things to do, or of records and books we most want to buy, or videos we intend to rent, we are categorizing—we are engaging in rudimentary ontology. By prioritizing items in a list, we are assigning relationships among various things. Ontology can be relatively simple, or it can be quite complex.

Ontology becomes more complex, and even daunting, when we begin to grapple with large domains of objects with complex relationships among them. For instance, anyone who has attempted to outline the processes and components of even a relatively small enterprise has experienced the brain-cramps that can come with complex ontology."

—David Koepsell, Center for Commercial Ontology: Prospectus
http://www.acsu.buffalo.edu/~koepsell/center.htm

Ontologies are about vocabularies and their meanings, with explicit, expressive, and well-defined semantics—possibly machine-interpretable. So what does this statement mean? What's a vocabulary? What's a meaning? What is semantics? What does machine-interpretable mean? What is ontology and what are ontologies? In this chapter, we define what ontology is and what ontologies are in clear and simple language, with meaningful examples. You may discover many ideas that are strange at first, such as semantics, knowledge representation, domain, reference, truth-function, intension, extension, axiom, theorem, theory, but you will be given useful, incisive, and simple explanations of what those ideas are, how they can be used in practice in your information technology projects, and where semantic technologies are heading.

You will also be happy to know that ontologies do have something to do with taxonomies, discussed in the previous chapter. In fact, ontologies extend taxonomies quite some way. Ontologies are to taxonomies as two-dimensional space is to three- (or more) dimensional space. In other words, ontologies enable you to specify the semantics of your domain, your enterprise, or your community, or across many communities, in great and arbitrarily greater detail. You'll also learn a bit about some languages used to express ontologies, including the W3C's emerging Web Ontology Language (OWL).

Overview of Ontologies

So what is ontology, and what are ontologies? Before looking at some definitions, let's take a look at an actual ontology.

Ontology Example

Figure 8.1 shows a simple human resources ontology created in the ontology management tool called Protégé (http://protégé.stanford.edu). You'll notice that there are classes such as Person, Organization, and Employee. In an ontology, these are really called *concepts*, because it is intended that they correspond to the mental concepts that human beings have when they understand a particular body of knowledge or subject matter area or domain (these phrases are all used interchangeably; they are intended to be synonymous), such as the human resources domain.

These concepts and the relationships between them are usually implemented as classes, relations, properties, attributes, and values (of the properties/attributes). So what Figure 8.1 depicts primarily are concepts of the important entities of the domain, which are implemented as classes. Examples are Person, Organization, and Employee. Also depicted are the relations between these entity-focused concepts, such as employee_of, managed_by, and manages. Finally, properties or attributes are depicted. Examples include address, name, birthdate, and ssn under the Person class. These properties or attributes have either explicit values or, more often, have value ranges. The value range for the property/attribute of employee_of, a property of the class Employee, for example, is the class Organization. By *range* we mean that the only possible values for any instances of the property employee_of defined for the class Employee must come from the class Organization.

Immediately we see that an ontology tries to capture the *meaning* (what we will call *semantics*) of a particular subject area or area of knowledge that corresponds to what a human being knows about that domain. An ontology also characterizes that meaning in terms of *concepts* and their relationships. Furthermore, an ontology is often represented as classes, relations, properties, attributes, and values.

Figure 8.1 is a graphical fragment of a simple ontology attempting to model the human resources domain (person, employee, organization), their subclasses (staff employee, management employee, company, group, division, and department), their properties, and the relationships among those concepts.

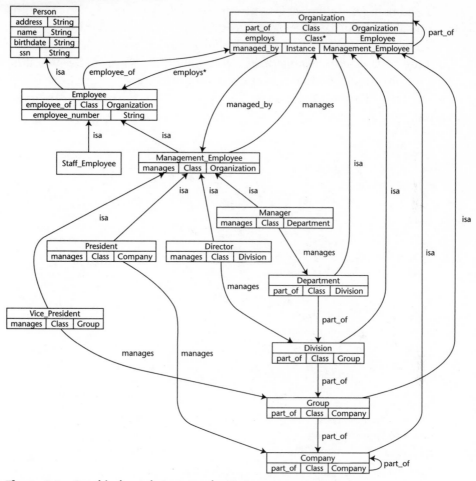

Figure 8.1 Graphical ontology example: Human resources.

Listing 8.1 is a fragment of the textual view of the same ontology—see the companion Web site (http://www.wiley.com/compbooks/daconta) for the equivalent of the same ontology represented in RDF/S. In the case of Listing 8.1, the language used is the Open Knowledge Base Connectivity Language (OKBC, http://www.ai.sri.com/~okbc/). Both underscore an important point: *There is no logical difference between a graphical and a textual rendition of an ontology* (or any other model, for that matter).

This fact is important, because a key point of this chapter is that an ontology is represented in a *knowledge representation language* (such as a Semantic Web language like RDF/S, DAML+OIL, OWL, or in an ontology language that predates the Semantic Web, such as Ontolingua/KIF/Common Logic, OKBC, CycL, or Prolog). Furthermore, such ontology languages are in turn typically based on a particular *logic*, with the logic itself being a language with a syntax and a semantics (these latter concepts are explained later in this chapter). Sometimes, therefore, we call the language in which the ontology is represented a *logic-based language*. So ultimately it does not matter whether you see a graphical or a textual rendition of an ontology; both are exactly equivalent. The important issue is that of the power of the underlying language used to represent the ontology.

```
(defclass
     (is-a USER)
     (role concrete)
     (single-sot managed_by
          (type SYMBOL)
;+        (allowed-classes Management_Employee)
;+        (cardinality 1 1)
          (create-accessor read-write))
     (single-slot part_of
          (type SYMBOL)
;+        (allowed-parents Organization)
;+        (cardinality 0 1)
          (create-accessor read-write))
     (multislot employs
          (type SYMBOL)
;+        (allowed-parents Employee)
          (cardinality 1 ?VARIABLE)
          (create-accessor read-write)))

(defclass Department
     (is-a Organization)
     (role concrete)
     (single-slot part_of
          (type SYMBOL)
;+        (allowed-parents Division)
;+        (cardinality 0 1)
          (create-accessor read-write)))


(defclass Company
     (is-a Organization)
     (role concrete)
     (single-slot part_of
          (type SYMBOL)
;+        (allowed-parents Company)
;+        (cardinality 0 1)
          (create-accessor read-write)))

(defclass Person
```

Listing 8.1 Textual ontology example: Human resources.

```
        (is-a USER)
        (role concrete)
        (single-slot birthdate
            (type STRING)
;+          (cardinality 1 1)
            (create-accessor read-write))
        (single-slot name_
            (type STRING)
;+          (cardinality 1 1)
            (create-accessor read-write))
        (single-slot address
            (type STRING)
;+          (cardinality 1 1)
            (create-accessor read-write))
        (single-slot ssn
            (type STRING)
;+          (cardinality 1 1)
            (create-accessor read-write)))

... some classes omitted for brevity
(see companion website for complete listing)...
```

Listing 8.1   *(continued)*

A corollary issue is that high-end ontology languages are backed by a rigorous formal logic, which thereby makes the ontology machine-interpretable. By *machine-interpretable* we mean that the semantics of the model is *semantically interpretable* by the machine; in other words, the computer and its software can interpret the semantics of the model directly—*without direct human involvement*. Software supported by ontologies moves up to the human knowledge/conceptual level; humans do not have to move down to the machine level. Interaction with computers takes place at our level, not theirs. This is an extremely important point, and it underscores the value of ontologies. In the following sections, we elaborate these issues so that you understand the importance of ontologies in the coming Semantic Web.

Ontology Definitions

The description and the picture and the code are nice, but just what is an ontology? An *ontology* defines the common words and concepts (the meaning) used to describe and represent an area of knowledge. But what does that definition mean? Let's delve into just what ontology is and what ontologies are. If you look up *ontology* in the dictionary, you'll find the following definition (from Merriam-Webster OnLine: http://www.m-w.com/):

1. A branch of metaphysics concerned with the nature and relations of being

2. A particular theory about the nature of being or the kinds of existents

This definition indicates that the term originates in philosophy—specifically, a part of metaphysics that is the systematic study of the principles underlying a particular subject, most often the nature of being and the nature of experience. Often these days, the distinction is made between "big O" Ontology and "little o" ontology. "Big O" Ontology is the philosophical discipline. "Little O" ontology is the information technology engineering discipline that has emerged over the past eight or so years. Much like the distinction between ordinary taxonomies and taxonomies as used in information technology, there is a comparable distinction for ontologies. IT offers the following definitions. The first definition is really a simple paraphrase in everyday language of the more technically jargonistic second definition, but to understand the second, it helps to build on an elucidation of the first definition:

- An ontology defines the common words and concepts (the meaning) used to describe and represent an area of knowledge.

- An ontology is an engineering product consisting of "a specific vocabulary used to describe [a part of] reality, plus a set of explicit assumptions regarding the intended meaning of that vocabulary"[1]—in other words, the specification of a conceptualization.[2]

Let's try to unpack these definitions. The first definition has two parts:

- Describing and representing an area of knowledge
- Defining the common words and concepts of the description

Recall from the previous chapter what we learned about a domain: A domain is a subject matter area or area of knowledge. Some examples of areas of knowledge or domains are medicine, automobile repair, financial planning, machine tooling, business management, physics, textiles, and geopolitics. Describing an area of knowledge is the act of expressing, in either written or spoken words, the important points about a specific area of knowledge. For example, in describing *automobile repair*, we would probably talk about the following:

- The kinds of cars there are (sedans, station wagons, sports cars, luxury cars, compacts, domestic and foreign cars)
- The types of engines (corresponding perhaps to the types of fuel used: gasoline, diesel, electric-powered, hybrid)

[1]Guarino (1998, p. 4).
[2]Gruber (1993).

- The particular engines (for example, a 1995–96 V-6 Ford Taurus 244/4.0 Aerostar Automatic with Block Casting # 95TM-AB, Head Casting 95TM)

- The manufacturers (Ford, General Motors, Chevrolet, Nissan, Honda, Volvo, Volkswagen, Saab, Hyundai, and so on)

- The things that constitute cars (engines, brake systems, cooling systems, electric systems, suspension, body, and so on) and their properties (an engine has 4, 6, 8, or 12 cylinders; brake pads have different compositions such as semimetallic or nonferrous material)

We'll see in the next section a more complicated, technical definition of *description*, one that brings into our discussion the semantic notion of *intension*.

An important part of automobile repair is elaborating how to repair various cars, subsystems of cars, diagnosis, tools to use in diagnosis and repair, parts to use in the repair process, costing and estimating of repairs, how to manage an automobile repair facility, certification of excellence in automobile repair, and so on. When describing an area of knowledge—a domain—we describe the important *things* in the domain, their *properties*, and the *relationships* among the things. If we were to elaborate our description (because, say, we were writing a paper or a book on automobile repair), we may even include *rules* about the domain, such as the following *diagnosis rule*, which specifies how to determine what is wrong with an automobile system in order to repair it: If the car won't start and it doesn't turn over, check and clean the battery connections.

Therefore, a description is or can be an ontology. As we saw in Chapter 7, it includes the same kinds of concepts:

- Classes (general things) in the many domains of interest
- Instances (particular things)
- The relationships among those things
- The properties (and property values) of those things
- The functions of and processes involving those things
- Constraints on and rules involving those things

In addition to *describing* an area of knowledge, we also need to *represent* that description. What does *representation* mean? Representing means that we encode the description in a way that enables someone to use the description. A description consists of words and phrases in a natural language (such as English or Chinese), that is, vocabulary/terminology and sentences that combine terminologies to express relationships among the terms (we'll use *vocabulary* and *terminology* as equivalent here and use *term* for the individual word). So representing means that we represent the description using terms and sentences. We define the terms (or we already have the terms defined in our mental lexicon), and then we combine those defined terms in ways that elaborate more of the *meaning* about the area of knowledge.

In information technology, however, we use a slightly more complicated notion of representing. We represent in order to use the description in information technology; in other words, we create a model that software will be able to utilize. We represent the classes, instances, relationships, properties, and rules for the area of knowledge. We use the terms of the natural-language description as *labels* for the underlying concepts—that is, the meaning of the area of knowledge consisting of classes, properties, and relationships. Typically, we represent or codify the ontology in a logical, knowledge representation language (which we discuss a bit later) rather than a natural language, because we want to represent our description as clearly, precisely, and unambiguously as possible, and natural language can be very ambiguous. We also want to make its meaning available for information technology use. Representation thus has to do with defining the terms (the vocabulary that acts as labels for the concepts), and that means also defining the concepts and their relationships that are behind the labels and that constitute the meaning of the model of the knowledge area we are interested in.

The first definition dealt with describing and representing an area of knowledge. What about the second definition of ontology? What does the specification of a conceptualization mean? Let's try to clarify that definition by referring to the different parts of the first definition.[3]

A *conceptualization* is a way of thinking about part of the world. When we *conceive* of the world or a part of the world, we have in mind, literally, a mental model of that part of the world. For example, when we conceive of automobile repair, we probably have a set of mental images of automobiles, their subsystems and parts, an automobile garage or repair shop, mechanics in uniforms, and so on. If we were to describe these images, we would probably do so according to the first definition—in terms of the things that are important to the notion of automobile repair, and their properties and relationships. Given a particular way of thinking about a part of the world (a subject area or domain), in other words, a conceptualization (we conceive it to be this way or that way, and not some other way), when we seek to describe it to ourselves or another person in a fairly detailed and precise way, we say we are *specifying* it.

Table 8.1 displays some of the key terminology you'll learn about in this chapter, along with shorthand definitions. You may want to refer back to this table periodically as you encounter one of the terms in the text.

---

[3]See Guarino and Giaretta (1995) for elaboration of various definitions of ontology.

Table 8.1 Terminology

TERM	DEFINITION
Common Logic (CL)	The name for the ISO standard knowledge representation language based on KIF.
Cyc and OpenCyc	The first ontology-based knowledge representation system, whose development began in 1984 at the Microelectronics & Computer Technology Corporation (MCC) in Austin, Texas, and that is now commercialized by Cycorp (http://www.cyc.com/). Cyc is a repository of machine-interpretable commonsense knowledge represented as mostly first-order predicate logic-based ontologies (with some second-order logic extensions) and a reasoning engine. OpenCyc is the open source version of the Cyc technology (http://www.opencyc.org/).
DAML+OIL	DARPA (Defense Advanced Research Program) Agent Markup Language-Ontology Inference Layer: These are two XML- and Web-based languages to support the Semantic Web, which have recently fused. DAML originated from a US DARPA-sponsored program; OIL originated from a European Union-sponsored program. Together they constitute the most semantically expressive language available for WWW documents. The combined language is now supported by the W3C Web standards consortium.
Description logic	A knowledge representation formalism (sometimes called a terminological logic, classification logic, concept logic, or term subsumption logic) based on a subset of first-order predicate logic that is a declarative formalism for the representation and expression of knowledge and sound, tractable reasoning methods founded on a firm theoretical (logical) basis.
Frame-based knowledge representation	A knowledge representation formalism for expressing ontological information derived originally from the artificial intelligence (AI) language called KL-1, which itself is one of the earliest formalizations of the notion of semantic network. The notion of a frame comes from the early LISP programming language terminology used by early KR languages. In frame terminology, a concept is a class, and a relation is a slot. Attributes (sometimes called properties) are just slots defined on a domain (a specific class subtree) or one of its subdomains (a subclass of a domain class).

(continued)

Table 8.1 *(continued)*

TERM	DEFINITION
Knowledge Interchange Format (KIF)	This is a knowledge representation language developed prior to the emergence of the Semantic Web. KIF is based on first-order predicate logic, with a slight extension into second-order logic (because it includes quantifying over sequence variables, i.e., predicates in a sequence). KIF has a LISP-like syntax. There is now an ISO-KIF standard called Common Logic (CL). CL has multiple syntaxes, including an XML and a Conceptual Graph syntax.
Open Knowledge Base Connectivity (OKBC) language	This is a language for knowledge access and interchange (an API) derived from the Generic Frame Protocol, developed in the early 1990s by knowledge representation technologists under the support of the DARPA Knowledge Sharing Effort (Patil et al., 1992). This protocol became the OKBC under the support of the DARPA High Performance Knowledge Base (HPKB) program, 1996–1999 (Cohen et al., 1998).
Ontolingua	A knowledge representation language based on KIF that is used for expressing ontologies (http://www.ksl.stanford.edu/software/ontolingua/). See Gruber (1993). Ontolingua was the first ontology language. It is currently also an ontology system with reasoning methods and is supported by the Knowledge Systems Laboratory at Stanford University.
Ontology	An ontology models the vocabulary and meaning of domains of interest: the objects (things) in domains; the relationships among those things; the properties, functions, and processes involving those things; and constraints on and rules about those things.
Protégé	Protégé is an ontology management tool developed and maintained by the Medical Informatics Laboratory at Stanford University based on the OKBC knowledge model and is recognized as an exemplary tool for managing ontologies (http://protege.stanford.edu/).

Table 8.1 *(continued)*

TERM	DEFINITION
Resource Definition Framework/Schema (RDF/S)	These are two languages. The first (RDF) expresses instance-level semantic relations phrased in terms of a triple: <subject, verb, object>, i.e., <object1, relation1, object2>. The second (RDFS) expresses class-level relations describing acceptable instance-level relations.
OWL	Web Ontology Language (sometimes called Ontology Web Languagea language developed by the W3C's Web Ontology Working Group and intended to be the successor of DAML+OIL. OWL is the most expressive knowledge representation for the Semantic Web so far.

In the next section, we build on the foundation laid in the previous chapter with the discussion on the Ontology Spectrum, and we also try to differentiate an ontology from a thesaurus.

Syntax, Structure, Semantics, and Pragmatics

This section discusses the levels of representation needed for models: syntax, structure, semantics, and pragmatics. This will assist you in understanding ontologies and what they provide to information technology. We will describe each simply and illustrate each with an example. Our intention in this section is to help you understand the following:

- The critical issues in creating ontologies: what makes one ontology better than another, and what features ontologies (especially those characterized as *conceptual models* and *logical theories*) provide and how they provide them — that other models on the Ontology Spectrum do not and cannot.

- The importance of ontologies from the perspective of an information technology manager or technical lead who must address emerging Semantic Web technologies for incorporation into the systems and practices of your company's infrastructure and their impact on your information strategies for the future.

Syntax

Syntax is usually identified with *form*, *format*, and *structure*, and that is how we will portray it here. More formally, every language has a syntax and a semantics: Cobol, Fortran, C, Java, English, Chinese, SQL, XML, RDF, and OWL. A language can be considered a formal system that has an alphabet or a vocabulary set (or both), a set of rules for defining how the alphabet and vocabulary can be combined into legitimate *statements* or *sentences* in the language, and then a *semantics* for the alphabet, the vocabulary, and the statements/sentences. We will talk about syntax first in order to lead up to the discussion on semantics (and pragmatics).

We are all probably very familiar with the syntax of programming languages and database languages, so the discussion will focus primarily on these. A programming language, just like a natural language like English, has a formal syntax. Think of the C or Java programming languages. When you learn C, a large part of what you learn is the syntax of the C programming language—for instance, that #include statements go before other programming statements near the beginning of the file, that a FOR loop has a certain number of components (a count, index, or boolean variable that has an initial value, possibly gets incremented or has its value changed during the execution of the program, and a check of the variable's value to determine whether exiting of the loop is required). These components must be present in a particular order.

Furthermore, the components must obey certain simple typing constraints. For example, if a variable is declared to be of type Integer, then the only possible value for that variable is an integer (or possibly some other value that is *coerced* into an integer). There may also be restrictions on the length of user-defined variable names. The *operators* (numeric operators such as + or -, boolean exclusive OR) and object accessors (if the language is an object-oriented language such as C++ or Java) are either reserved symbols or words in the programming language and have their own required syntax.

So syntax is about order and format. If the program you develop is syntactically correct, then the compiler—which initially parses and confirms the syntax—will not generate warning or error messages. Once all the syntactic errors (errors in formatting, order, and simple typing) are corrected, then the compiler will continue the rest of its work, creating symbol tables, transformations, and optimizations of the code—in other words, begin to deal with at least the rudimentary semantics of the program. It remains rudimentary because the compiler will not know how you intend the particular logical flow of programming to be and what you mean by it, which is why these kinds of *semantic* programming errors are sometimes called *logical* errors. Currently, it requires a human or an extremely smart compiler (perhaps driven by an expert system that uses knowledge) to detect and correct semantic errors, because, in general, computers and their software are not semantically aware—and changing that state of affairs, at least with respect to the Internet, is what this book is all about.

In the Web world, we typically deal with documents, so the syntax of documents, along with the markup languages that structure documents and data, are our primary interest. The syntax of documents involve strings of characters from some alphabet (for text) or some set of defined binary encodings (for graphics, video, and so on). The semantics is what those symbols are intended to mean in a human-defined domain (sometimes called, more formally, part of a universe of discourse)—that is, what the documents mean. Syntactic symbols are meaningless unless they are given a *semantic interpretation*, in other words, mapped to objects in a model where that meaning is represented. Semantic interpretation is semantics: It is interpreting the syntactic symbols with respect to their intended meaning. In the Web work, XML has a syntax. A document that is marked up using XML is either syntactically correct or not, with respect to the syntax of XML. That means that certain constructs have to appear in a certain order, XML tags have to be closed by a delimiter, and so on.

Structure

Syntax is order and format, but it is also structure. Databases, Web objects, objects in the coming Semantic Web, models, and ontologies require structure.

Models generally require structure, a way of organizing and containing elements of the model. A database schema, for example, is primarily a way to both describe and prescribe the structure of a database. We understand the notion of description better now, after our discussion in the previous section. By *prescribe*, we mean that the objects of the database—the tables, columns, rows, and values—are required to adhere to the structure of the schema, the way the elements of the schema are organized and the way that certain elements are contained within other elements. This prescription is enforced typically by the Database Management System (DBMS), which we can think of, at least partially, as the *interpreter* or *validator* of the data with respect to the database schema. DBMSs typically do much more than this; however, here it functions much like an XML parser/validator, parsing XML files (checks them against the syntactic specification of the requisite XML language version) and then validating them with respect to a particular, structure-defining DTD or a schema based on the XML Schema language.

Conceptual models, such as those written in UML, are also concerned with structure. The structure in conceptual models is reflected partially in the inheritance hierarchies of the subclass relation: One class is a subclass of another class. Structure is also reflected in the part-of relation: One class is a part of or constitutes another class. Structure is also reflected in other arbitrary relations. In a UML model of a human resources application; for example, two classes may be in an employee-of relation (similar to the relation in a database conceptual schema, which is usually constructed in an entity-relation or extended-entity-relation model), as in Figure. 8.2. Note that this is roughly the UML equivalent of the OKBC ontology in Figure 8.1 (though without the underlying logical richness and precision of the latter; richness and precision enables machine semantic interpretability).

Structure can typically be represented by a *node-and-edge* graphical notation—in other words, using a node and edge or link, the latter of which can be directed (symbolized by an arrowhead pointing at the node the relation is directed toward, as in Figure 8.3). The general study of such node-and-edge models is called *graph theory*, where a graph is a more complicated data structure than a tree, which is a simpler hierarchic structure such as we saw in the previous chapter on taxonomies. A graph (think of a complex network) is more complicated than a tree because it is a tree with either *directed* or *undirected* links arbitrarily connecting nodes, whereas a tree is a data structure that just has edges or links (branches), a distinguished node called the *root* (as we saw in the last chapter) into which no edge enters, and from the root there is a unique path to every node.

The main difference between a graph and a tree is that a graph may have multiple paths to nodes. A *directed graph* is a graph in which the edge is directed from one node to another (think of a relation like father-of, where the edge from John to Harry signifies that John is the father-of Harry). An *undirected graph* means that there is no arrow, but only a simpler edge (think of the relation friend-of between John and Sue: John is the friend-of Sue and Sue is the friend-of John). A graph without *cycles* (links between a child node and one of its ancestors) is called an *acyclic graph*. A graph with cycles (links between a child node and one of it parents) is called a *cyclic graph*. Directed graphs with cycles are called *directed cyclic graphs*; directed graphs without cycles are called *directed acyclic graphs* (DAGs) and are typically the data structure used for most complex structures, such as ER, UML, and ontology models. There is an implementation cost incurred with cycles (i.e., you have to *detect cycles* and so must keep additional bookkeeping information around when traversing your graph as, for example, in a search), so in general most, but not all, models do not permit them.

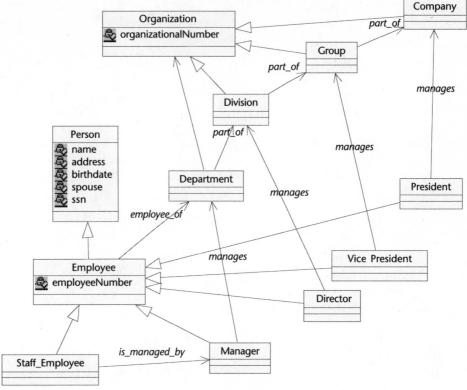

Figure 8.2 UML Human Resources model fragment.

Structure itself, though important, is not the crucial determining or characteristic factor for models; semantic interpretation is. Structure is a side effect of the degree of semantic interpretation required. Knowledge (as encoded in ontologies, for example) is the relatively complex symbolic modeling (representation) of some aspect of a universe of discourse (i.e., what we are calling subject areas, domains, and that which spans domains).

Semantics

Semantic interpretation is the mapping between some structured subset of data and a model of some set of objects in a domain with respect to the intended meaning of those objects and the relationships between those objects.

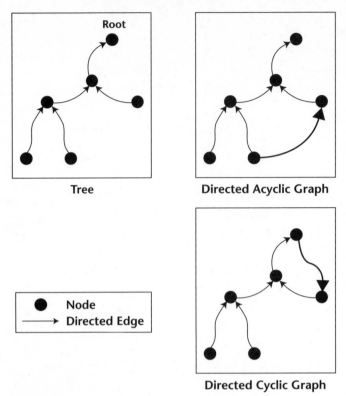

Figure 8.3 Trees and graphs.

Typically, the model lies in the mind of the human. We as humans "understand" the semantics, which means we symbolically represent in some fashion the world, the objects of the world, and the relationships among those objects. We have the semantics of (some part of) the world in our minds; it is very structured and interpreted. When we view a textual document, we see symbols on a page and interpret those with respect to what they mean in our mental model; that is, we supply the semantics (meaning). If we wish to assist in the dissemination of the knowledge embedded in a document, we make that document available to other human beings, expecting that they will provide their own semantic interpreter (their mental models) and will make sense out of the symbols on the document pages. So, there is no knowledge in that document without someone or something interpreting the semantics of that document. Semantic interpretation makes knowledge out of otherwise meaningless symbols on a page.[4]

If we wish, however, to have the computer assist in the dissemination of the knowledge embedded in a document—truly realize the Semantic Web—we

---

[4]For an extended discussion of these issues, including the kinds of interpretation required, see Obrst and Liu (2003).

need to at least partially automate the semantic interpretation process. We need to describe and represent in a computer-usable way a portion of our mental models about specific domains. Ontologies provide us with that capability. This is a large part of what the Semantic Web is all about. The software of the future (including intelligent agents, Web services, and so on) will be able to use the knowledge encoded in ontologies to at least partially understand, to semantically interpret, our Web documents and objects.

In formal language theory, one has a syntax and a semantics for the objects of that syntax (vocabulary), as we mentioned previously in our discussion of the syntax of programming languages and database structures. Ontologies try to limit the possible formal models of interpretation (semantics) of those vocabularies to the set of meanings you intend. None of the other model types with limited semantics—taxonomies, database schemas, thesauri, and so on—does that. These model types assume that humans will look at the "vocabularies" and magically supply the semantics via the built-in human semantic interpreter: your mind using your mental models.

Ontologists want to shift some of that "semantic interpretative burden" to machines and have them eventually mimic our semantics—that is, understand what we mean—and so bring the machine up to the human, not force the human to the machine level. That's why, for example, we are not still programming in assembler. Software engineering and computer science has evolved higher-level languages that are much more aligned with the human semantic/conceptual level. Ontologists want to push it even farther.

By *machine semantic interpretation*, we mean that by structuring (and constraining) in a logical, axiomatic language (i.e., a knowledge representation language, which we discuss shortly) the symbols humans supply, the machine will conclude via an inference process (again, built by the human according to logical principles) roughly what a human would in comparable circumstances.

NOTE

For a fairly formal example of what's involved in trying to capture the semantics of a knowledge representation language such as the Semantic Web languages of RDF/S and DAML+OIL in an axiomatic way, see Fikes and McGuinness (2001). For an example that attempts to capture the semantics of a knowledge representation language with the semantic *model theory* approach, see Hayes (2002), who presents a model-theoretic semantics of RDF/S. In principle, both the axiomatic and the model-theoretic semantics of these two examples should be equivalent.

This means that given a formal vocabulary—alphabet, terms/symbols (logical and nonlogical), and statements/expressions (and, of course, rules by which to form expressions from terms)—one wants the formal set of interpretation models correlated with the symbols and expressions (i.e., the semantics) to approximate those models that a human would identify as those he or she intended (i.e., close to the human conceptualization of that domain space). The syntax is addressed by proof theory, and the semantics is addressed by model theory. One way of looking at these relationships is depicted in Figure 8.4. In this figure, the relationship between an alphabet and its *construction rules* for forming words in that alphabet is *mapped* to formal objects in the semantic model for which those symbols and the combinatoric syntactic rules for composing those symbols having a specific or composed meaning. On the syntactic side, you have symbols; on the semantic side, you have rules. In addition, you have rules mapping the constructs on the syntactic side to constructs on the semantic side.

The important issue is that you have defined a specification language that maps to those semantic objects that you want that language and its constructs to *refer to* (i.e., to mean). If those syntactic constructs (such as Do or While or For or Goto or Jump or Shift or End or Catch or Throw) do not correspond (or map) to a semantic object that corresponds to what you want that syntactic object to mean. "Do" in a programming language such as C means that you enter a finite state automaton that enforces particular transitions between states that:

- Declare what input values enable the state transition; what values are used, consumed, and transformed; and what values are output (think of a procedure or function call that passes arguments of specific types and values and returns results of specific types and values).

- Performs other tasks called *side effects*, or arbitrary other things that are not directly functions of the input.

Figures 8.4 to 8.6 illustrate a specific example of the mapping between the syntax and semantics of a programming language. Syntactic objects are associated with their *semantic interpretations*, each of which specifies a formal set-theoretic domain and a mapping function (that maps atomic and complex syntactic objects to semantic elements of the formal domain). Figures 8.4 to 8.6 display, respectively, the mapping between syntactic objects and a simple semantics for those objects, then a mapping between a simple semantics and a complex semantics for those objects, and finally between a complex semantics and an even more complex semantics for those objects. The mappings between semantics levels can also be viewed as simply the expansion of the semantics from more simple to more complex elaborations

In Figure 8.4, the syntactic objects are mapped to a descriptive shorthand for the semantics. "zDLKFL" is a *string constant*, "4+3" is an *addition* operation, and so on.

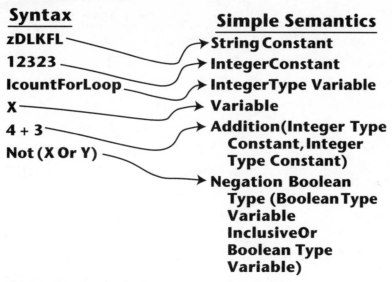

Syntax

zDLKFL

12323

IcountForLoop

X

4 + 3

Not (X Or Y)

Simple Semantics

String Constant

IntegerConstant

IntegerType Variable

Variable

Addition(Integer Type Constant, Integer Type Constant)

Negation Boolean Type (Boolean Type Variable InclusiveOr Boolean Type Variable)

Figure 8.4 Mapping between syntax and semantics.

Figure 8.5 expands that simple shorthand for the semantics to a more complex semantics based on set theory from mathematics. "zDLKFL," which is a string constant, is elaborated to be a specific string that is an element from the set of all possible strings (an infinite set) composed of ordinary English letters (we loosen our formal notation here some, but you should understand *S* to be the infinite expansion of all possible strings from the English alphabet). In both Figures 8.5 and 8.6, we have attached the note "* Where [[X]] signifies the semantic or truth value of the expression X." The next section on logic discusses *truth values* (a value that is either true or false). The *semantic value* is a little more complicated than that, and we will not get into it in much detail in this book.[5] Suffice it to say that the semantic value of a term is formalized as a function from the set of terms into the set of formal objects in the domain of discourse (the knowledge area we are interested in).

Figure 8.6 elaborates the semantics even more. The syntactic object X that is a *variable* in Figure 8.4 is shown to be an element of the entire Universe of Discourse (the domain or portion of the world we are modeling) of Figure 8.5. This means that X really ranges over all the classes defined in the model in Figure 8.6; it ranges over the disjunction of the set Thing, the set Person, and so on, all of which are subsets of the entire Universe of Discourse. Again, the formal notation in these figures is simplified a bit and presented mainly to give you an appreciation of the increasingly elaborated semantics for simple syntactic objects.

[5]A formal introduction to semantic value can be found at http://meta2.stanford.edu/kif/Hypertext/node11.html.

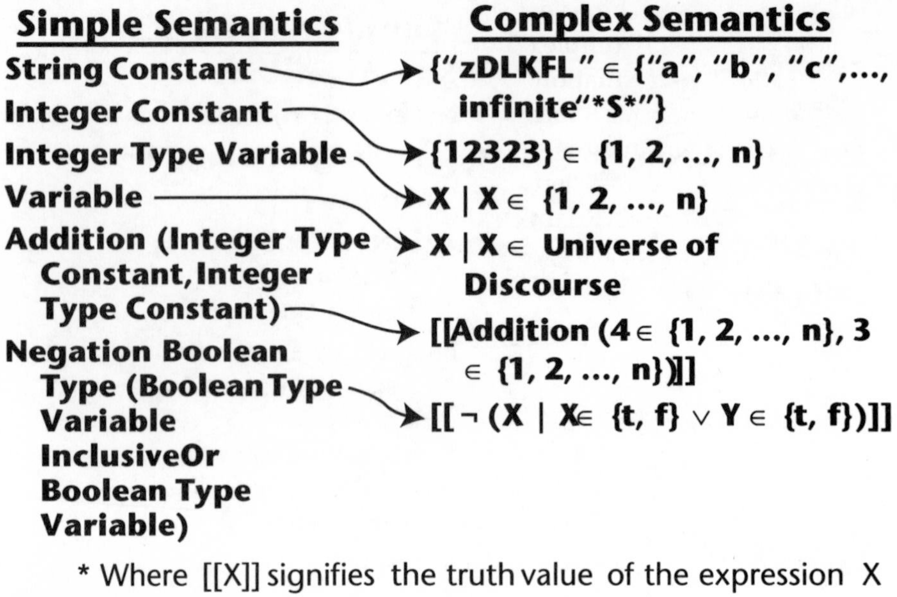

Simple Semantics

String Constant

Integer Constant

Integer Type Variable

Variable

Addition (Integer Type Constant, Integer Type Constant)

Negation Boolean Type (Boolean Type Variable InclusiveOr Boolean Type Variable)

Complex Semantics

{"zDLKFL" ∈ {"a", "b", "c",..., infinite"*S*"}

{12323} ∈ {1, 2, ..., n}

X | X ∈ {1, 2, ..., n}

X | X ∈ Universe of Discourse

[[Addition (4 ∈ {1, 2, ..., n}, 3 ∈ {1, 2, ..., n})]]

[[¬ (X | X∈ {t, f} ∨ Y ∈ {t, f})]]

* Where [[X]] signifies the truth value of the expression X

Figure 8.5   From simple to complex semantics.

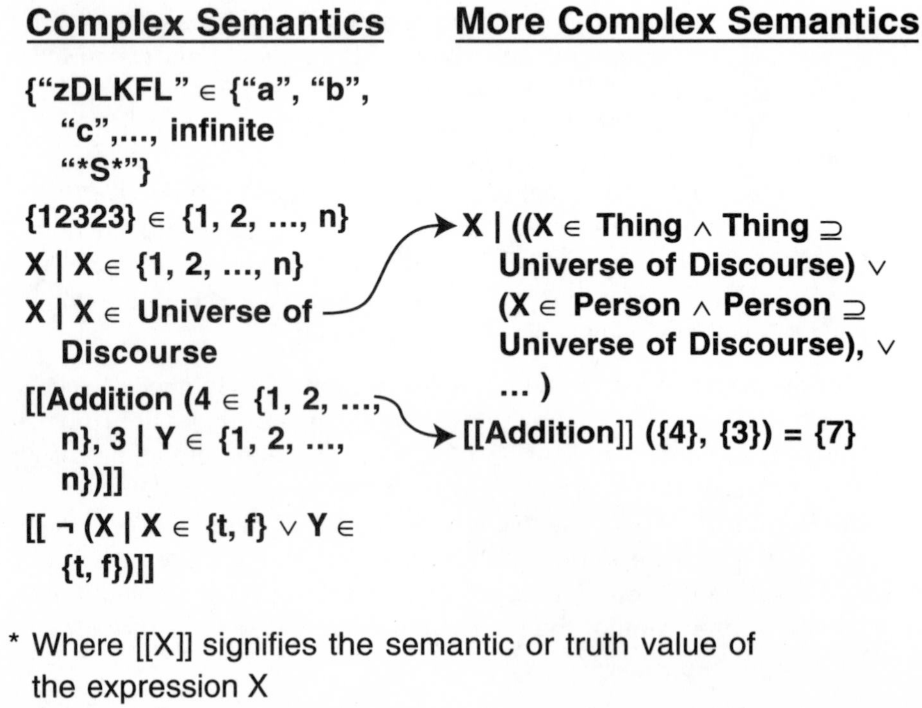

Complex Semantics

{"zDLKFL" ∈ {"a", "b", "c",..., infinite "*S*"}

{12323} ∈ {1, 2, ..., n}

X | X ∈ {1, 2, ..., n}

X | X ∈ Universe of Discourse

[[Addition (4 ∈ {1, 2, ..., n}, 3 | Y ∈ {1, 2, ..., n})]]

[[¬ (X | X ∈ {t, f} ∨ Y ∈ {t, f})]]

More Complex Semantics

X | ((X ∈ Thing ∧ Thing ⊇ Universe of Discourse) ∨ (X ∈ Person ∧ Person ⊇ Universe of Discourse), ∨ ...)

[[Addition]] ({4}, {3}) = {7}

* Where [[X]] signifies the semantic or truth value of the expression X

Figure 8.6   More elaborated semantics.

Obviously, the machine semantics is very primitive, simple, and inexpressive with respect to the complex, rich semantics of humans, but it's a start and very useful for our information systems. The machine is not "aware" and cannot reflect, obviously. It's a formal process of semantic interpretation that we have described—everything is still bits. But by designing a logical knowledge representation system (a language that we then implement) and ontologies (expressions in the KR language that are what humans want to model about our world, its entities, and the relationships among those entities), and getting the machine to infer (could be deduce, induce, abduce, and many other kinds of reasoning) conclusions that are extremely close to what humans would in comparable circumstances (assertions, facts, and so on), we will have imbued our systems with much more human-level semantic responses than they have at present. We will have a functioning Semantic Web.

Pragmatics

Pragmatics sits above semantics and has to do with the intent of the semantics and actual semantic usage. There is very little pragmatics expressed or even expressible in programming or databases languages. The little that exists in some programming languages like C++ is usually expressed in terms of *pragmas,* or special directives to the compiler as to how to interpret the program code. Pragmatics will increasingly become important in the Semantic Web, once the more expressive ontology languages such as RDF/S and OWL are fully specified and intelligent agents begin to use the ontologies that are defined in those languages. Intelligent agents will have to deal with the pragmatics (think of pragmatics as the extension of the semantics) of ontologies. For example, some agent frameworks, such as that of the Foundation for Intelligent Physical Agents (FIPA) standards consortium,[6] use an Agent Communication Language that is based on *speech act theory,*[7] which is a pragmatics theory about human discourse that states that human beings express their utterances in certain ways that qualify as acts, and that they have a specific intent for the meaning of those utterances. Intelligent agents are sometimes formalized in a framework called BDI, for Belief, Desire, and Intent.[8]

In these high-end agents, state transition tables are often used to express the semantics and pragmatics of the communication acts of the agents. A communication act, for example, would be a request by one agent to another agent concerning information (typically expressed in an ontology content language

---

[6]See the FIPA home page (http://www.fipa.org/), especially the specification on Communicative Acts under the Agent Communication Language (http://www.fipa.org/repository/cas.php3).

[7]See Smith (1990) for a philosophical history of speech act theory in natural language.

[8]See Rao and Georgeff (1995).

such as Knowledge Interchange Format [KIF])[9]—that is, either a query (an ask act, a request for information) or an assertion (a tell act, the answer to a request for information). When developers and technologists working in the Semantic Web turn their focus to the so-called web of proof and trust, pragmatic issues will become much more important, and one could then categorize that level as the Pragmatic Web. Although some researchers are currently working on the Pragmatic Web,[10] in general, most of that level will have to be worked out in the future.

Table 8.2 displays the syntactic, semantic, and pragmatic layers for human language; Table 8.3 does the same for intelligent agent interaction. In both cases, the principles involved are the same. Note that the levels are numbered from the lower syntactic level upward to the semantic and then pragmatic levels, so both tables should be read from bottom to top. In all the examples (1 to 3), you should first focus on the question or statement made at the top row. In Example 1 in Table 8.2, for example, you ask the question "Who is the best quarterback of all time?" The answer given to you by the responder is the string represented at the *syntactic level* (Level 1), that is, the string "Joe Montana". The literal meaning of that answer is represented at the *semantic level* (Level 2), in other words, *The former San Francisco quarterback named Joe Montana*. The *pragmatic level* (Level 3) shows that the response is a straight-forward *answer* to your question "Who is the best quarterback of all time?" This seems simple and reasonable. However, looking at Example 2, we see that there are some complications.

In Example 2, you ask the same question—Who is the best quarterback of all time? —but the response made to you by the other person as represented at the *syntactic level* (Level 1) is "Some quarterback." The literal meaning of that answer is represented at the *semantic level* as *There is some quarterback*. The *pragmatic level* (Level 3) describes the pragmatic *infelicity* or strangeness of the responder's response; in other words, *either the person doesn't know anything about the answer except that you are asking about a quarterback, or the person knows but is giving you less specific information than you requested, and so, is in general not to be believed* (this latter condition is a pragmatic violation).

---

[9]See the KIF [KIF] or Common Logic [CL] specification.
[10]See Singh (2002).

Table 8.2 Natural Language Syntax, Semantics, and Pragmatics

LANGUAGE LEVEL	EXAMPLE 1: YOU ASK: "WHO IS THE BEST QUARTERBACK OF ALL TIME?"	EXAMPLE 2: YOU ASK: "WHO IS THE BEST QUARTERBACK OF ALL TIME?"	EXAMPLE 3: YOU MAKE STATEMENT: "THE BKFKHDKS IS ORANGE."
3) Pragmatics: Intent, Use (speech act)	Answer to your question: "Who is the best quarterback of all time?"	Answer to your question: "Who is the best quarterback of all time?" ***Pragmatic anomaly:** Either the person doesn't know anything about the answer except that you are asking about a quarterback, or the person knows but is giving you less specific information than you requested, and so, is in general not to be believed (this latter condition is a pragmatic violation).[11]	Observation
2) Semantics: Meaning	The former San Francisco quarterback named Joe Montana	There is some quarterback.	Something named or characterized as the "BKFKHDKS" is a nominal (so probably an entity, but uncertain whether it is a class- or instance-level entity), and it has the color property value of orange.

(continued)

[11]This is a violation of the so-called Gricean conversational (i.e., pragmatic) maxim of cooperation (Grice, 1975): the "implicature" (i.e., implication) is that you know what you are talking about, and you understand the level of detail required to legitimately answer the question, and so, if you reply with something more general than the question asked (e.g., here, restating the given information), you either do not know the answer and are trying to "hide" that fact or you do know the answer and are trying to "mislead."

Table 8.2 *(continued)*

LANGUAGE LEVEL	EXAMPLE 1: YOU ASK: "WHO IS THE BEST QUARTERBACK OF ALL TIME?"	EXAMPLE 2: YOU ASK: "WHO IS THE BEST QUARTERBACK OF ALL TIME?"	EXAMPLE 3: YOU MAKE STATEMENT: "THE BKFKHDKS IS ORANGE."
1) Syntax: Symbols, Order, Structure	The answer: "Joe Montana"	The answer: "Some quarterback"	The statement: "The BKFKHDKS is orange"

Listing 8.2 displays an example of two messages between intelligent agents in the FIPA agent framework (highlighted in bold are the two message types). The first message is a request by Agent J to Agent I for the delivery of a specific package to a specific location. The second is an agreement by Agent I to Agent J concerning that delivery; it agrees to the delivery and assigns the delivery a high priority. Table 8.3 displays the syntactic, semantic, and pragmatic levels of the two agent messages. In Table 8.3, the *Request* and the *Agreement* actions, respectively, are only represented at the *pragmatic level* (Level 3); you'll note that at both the syntactic and the semantic levels (Levels 1 and 2), the description is nearly the same for both Examples 1 and 2. It is only at the pragmatic level (indicated in the FIPA message by the *performative* or speech act *type keyword* request *or* agree) that there is any distinction. But the distinction as represented at the pragmatic level is large: Example 1 is a *request*; Example 2 is an *agreement* to the request.

```
(request
    :sender (agent-identifier :name i)
    :receiver (set (agent-identifier :name j))
    :content
    "((action (agent-identifier :name j)
        (deliver package234 (location 25 35))))"
    :protocol fipa-request
    :language fipa-sl
    :reply-with order678)
(agree
    :sender (agent-identifier :name j)
    :receiver (set (agent-identifier :name i))
    :content
    "((action (agent-identifier :name j)
        (deliver package234 (location 25 35)))
        (priority order678 high))"
    :in-reply-to order678
    :protocol fipa-request
    :language fipa-sl)
```

Listing 8.2 FIPA agent messages: Request and agree.

Table 8.3 Intelligent Agent Syntax, Semantics, and Pragmatics

LANGUAGE LEVEL	EXAMPLE 1: AGENT IS REQUESTED TO PERFORM AN ACTION BY ANOTHER AGENT	EXAMPLE 2: AGENT AGREES TO PERFORM AN ACTION REQUESTED BY ANOTHER AGENT
3) Pragmatics: Intent, Use (speech act)	Agent J Requests an action by Agent I and the content is identified by order678.	Agent I Agrees to action requested by Agent J and the content is identified by order678.
2) Semantics: Meaning	Agent J's action is about the delivery of a specific package package234 to a specific location identified by 25 35. Note: Terms such as "action," "deliver," "location," and possible location values, units of measure, etc. have to be defined in an ontology that both agents know about. The ontology represents the meaning for these terms.	The Agent J action about the delivery of a specific package package234 to a specific location identified by 25 35, has high priority. Note: Terms such as "action," "deliver," "location," and possible location values, units of measure, etc. have to be defined in an ontology that both agents know about.

1) Syntax: Symbols, Order, Structure	`"((action (agent-identifier :name j)`
	
	`(deliver package234 (loc 25 35))))"`
		`"((action (agent-identifier :name j)`
		
		`(deliver package234 (loc 25 35)))`
		
		`(priority order678 high))"`

Expressing Ontologies Logically

As mentioned in the previous section, ontologies are usually expressed in a logic-based knowledge representation language, so that fine, accurate, consistent, sound, and meaningful distinctions can be made among the classes, instances, properties, attributes, and relations. Some ontology tools can perform automated reasoning using the ontologies, and thus provide advanced services to intelligent applications such as conceptual/semantic search and retrieval (non-keyword based), software agents, decision support, speech and natural language understanding, knowledge management, intelligent databases, and electronic commerce.

As we saw in Chapter 7, an ontology can range from the simple notion of a taxonomy (knowledge with minimal hierarchic or parent/child structure), to a thesaurus (words and synonyms), to a conceptual model (with more complex knowledge), to a logical theory (with very rich, complex, consistent, meaningful knowledge).

More technically, an ontology is both the vocabulary used to describe and represent an area of knowledge and the meaning of that vocabulary—that is, it is syntactically a language of types and terms that has a corresponding formal semantics that is the intended meaning of the constructs of the language and their composition. The recent computational discipline that addresses the development and management of ontologies is called *ontological engineering*.

Ontological engineering usually characterizes an ontology (much like a logical theory) in terms of an *axiomatic system*, or a set of axioms and inference rules that together characterize a set of theorems (and their corresponding formal models)—all of which constitute a theory (see Figure 8.7 and Table 8.4). In the technical view of ontological engineering, an ontology is the vocabulary for expressing the entities and relationships of a conceptual model for a general or particular domain, along with semantic constraints on that model that limit what that model means. Both the vocabulary and the semantic constraints are necessary in order to correlate that information model with the real-world domain it represents.

Figure 8.7 schematically attempts to show that theorems are proven from axioms using inference rules. Together, axioms, inference rules, and theorems constitute a theory.

Table 8.4 displays a portion of an ontology represented as axioms and inference rules. This table underscores that an ontology is represented equivalently either graphically or textually. In this fragment, the ontology is represented textually. The class-level assertions are in column one, labeled *Axioms*; these are asserted to be true. The representative *Inference Rules* (by no means all the inference rules available) are in column two. Finally, the *Theorems* are in column three. Theorems are hypotheses that need to be proved as being true. Once proved, theorems can be added to the set of axioms. Theorems are proved true by a process called a *proof*. A proof of a theorem simply means that, given a set of initial assertions (axioms), if the theorem can be shown to follow by applying the inference rules to the assertions, then the theorem is derived (validated or shown to be true).

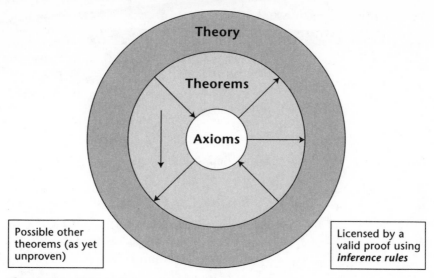

Figure 8.7 Axioms, inference rules, theorems, theory.

The set of axioms, inference rules, and valid theorems together constitute a theory, which is the reason that high-end ontologies on the Ontology Spectrum are called *logical theories*. Table 8.4 displays axioms at the universal level, that is, the level at which class generalizations hold. Of course, we realize that part of an ontology is the so-called knowledge base (sometimes called fact base), which contains assertions about the instances and which thus constitutes assertions at the individual level.

Also in this example, we note that there are probably many more axioms, inference rules, and theorems for this domain. Table 8.4 just represents a small fragment of an ontology to give you an idea of its logical components.

Table 8.5 gives another example of an ontology, one that is probably of interest in electronic commerce. In this example, the ontology components are expressed in English, but typically these would be expressed as textually or graphically in a logic-based language as in the previous example. Note in particular that the single-rule example looks very similar to the last axiom in the first column of Table 8.4. This ontology example comes from electronic commerce: the general domain of machine tooling and manufacturing. Note that these are expressed in English but usually would be in expressed in a logic-based language.

Table 8.4 Axioms, Inference Rules, Theorems: A Theory

AXIOMS	INFERENCE RULES	THEOREMS
Class(Thing)	**And-introduction**: Given P, Q, it is valid to infer $P \wedge Q$.	If $P \wedge Q$ are true, then so is P (Q.
Class(Person)	**Or-introduction**: Given P, it is valid to infer $P \vee Q$.	If X is a member of Class(Parent), then X is a member of Class(Person).
Class(Parent)	**And-elimination**: Given $P \wedge Q$, it is valid to infer P.	*If X is a member of Class(Child), then X is a member of Class(Person).*
Class(Child)	**Excluded middle**: $P \vee \neg P$ (i.e., either something is true or its negation is true)	If X is a member of Class(Child), then NameOf(X, Y) and Y is a String.
If SubClass(X, Y), then X is a subset of Y. This also means that if A is a member of Class(X), then A is a member of Class(Y).		If Person (JohnSmith), then $\neg$ ParentOf(John Smith, JohnSmith).
SubClass(Person, Thing)		
SubClass(Parent, Person)		
SubClass(Child, Person)		
ParentOf(Parent, Child)		
NameOf(Person, String)		
AgeOf(Person, Integer)		
If X is a member of Class (Parent) and Y is a member of Class(Child), then $\neg$ (X =Y).		

Term versus Concept: Thesaurus versus Ontology

To help us understand what an ontology is and isn't, let's try to elaborate one of the distinctions we made in the last chapter: that between a term and a concept.[12] One way to illustrate this distinction is to differentiate between a thesaurus and an ontology (specifically, a high-end ontology or logical theory, i.e., on the upper right in the Ontology Spectrum of Figure 7.6).

[12]For further discussion of the distinction between terms and concepts, refer to (ISO 704, 2000).

Table 8.5 Ontology Example

CONCEPT	EXAMPLE
Classes (general things)	Metal working machinery, equipment, and supplies; metal-cutting machinery; metal-turning equipment; metal-milling equipment; milling insert; turning insert, etc.
Instances (particular things)	An instance of metal-cutting machinery is the "OKK KCV 600 15L Vertical Spindle Direction, 1530x640x640mm 60.24"x25.20"x25.20 X-Y-Z Travels Coordinates, 30 Magazine Capacity, 50 Spindle Taper, 20kg 44 lbs Max Tool Weight, 1500 kg 3307 lbs Max Loadable Weight on Table, 27,600 lbs Machine Weight, CNC Vertical Machining Center" (http://www.okkcorp .com/kcvseries.html)
Relations: subclass-of, (kind_of), instance-of, part-of, has-geometry, performs, used-on, etc.	A kind of metal working machinery is metal cutting machinery. A kind of metal cutting machinery is milling insert.
Properties	Geometry, material, length, operation, ISO-code, etc.
Values:	1; 2; 3; "2.5", "inches"; "85-degree-diamond"; "231716"; "boring"; "drilling"; etc.
Rules	If milling-insert(X) & operation(Y) & material(Z)=HG_Steel & performs(X, Y, Z), then has-geometry(X, 85-degree-diamond). [Meaning: If you need to do milling on high-grade steel, then you need to use a milling insert (blade) that has an 85-degree diamond shape.]

Figure 8.8 displays the *triangle of signification* or *triangle of meaning*. It attempts to display in an abbreviated form the three components (the angles) of the meaning of natural languages like English. The first component, at the lower left, is the terms, that is, the symbols (the labels for the concepts) or the words of English and the rules for combining these into phrases and sentences (the syntax of English). In themselves, they have no meaning until they are associated with the other components, such as other angles of "Concepts" and "Real-World Referents."

For example, if asked for the meaning of the term "LKDF34AQ," you would be at a loss, as there is no meaning for it. If asked, however, for the meaning of "automobile," you would know what is meant because there is an associated thing in the world (the real-world referent that has four tires, an engine, is manufactured by Ford or Honda, gets particular miles to the gallon, and so on) and there is a concept in our human mental model that stands for (or "represents") that real thing in the world. That is why there is a dotted line between Term and Real-World Referent in Figure 8.8; there is no direct link. Humans need a concept to mediate between a term and the thing in the world the term refers to.

A thesaurus generally works with the left-hand side of the triangle (the terms and concepts), while an ontology in general works more with the right-hand side of the triangle (the concepts and referents), as depicted in Figure 8.9.

Recall from the previous chapter that a thesaurus is developed primarily as a classification space over a domain, a set of domains, or even over the entire world, such as Roget's 1916 thesaurus—for the purpose of conceptual navigation, search, and information retrieval. Therefore, the semantics of the classification space can remain relatively weak, characterizing the simple semantic relations among conceptual labels (terms), and so structured mostly taxonomically by broader-than and narrower-than relations. All you really need to know about a term node in a thesaurus is that it is semantically distinct from other nodes (hence, removing ambiguity), and it is broader than or narrower than certain other terms. No complicated notion of the meaning has to be captured and represented.

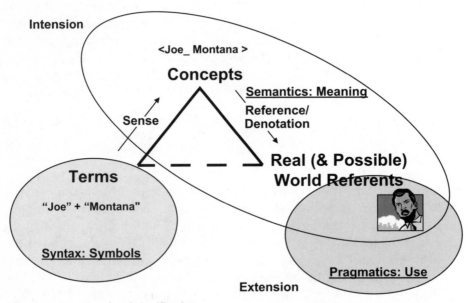

Figure 8.8 Triangle of signification.

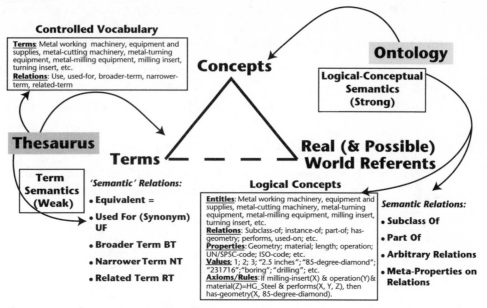

Figure 8.9 Thesaurus versus ontology.

An ontology, however, does try to represent the complex semantics of concepts and the relations among concepts, their properties, attributes, values, constraints, and rules. But then, the purpose of an ontology is quite distinct from that of a thesaurus. An ontology does try to capture and represent the meaning of a domain, a set of domains, or the entire world, because it attempts to explicitly simulate the meaning that a human being has in his or her mental model of the domain, set of domains, or the world. Furthermore, an ontology is meant to be used directly by many kinds of software applications that have to operate on and so have knowledge about the domains represented by the ontology—including sometimes applications that have not yet been thought of. Finally, an ontology is meant to be extended, refined, and reused, traits that it shares with its semantically weaker cousin, the thesaurus. Unlike the thesaurus, however, an ontology tries to express precise, complex, consistent, and rich conceptual semantics.

Given this distinction between terms and concepts, how do ontological engineers actually develop the ontologies that contain the concepts? How do they decide what the concepts and relations of a particular domain are? How do they discover the principles holding for those concepts and relations?

Troelstra (1998) asks those same questions about mathematics. Since ontological engineering generally adopts the formal methods of mathematics and logic, we think the following quotation from Troelstra (1998, pp. 1–2) is appropriate here.

Given an informally described, but intuitively clear concept, one analyzes the concept as carefully as possible, and attempts to formulate formally precise principles characterizing the concept to a greater or lesser extent.

Although space precludes us from delving too deeply into ontological engineering as a technical discipline, we will introduce some semantic concepts related to ontologies that are important to ontological engineers.

Important Semantic Distinctions

This section is an introduction to some of the semantic distinctions and issues that are useful to know when learning about ontologies:

- Extension
- Intension
- Meta and object levels of representation
- Ontology and semantic mapping

Extension and Intension

Typically, ontologies make a distinction between *intension* and *extension*. The same distinctions hold of other models in other modeling languages; however, other models typically don't make these formal distinctions—though they should.

Ontologies provide two kinds of knowledge:

- About the class or generic information that describes and models the problem, application, or, most usually, the domain
- About the instance information—that is, the specific instantiation of that description or model

In the database and formal/natural language worlds, the first type of knowledge is the *intension* and the second is the *extension*. In the database world, a schema is the *intensional* database, whereas the tuples of the database constitute the *extensional* database. In the formal/natural language worlds, a description or specification is an intension, whereas the actual objects (instances/individuals) in the model (or world) for which the description is true are in the extension.

A definite description in natural language, for example, is a nominal—that is, a noun compound, such as "the man in the hat" or "the current President of the United States," which is a description that seemingly picks out a *definite* individual in the world or a particular context, indicated by the use of the definite article "the." The definite description "the man in the hat" therefore picks out the man, whoever he is, who happens to be wearing a hat in the current context of our conversation in a particular room. Let's say that we are at a party. I am in a conversation with you when I suddenly point to an individual across the room and say, "I think you know the man in the hat over there." You look, perhaps squinting your eyes, and reply, "Is that Harry?" If the man in the hat is indeed our mutual friend Harry Jones, I'll respond, "Yes." The *intension* in this case is "the man in the hat." The *extension* is "Harry Jones." Harry Jones is the individual for which it is true that he is "the man in the hat." The property of being the man in the hat could actually apply to countless individuals in other contexts. That *intensional* description, "there is someone who has the property of being a man wearing a hat," could pick out many specific individuals in different contexts. Whichever individuals that description applies to in a specific context is said to constitute the *extension* of that intensional description.

Even in the context of the party, Harry Jones could have other properties (we also sometimes call these properties *predicates*, meaning they are predications or statements/descriptions that hold or synonymously are true of a particular individual). He could be "the drummer for the CyberHogs" or "the husband of that woman who works in the Accounting Department who is always complaining at our staff meetings about the lack of microwaves available to employees." The same individual can have multiple properties at the same or different times. Conversely, the same properties can apply to different individuals at the same or different times.

Developing an Ontology (Theory) of Interesting Things

In this section, we describe the difference between an intension and an extension by giving an extended example. A simple example of the distinction between intension and extension in a pseudo-formal/natural language is the following.

```
Class Father:
Subclass_of: Person
Subclass_of: Male
Father_of: <default: none>, <range: Person>, constraints: <non-reflex-
ive, anti-symmetric>
```

This roughly means that no Father is his own Father (nonreflexive). If X is the Father_of Y, Y is not the Father_of X (antisymmetric), though of course if X is a Father and the Father_of Y, Y can be a Father.

There will probably be additional properties inherited from the Person and Male classes, such as:

```
Lives_at:<location>,
Works_at: <company>, etc.
```

This is a formal description/specification of what a Father is and what properties a Father has. Following is a formal description/specification of what a specific instance of the class Father is (John Q. Public) and what specific property values that instance of a Father has:

```
Instance John Q. Public
Instance_of: Father
Father_of: <person instances: <Ralph R. Public>, <Sally S. Public>>
Lives_at: <location instance: <123 Main St.>>
Work_at: <company instance: <Very Big Company, Inc.>>, etc.
```

A simplified way to state this is as follows:

Intension.   Father(X), where X is a variable for the domain (Male Person)

Extension.   {John Q. Public, ...}, that is, the actual set of instances/individuals who are X for whom it is true that Father(X)

The important point here is that an intension is a description I, and an extension E is the set of things that actually have those properties of I (in a given database, object model, universe of discourse, world)—that is,

Some description I holds of (is true of) some set of individuals E. For example:

```
I: The current President of the United States
E: {George W. Bush}
```

The same I a few years ago would have had a different E: {Bill Clinton}:

```
I: The man in the hat over there
E: {Harry Jones}
```

The same I yesterday would have had a different E: {Joe}.

Now, the various technical communities will call I the following: a taxonomy, a schema, a conceptual/object model, an intensional semantics, an ontology. They will call E the following, respectively: leaves of the taxonomy (meaning: the bottommost objects in a taxonomy), tuples, instances, the extension, instances/individuals.

So what does all of this mean to you? It means that in an ontology (or its correlate), you describe a set of structured, generic properties that have a particular semantics (meaning). This is called a model, meaning that it defines and represents information about some aspects of the world that you (as the modeler) care to model.

For example, in an ontology, you could represent information describing the semantics of many domains: person, location, event, and so on, and the relationships among them (a person is at a location when an event occurs, a person causes an event to occur at a location, a person is in some relation to an event that occurs at a location, and so on).

Let's say you're a marketing analyst and you'd like to develop an ontology that would represent the things you are currently interested in. This ontology (if it's a high-end ontology, we would call it a *logical theory*) would use the usual domain ontologies (or correlates), in other words, the usual generic knowledge/semantics about persons, locations, events—assuming you had such, which unfortunately we don't have much of today. It would be a model of My Theory of Interesting Things; at the top that might consist of the following description/specification. Let's give an example of this kind of intension *I*:

```
I_1: Person P at Location L while Event E occurs is Interesting:
where P is any Person, Location L ranges over {US_Cities, Canada_Cities,
Mexico_Cities} and Event Ev ranges over the conjunction of the following
event types: {Credit_Card_Purchases_of_Sporting_Events AND
Credit_Card_Purchases_of_Book_Merchandise AND
Credit_Card_Purchases_of_Clothing_Merchandise}
```

This means that we are interested only in those persons who purchased sporting events, book merchandise, and clothing merchandise using credit cards. Now, let's assume that this *I* is defined at a specific Time *T*, December 19, 2002. At that time, *I* had an extension consisting of the following:

```
E_1:
{{Person Instance: {John Q. Public},
Location Instances (constrained to US_Cities):
{US_Cities: Akron_Ohio},
Event Instances (constrained to
Credit_Card_Purchases_of_Sporting_Events,
Credit_Card_Purchases_of_Book_Merchandise,
Credit_Card_Purchases_of_Clothing_Merchandise):
{Purchase1234_of_12-19-02, Purchase456789_of_12-19-02,
Purchase556677_of_12-19-02}
{Person Instance: {Cynthia A. Citizen},
Location Instances (constrained to US_Cities):
{US_Cities: Peoria_Illinois},
Event Instances (constrained to
Credit_Card_Purchases_of_Sporting_Events,
Credit_Card_Purchases_of_Book_Merchandise,
Credit_Card_Purchases_of_Clothing_Merchandise):
{Purchase890_of_12-19-02, Purchase13579_of_12-19-02,
Purchase112233_of_12-19-02}}
```

In this example, John Q. Public in Akron, Ohio, and Cynthia A. Citizen in Peoria, Illinois, are the only individuals who had all three kinds of specific purchases (sporting events, books, clothing) using a credit card in any U.S. city on December 19, 2002.

Now, what if the My Theory of Interesting Things changes? What if tomorrow a marketing analyst has to add a new description of what constitutes Interesting Things? Let's assume that the new description just adds an additional property, for instance, Intension *I*'s Events *Ev* now also range over {Started_Flight_from_LaGuardia_Airport}.

The description *I* now changes to *I'* that is the same as *I* with the additional assertion that the Started_Flight_from_LaGuardia_Airport is also possible.

This means that if My Theory of Interesting Things changes (with the addition of a new property, for example), a new query could be generated that finds the extension of the new intension in the database. Correspondingly, the old extension could be evaluated with respect to the new intension and seen as to whether it holds or has a relation to the new extension of the new intension (that is, the new set for which the new description holds). Two intensions may have the same extensions; this is known as *extensional equivalence*. It can help you to know that the same individual has two different descriptions: Clark Kent and Superman. The man who saw Billie B's magic show at the Hyatt on 22nd St. yesterday and the man who charged an Aeroflot ticket with destination Rasputania at LaGuardia this morning could be the same person My Theory of Interesting Things could be modeled in the ontology (set of integrated ontologies) in the same way as any other domain ontology; it's a theory just as they are. A modeler can use the same mechanisms to model My Theory of Interesting Things as any other theory in the ontology—for instance, specialize it, inherit from it, modify it, and so on. A generic model of My Theory of Interesting Things could be created, which an individual analyst could specialize according to a set of new properties. Other marketing analysts could in turn specialize from that.

This means that the description changes. Things for which the old description held are updated. Things for which the new description holds are found. Links between the things described by the two descriptions are also found. You can model Things That Are of Interest to You (or My Theory of Interesting Things). In fact, you absolutely should. Your model can change, and it no doubt will.

Of course, the devil is in the details of the implementation. But if you are model-driven (meaning here ontology- or knowledge-driven), that just means you can change your model, regenerate the implementation, or find the delta, and continue.

Everything should be model-driven. It's much simpler to change the model (the description) than the thing that, without the model, has no well-defined semantics. Without a model, you are perpetually doomed to try to correlate tuples in multiple databases that have no accompanying semantics. This is why data mining and its parent, knowledge discovery, are such hot technologies now—this is the way we usually do things. No model, no semantics. So we try to infer the semantics, or what the data means. It's tough to do.

Levels of Representation

When discussing ontologies, you need to make distinctions among a number of representation levels. These distinctions are necessary because ontologies can be viewed as languages, or syntactic vocabularies with accompanying semantics. Furthermore, because ontologies are content and content can only be expressed using a *content language*, which is usually called a *knowledge representation language* (we discuss these in more detail in the next section), we are therefore talking about at least two levels of representation: the *knowledge representation language level*, typically called the *meta level* with respect to the underlying level, and the *object level*, which is the underlying content level, the level at which ontologies are expressed. But the notions of meta and object level are really relative to the particular levels one is talking about. We also know that we need a third level, the level of *instances*. This is the level at which instances of the ontology classes exist.

So if you are focused on the instance level, then that level can be viewed as the object level, and its meta level is the level at which class or universal knowledge is asserted (the concepts of the ontology). If instead one is focused on the class or universal level, then that level can be viewed as the object level, and its meta level is the level of the knowledge representation language.

Table 8.6 displays the three levels of representation required for ontologies and the kinds of constructs represented at the individual levels.

- Level 1—The knowledge representation level
- Level 2—The ontology concept level
- Level 3—The ontology instance level

The knowledge representation language level (the highest meta level) defines the constructs that will be used at the ontology concept level. These constructs include the notions of Class, Relation, Property, and so on. Examples of KR languages (which we talk about in more detail in the next section) include languages that preceded the Semantic Web—such as KL-ONE, Ontolingua, Classic, LOOM, Knowledge Interchange Format (KIF), CycL, and Unified Modeling Language (UML)—and Semantic Web languages, including RDF/S, DAML+OIL, and OWL.[13]

---

[13]KL-ONE: Brachman and Schmoltze (1985), CLASSIC: Patel-Schneider et al. (1991); LOOM: MacGregor (1991); Knowledge Interchange Format (KIF): [KIF]; Ontolingua: Gruber (1993); Cyc and CycL: Lenat and Guha (1990, 1991) and [CYC]; Unified Modeling Language: [UML]; DAML+OIL: [DAML+OIL]; OWL: Dean et al. (2002), Smith et al. (2002), McGuinness and van Harmelen (2002).

Table 8.6 Ontology Representation Levels

LEVEL	EXAMPLE CONSTRUCTS
Knowledge representation (KR) language (Ontology Language) level: Meta level to the ontology concept level	Class, Relation, Instance, Function, Attribute, Property, Constraint, Axiom, Rule
Ontology concept (OC) level: Object level to the KR language level, meta level to the instance level	Person, Location, Event, Parent, Hammer, River, FinancialTransaction, BuyingAHouse, Automobile, TravelPlanning, etc.
Ontology instance (OI) level: Object level to the ontology concept level	Harry X. Landsford III, Ralph Waldo Emerson, Person560234, PurchaseOrder TransactionEvent6117090, 1995-96 V-6 Ford Taurus 244/4.0 Aerostar Automatic with Block Casting # 95TM-AB and Head Casting 95TM

NOTE

Web Ontology Language is nicknamed OWL in honor of Owl in Winnie the Pooh (Milne, 1996), who spells his name "WOL." Examples of OWL documents can be found at http://www.w3.org/2001/sw/WebOnt/.

At the second level, the ontology concept (OC) level, ontologies are defined using the constructs of the KR level. At this level, you are interested in modeling the generic or universal content, the domain knowledge about Persons, Locations, Events, Parents, Hammers, and FinancialTransactions.

At the third and lowest level, the ontology instance level, the constructs are instances of ontology concept level constructs. So this level concerns the knowledge base or fact base, the assertions about instances or individuals such as Harry X. Landsford III, an instance of the class Person, and PurchaseOrder-TransactionEvent6117090, an instance of the class PurchaseOrderTransaction-Event.

Ontology and Semantic Mapping Problem

One important issue in understanding and developing ontologies is the *ontology or semantic mapping problem*. We say "or semantic mapping problem" because this is an issue that affects everything in information technology that must confront semantics problems—that is, the problem of representing *meaning* for systems, applications, databases, and document collections. You must always consider mappings between whatever representations of semantics you currently have (for system, application, database, document collection) and some other representation of semantics (within your own enterprise, within your community, across your market, or the world). And you must consider semantic mappings within your set of ontologies or whatever your semantic base representation is (if it's not ontologies, it's probably hard-coded in the procedural code that services your databases, and that means it's *really* a problem).

This semantic problem exists *within* and *without* ontologies. That means that it exists *within* any given semantic representation such as an ontology, and it exists *between (without)* ontologies. Within an ontology, you will need to focus on a specific *context* (or view) of the ontology, given a specific purpose or rationale or use of the ontology. And without (between) ontologies, you will need to focus on the semantic equivalence between different concepts and relations in two or more distinct ontologies. These ontologies may or may not be about approximately the same things. Chances are, the two distinct ontologies that you need to map together say similar but slightly different things about the same domain. Or you may need to map your reference ontology or ontology lattice to another standard represented as a taxonomy, thesaurus, or ontology. And you need to *avoid semantic loss* in the mapping.

Figure 8.10 displays mappings from an ontology to an electronic commerce taxonomy (for example, a portion of the UNSPSC product and service taxonomy). On the right in the figure is the reference ontology with its semantically well-defined relationships; on the left is the taxonomy to be used for an electronic commerce application with its less well-defined relationships. In practice, you may need to maintain mappings between ontologies (or, as in this example, between ontologies and taxonomies) simply because each knowledge representation system may be managed by separate organizations and need to evolve separately. In general, determining the semantic equivalence (mappings) between concepts in two ontologies is hard and requires human knowledge of the semantics of the two sides and thus human decision making (though current ontology management tools do have some automated support) to make the correct mappings. Although the names (labels) of two concepts may be the same (or completely different) in the two ontologies, there is no guarantee that those concepts mean the same thing (or mean different things). We've seen earlier that *terms* (words or labels) have very weak semantics in themselves; string identity cannot be relied on to provide semantic identity or equivalence. Similarly, structural correspondence cannot be relied on to ensure semantic correspondence. Determining semantic equivalence and then creating mappings between two ontologies will remain only a semi-automated process for quite some time in the future.

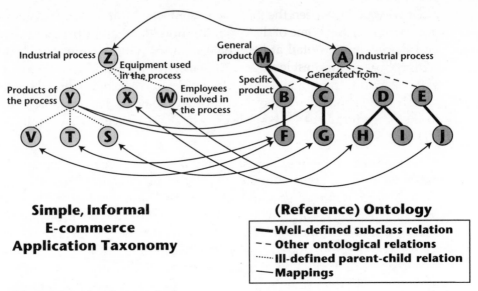

Figure 8.10 Mapping ontologies.

Most ontology languages and their supporting tools have some facility for defining mappings between ontologies. The simplest mechanism is an *include* or *import* statement, whereby one ontology includes or imports another ontology. This is the simplest mechanism, because you just bring in the entire ontology into your current ontology and all the concepts and relations of the imported ontology are available to the new expanded ontology space. However, these new imported concepts and relations are not really semantically rectified (made semantically meaningful with respect to the preexisting ontology which included them).[14] After importing, a tighter semantic rectification can be undergone, by *merging* or *mapping* the old and new concepts and relations. Merging will result in consolidated concepts and relations; mapping will keep the concepts and relations from both ontologies distinct but linked. Tools such as Protégé and Ontolingua/Chimaera support the merging process better than they support the mapping process. Semantic Web languages such as DAML+OIL and OWL have constructs that enable you to import an ontology, but also to declare that two concepts (represented as classes) are the same semantically. In addition, OWL enables you to declare that two individuals (instances) are the same semantically—a good step toward greater support for semantic mapping.

---

[14]The OWL:imports statement actually does semantically rectify insofar as it both *includes* an ontology and declares that the assertions defining the meaning of the included ontology are to be included too. This *imports* is stronger than most *includes* and may in fact fail because of semantic disagreement between the two ontologies.

Now that we have seen the primary representation levels needed for expressing ontologies and some of the issues involved in mapping between ontologies, let's look in more detail at knowledge representation languages, formalisms, and logics—the highest level of representation.

Knowledge Representation: Languages, Formalisms, Logics

This section introduces some background material on knowledge representation, a technical discipline from the field of artificial intelligence, to assist in our understanding of ontologies and the ontology languages of the Semantic Web. We will try to keep our discussion brief, but yet provide enough detail so that technical managers and leads have some scaffolding on which to support the ontological notions we have presented in this chapter.

A wealth of material is already available on knowledge representation. This section provides some references for those who are interested in obtaining more detail, but we will focus on just a few questions: What is knowledge representation, what are the important principles and components of knowledge representation, and how is knowledge representation related to ontologies and the Semantic Web?

Semantic Networks, Frame-Based KR, and Description Logics

Knowledge representation is a branch of artificial intelligence that focuses on the design and implementation of languages and systems that represent knowledge about the world. A knowledge representation therefore is a stand-in for real objects in the world, and the events and relationships those real things participate in. In our earlier discussion about representation, we saw that one of the important issues is that representation is a means for both expressing and using information. So knowledge representation is a means for both expressing and using semantic information, that is, knowledge about the world or specific domains of the world, with the additional qualification that the use of that knowledge should be used for intelligent reasoning and be computationally efficient.[15]

In general, the language used for knowledge representation determines the kind of reasoning that can take place on the knowledge; the representation precedes reasoning. A knowledge representation language with limited

---

[15]See Davis, Shrobe, Szolovits (1993). Also see John Sowa's (2001, p. 135) discussion based on the Davis et al. article.

expressivity (in the kinds of knowledge it is possible to represent) cannot directly be used for automatic reasoning methods that require more complex expressiveness. This issue will become clearer in our discussion of logic.

Knowledge representation is derived from the semantic networks developed during the 1960s and 1970s. It is generally accepted that the first elaboration of the notion of a semantic network was by Quillian's chapter in Minsky's (1968) book describing emerging artificial intelligence research at MIT.[16] A *semantic network* was just that: a network structure (typically represented as directed acyclic graphs) for the expression of semantics, or a node-and-link representation of knowledge constructs (now we would typically called them *concepts*) and their relationships. What are currently known as *knowledge maps* would probably correspond to semantic networks. One problem with semantic networks is that, in general, they were ad hoc, heterogeneously structured and represented, with their semantics dependent only on the particular researchers who developed them and the particular systems that used them. The reasoning methods of semantic networks were based on particular implementation strategies, not on a formal language.

Developing a semantic network was not recognized as really being about the design and implementation of a knowledge representation *language.* In fact, it was only in the late 1970s and early 1980s that the knowledge representation community began to formalize consistently and coherently the notion of a semantic network as a logic-based language for representing knowledge.[17] The first formalization of a semantic network based on logic was the frame-based language KL-ONE (Brachman & Schmolze, 1985).

A *frame-based* knowledge representation language is a language for representing knowledge based on frames, which are simply data structures for representing concepts (called *classes*) and relations (called *slots*). The notion of a frame corresponds to early LISP programming language terminology: A slot and filler data structure was a representation for records in LISP. Attributes (sometimes called properties) are just slots defined on a domain (a specific class subtree). Frame-based systems are close to the object-oriented modeling paradigm, insofar as the knowledge of a domain is centered on the primary *entities* (represented as classes and instances of those classes) of the domain. A class or an instance in a frame-based language has many properties nowadays considered standard for both object models and ontologies: multiple parents, inheritance of relations and attributes (slots in frame systems), default values

[16]For additional information on semantics networks and the frame-based languages that were descendants of them, see Minsky (1975), Fahlman (1979), Brachman (1978), Brachman and Levesque (1985), and Brachman and Schmolze (1985).

[17]In addition to the Brachman citations in the previous footnote, see also the SIGART Bulletin of June 1991, which was a *Special Issue on Implemented Knowledge Representation and Reasoning Systems,* and Mylopoulos and Brodie (1989).

and the possibility of overriding values, and *facets*, the latter of which can be considered knowledge aspects or meta data associated with frames or slots (for example, sometimes the *unit of measure* of a slot will be attached to the slot as a facet; other uses of facets are to record origin, authoring, and descriptive information, i.e., meta data).

This frame perspective is different from the other major modeling perspective in knowledge representation languages—that based on logical *axioms* (logical expressions) and in which the knowledge of a domain is distributed across axiom set—as in *description logics* (which we talk about shortly). Most modern knowledge representation languages and systems based on the languages (such as KIF/CL, DAML+OIL, OWL), however, either explicitly or implicitly allow for both modeling perspectives and make the distinction transparent to the user/developer (though developers who wish to understand and use either perspective have access to the underlying constructs). The important point is that *frame-based representations are equivalent to logic-based representations.*

Listing 8.2 shows a frame-based representation. In this example, the class StationWagon is defined as being a subclass of the class Automobile and having a number of properties (or attributes): having doors, a model type, a manufacturer, and a certain weight—all of which will get inherited downward by any subclasses or instances of StationWagon. Note here (in our notation, words that begin with a capital letter signify classes) that Manufacturer and Weight-Measure are themselves classes. Then an instance of StationWagon class, identified by the identifier inst-345678, instantiates specific values for the properties defined at the class level. Those values can in fact override the default values (if any are defined) of the class level.

```
(defineClass StationWagon
     (superclass        Automobile)
     (doors          5)
     (model          *noDefault*)
     (manufacturer   Manufacturer)
     (weight         WeightMeasure))

(defineInstance    inst-345678
     (class          StationWagon)
     (doors          3)
     (model          Taurus)
     (manufacturer   Ford)
     (weight         1840 lbs.))
```

Listing 8.2 Example of frame-based knowledge representation.

Semantic networks evolved to frame-based systems. Frame-based systems led to the development of *description logics*. The frame-based language KL-ONE was also the first description logic because, in addition to supporting frame representation, it was formalized logically with description-forming structures (related to our previous discussion of general *descriptions*, but used in the more technical sense of intensional descriptions). A description in a description logic is an expression in a formal language that defines a set of instances or tuples (the extension, as we've seen). A description logic, therefore, is a language for representing knowledge that has a syntax and a semantics—a syntax for constructing descriptions and a semantics that defines the meaning of each description.

Description logics are sometimes called terminological logics, classification logics, or concept logics. They are based on a declarative formalism—a language—for defining concepts in multiple hierarchies/taxonomies that are organized in a subsumption framework. *Subsumption* is a special relation, such as the *subclass of* or *isa* relation in object models and ontologies, that organizes the entire model into a generalization/specialization hierarchy, with more general information as you go upward in the hierarchy and more specific information as you go downward. Mathematically, the subsumption relation generates a partially ordered set or poset. Because subsumption in the general case is *undecidable* (consider undecidability as meaning that a query may never terminate, since it will be searching an infinite space, and so no decision procedure can be constructed that can *decide* whether or not a given query will terminate and return with results), description logics try to get around that problem by limiting the knowledge representation language and other tricks.

Description logics as a technical thread of knowledge representation was founded to:

- Formalize the nature of knowledge representation logically, or develop a formalism based on logic for the representation and expression of knowledge.
- Provide for sound, tractable reasoning methods founded on a firm theoretical and logical basis.

Generally, description logics have tried to create knowledge representation languages that enable both expressivity of the knowledge (i.e., richness of the detail of the semantics of the world portion you want to model) *and* tractable reasoning—which, in general, means to develop a logical language that is less expressive (but perhaps expressive enough to represent useful knowledge?) and less formally powerful than *first-order logic* (the predicate calculus) and thus more tractable for machine interpretation and automated inference (to get around the decidability issue mentioned previously). Although we will talk briefly about first-order logic in the next section, we observe now that most description logics are defined in terms of a function-free first-order logic that uses at most three variables and are defined to be sound, complete, and decidable (these are formal properties of logics, which we will see shortly), and tractable (amenable to efficient computational use).

Listing 8.3 shows an example of some assertions in the LOOM description logic.[18] In this example, the first relation *At-Least-One-Son* logically defines the set of all persons that have at least one son. The second relation *More-Sons-Than-Daughters* logically defines the set of all persons for whom it is the case that they have more sons than daughters. The *:if-def* indicates that the definition is total, rather than partial (*:def*), and *:setof* indicates a set expression, that is, an unnamed relation with domain variables (here, *?c*) and definition (here, *(son ?p ?c)*).

```
(defrelation At-Least-One-Son (?p)
        :iff-def (and
                (Person ?p)
                (>= (cardinality
                        (setof (?c) (son ?p ?c)))
                        1))


(defrelation More-Sons-Than-Daughters (?pp)
        :iff-def (and
                (Person ?pp)
                (> (cardinality
                        (setof (?b) (son?pp ?b)))
                    (cardinality
                        (setof (?g) (daughter ?pp ?g))))))))
```

Listing 8.3   LOOM description logic example.

LOOM is among the class of description logic knowledge representation languages developed during the past 20 years. Others include Classic, KRIS, and more recently, FaCT—the description logic used as the back-end classifier and inference engine of OntoEdit, which enables you to build ontologies in DAML+OIL.[19] But now, let's shift into a brief description of logic, the formal substrate for all knowledge representation and Semantic Web languages (and perhaps even English!).

[18]MacGregor (1994), pp. 2-4.

[19]LOOM: MacGregor (1991); CLASSIC: Patel-Schneider et al. (1991); KRIS: Baader and Hollunder (1991); FaCT: Horrocks (2002). CycL: Lenat and Guha (1991) is another language that is based on logic, but more accurately on first-order predicate logic, a type of logic that we will discuss later in this chapter.

Logic and Logics

Logic is sometimes supposed to underlie all of mathematics and science. Some say that logic also underlies all of natural language. We will remain agnostic on these pronouncements and will just say that logic *usually* and *definitely should* underlie all models and modeling languages. Why? Because if we are serious about defining languages that can both represent the knowledge of the world according to the perspective of the human being *and* be machine-interpretable at the semantic level (i.e., machines and their software can interpret human semantics and knowledge at our human level of understanding), then those knowledge representation languages and the knowledge they represent must be supported by formally powerful tools only representable by logic. Otherwise our knowledge—if represented in nonlogically underpinned ways—will remain arbitrarily interpretable by our software, the condition that holds today, where the semantics of our data and systems are embedded indecipherably and inextricably in our imperative programming code.

This state of affairs is the primary reason, by far, why human beings are reduced to interacting with computers at the computer level rather than the human level: We sink to having to interpret 0s and 1s, UIDS, SchdUpdDs, GOTOs, and DO-LOOPS, for the semantics of our data and systems, rather than having our systems use data that is interpreted semantically and interact at *our* level, in terms of People, Places, Things, Events, and Locations.

The history of software in general is a history of the general evolution of our programming languages upward to our human level. Think about so-called third-, fourth-, fifth-, and sixth-generation languages. Our programming languages have been evolving upward to meet our human knowledge/conceptual level. *Structured programming languages*—languages to support ways of logically modularizing and encapsulating programming constructs according to ways humans decompose problems—and *object-oriented languages*—the last major shift in programming language to using surrogates of real-world human objects—and more recently *agent-oriented languages*—the shift upward from those programming language surrogates of real-world human objects to real-world human tasks—have demonstrated to all of us this nearly inexorable fact: Our programming languages and their representations have moved and *need* to move up to our human level, in order for us to get computers to do things as we want them to.

Going downward and adapting our human requirements and modes of operation and interpretation to the machine level makes us inefficient, misunderstood, and ineffective. Our software projects have to recapitulate each time the knowledge that could have been represented correctly or near-correctly the first time. We reinvent the wheel each day on each project, on every project, across the world. We have 10 million ways now of doing the same thing! Isn't that enough? Let's start to do things better. Let's shift to the explicit representation of knowledge about the world using ontologies, which are grounded in firm logics that enable knowledge to be interpreted directly by machines. Let's enable our machines to interact at our human conceptual level.

In this section, therefore, we will look at the kinds of logics that exist. These logics are the machinery behind our Semantic Web languages (and, as some folks propose, even human natural languages) that enable those languages to express a rigorous, unambiguous (depending on context), and semantically rich human-level knowledge that in turn is machine-interpretable.

Propositional Logic

The first type of logic we'll briefly look at is propositional logic. *Propositional logic* is the simplest kind of logic. It enables you to formally express simple semantic truths about the world—simple states of affairs usually called propositions. A *proposition* is just some expression (sometimes also called a statement) in logic about the world or some part of the world that is either true or false or, in certain logics, that has three truth values (true, false, unknown) unknown. Table 8.7 is a simple example of an expression in ordinary propositional logic with two truth values (refer back to Figure 8.1 to check these statements).

This example displays the English version of the propositions on the left and the propositions formalized in propositional logic on the right. We see that the proposition "John is a management employee" is formalized as p and the proposition "John manages an organization" as q in propositional logic. The entire structure on the left- (or the right-) hand side is called a *proof*, with *assertions* above the solid line and a *conclusion* below the line. The way to read a proof is this: If the assertions are held to be true, it follows logically from them that the conclusion is true—and true by reason of a logical inference rule, here the rule *modus ponens*.

Table 8.7 Propositional Logic Example

PROPOSITIONS IN ENGLISH	PROPOSITIONS IN PROPOSITIONAL LOGIC	
If John is a management employee, then John manages an organization.	$p \rightarrow q$	
John is a management employee.	p	
———————	———————	
John manages an organization.	q	Modus ponens
Modus ponens		

One limitation of propositional logic is that you cannot speak about individuals (instances like John, who is an instance of a management employee) because the granularity is not fine enough. The basic unit is the proposition, which is either true or false. More complicated propositions use compositions of propositions, composed by using the logical connectives such as *and*, *or*, and as earlier, *implication*. One cannot "get inside" the proposition and pull out instances or classes or properties. For these, one needs first-order predicate logic.

First-Order Predicate Logic

In *first-order predicate logic*, finer semantic distinctions can be made. In Table 8.8, distinct predicates p and q can refer to the same individual x. A *predicate* is a feature of language (and logic) that can be used to make a statement or attribute a property to something, in this case the properties of being *a management employee* and *managing an organization*. So both properties and individuals can be represented in predicate logic. We also note that an instantiated predicate is a proposition, for instance, *management_employee(john) = true*. An uninstantiated predicate—for example, *management_employee(x)*—is *not* a proposition because the statement does not have a truth value (and only propositions have truth values); in other words, we don't know what x refers to and so cannot tell if "x is a management_employee" is true or not. In this example, we have only two predicates, *management employee* and *managing an organization*; we have not yet teased apart the statement into three parts: a *management employee* part, a *managing an organization* part, and a *manages* part. But in Table 8.9, we will do just that.

Table 8.8 Predicate Logic Example

PROPOSITIONS AND PREDICATES IN ENGLISH	PROPOSITIONS AND PREDICATES IN FIRST-ORDER PREDICATE LOGIC	
If John is a management employee, then John manages an organization.	$p(x) \rightarrow q(x)$	
John is a management employee.	p(john)	
_____	_____	
John manages an organization.	q(john)	Modus ponens
Modus ponens		

In addition to predicates, predicate logic also has quantifiers. Quantifiers come in many flavors, but we are only interested in two simple kinds: the universal quantifier and the existential quantifier. A *quantifier* is a logical symbol that enables you to quantify over instances or individuals (most modeling languages use the term *instance;* usually logic uses the term *individual*). *The universal quantifier* means *All;* the *existential quantifier* means *Some.*

In fact, this is why ordinary predicate logic is called *first-order*: It only quantifies over instances. If you use a logic to quantify over both instances and predicates, then that logic is called *second-order logic.* The universal quantifier *binds* a designated instance variable in the expression so that wherever that variable occurs (in whatever predicate), *every possible substitution* of that variable by an instance must make the complex expression true. In Table 8.9, everyone and anyone who is a management employee also manages an organization (we don't know yet if the person is a manager or a director or a vice president or president, but in any case, we know that person manages some organization).

This final example may seem a bit complicated, but it demonstrates that fine logical (and semantic) distinctions can be made *and* formalized in predicate logic. High-end ontologies (ontologies that are logical theories in our Ontology Spectrum) are modeled in semantic languages such as DAML+OIL and OWL that have a logic behind them, a logic that is almost but not quite as complicated as first-order predicate logic (*description logics* explicitly try to achieve a good trade-off between semantic richness and machine tractability). This is the reason that ontologies modeled in those languages can be *machine-interpretable*: The machine knows exactly what the model means and how the model works logically, and can infer in a step-by-step fashion those inferences a human would make. But you need not worry about the formal logic behind those languages. You just use the languages like OWL to create your ontologies, and then the OWL interpreter will do the right thing. That is the power of using ontologies, especially those developed in a semantically rich language that expresses what you want to express.

Table 8.9 Example of Quantifiers in Predicate Logic

PROPOSITIONS AND PREDICATES IN ENGLISH	PROPOSITIONS AND PREDICATES IN FIRST-ORDER PREDICATE LOGIC
Everyone who is a management employee manages some organization.	$\forall x. [p(x) \rightarrow \exists y. [q(y) \wedge r(x,y)]\,]$
	"for all x, if x is a p,
Or:	
	then there is some y such that
For everyone who is a management employee, there is some organization that that person manages.	y is a q and x is in the r relation to y"

Ontologies Today

This section looks at ontologies today, including some of the tools that are available, some issues concerning ontologies, and the emerging Semantic Web ontology languages.

Ontology Tools

Ontology development tools are now entering the market. Most of the tools until recently were research tools, such as Ontolingua/Chimaera (McGuinness et al., 2000) and Protégé (Noy et al., 2000). Both of these tools use frame-based knowledge representation languages developed for artificial intelligence, such as the Open Knowledge Base Connectivity (OKBC) language (Chaudhri et al., 1998). Two exceptions are Cyc (Lenat and Guha, 1990, 1991), which has been a commercial product for a number of years, and OntologyWorks's tool suite; both use a first-order logic (FOL) based language, with OntologyWorks using KIF/CL (which has second-order logic extensions).

Also, the Cyc upper ontology itself is freely available. What's an *upper ontology*? It's an ontology (or more appropriately, a set of integrated ontologies) that tries to characterize very basic commonsense knowledge notions that humans know so well we typically don't know we know them: that is, distinctions between kinds of objects in the world, events and processes, how parts constitute a whole and what that means, and general notions of time and space.

Other newer tools for creating ontologies include the commercially available OntoEdit (http://ontoserver.aifb.uni-karlsruhe.de/ontoedit/) and the research tool OilEd (http://img.cs.man.ac.uk/oil/). Both of these tools use knowledge representation languages which are being developed as standards under the W3C (http://www.w3.org/) to support the Semantic Web. Other, more generic tools that can help build an infrastructure for ontologies include both Java and Common Lisp (e.g., Allegro Common Lisp). See our Web site at http://www.wiley.com/compbooks/daconta for additional pointers to tools.

Levels of Ontologies: Revisited

Earlier in this chapter, we looked at levels of knowledge representation. In this section we look at levels briefly again, but this time with respect to the kinds of knowledge represented at different levels within the overall content level (what we had called the ontology concept and instance levels previously). This is the level of ontologies.

Ontologies really exist at three general levels: top level, middle level, and lower domain level. At the top level, the ontological information represented concerns primary semantic distinctions that apply to every ontology under the sun: These concern primary distinctions between tangible and intangible objects (objects that can be touched or held and those that cannot; sometimes this distinction is called that between abstract and concrete objects), the semantics of parthood (i.e., what constitutes a part and what is the nature of those relations between parts and wholes; in many cases, there are multiple notions of *parthood*, some transitive, some not, some with other properties that need to be specified in an ontology and then inherited downward into the medium and lower domain levels of ontology representation.

In Figure 8.11, the three general levels of ontologies are depicted. At the top is the *upper ontology*. This represents the common generic information that spans all ontologies. In the middle is the *middle ontology*. This level represents knowledge that spans domains and may not be as general at the knowledge of the upper level. Finally, the lower levels represent ontologies at the domain or sub-domain level. This is typically knowledge about more or less specific subject areas. In the figure, we point out the probable electronic commerce areas of interest, though we caution: In general, electronic commerce will be interested in *all* the ontology levels and areas, simply because commerce involves nearly everything.

Although we do not have space here to present ontology methodologies and the ways the different levels of ontologies are designed and developed by ontological engineers, we assure you that there are such methodologies and that in fact distinct methodologies and knowledge are required for each level.

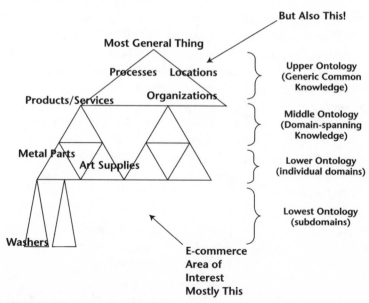

Figure 8.11 Ontology levels.

In general, ontologists and semanticists can address the upper and to some extent the middle ontology levels, but domain experts have to address the domain and lower levels, since only they know the specific knowledge about their domains. They can be guided by ontologists for semantic modeling issues, and in fact, must be guided by them. But the knowledge is theirs alone, and this knowledge must be provided to ontologists to represent their domains accurately.

Emerging Semantic Web Ontology Languages

This section introduces the emerging Semantic Web languages for representing ontologies. These languages include the Resource Description Framework (RDF) and RDF Schema (when referring to both, typically the abbreviation RDF/S or RDF(S) is used); Defense Advanced Research Projects Agency (DARPA) Agent Markup Language (DAML) + Ontology Inference Layer (OIL), usually abbreviated DAML+OIL; and the Web Ontology Language (OWL). Chapter 5 provided an introduction to RDF and RDFS, so we will not focus on RDF/S here.[20] Instead, we will talk primarily about DAML+OIL and OWL, both of which are the most semantically expressive languages for defining ontologies for the Semantic Web, with emphasis on OWL in particular, because it builds on and is intended to supersede DAML+OIL.

DAML+OIL

DAML is a Semantic Web ontology language that was developed as part of the DARPA DAML program, which originated in 2000 and continues to the present. Soon after the initial U.S.-based DAML language version had emerged, DAML researchers and the comparable European Union-based OIL language researchers became aware of each other's effort.[21] There have subsequently been two versions of the combined language, now called DAML+OIL: December 2000 and March 2001. More recently, the DAML-Service (DAML-S) extension has emerged.[22] DAML-S is really a collection of ontologies represented in DAML+OIL that address the semantics of Web services, including services modeled as processes, resources, service profiles, service models, and service groundings (i.e., the concrete realization of the abstractly specified service components, and comparable to the Web Service Description Language's notion of binding).

[20]For a good additional tutorial on RDF/S, see Manola and Miller (2002).

[21]The first official version of DAML (DAML-ONT) can be found at http://www.daml.org/2000/10/daml-ont.html. Also see OIL http://www.ontoknowledge.org/oil/, and Bechhofer et al. (2000).

[22]DAML-S v0.7: http://www.daml.org/services/daml-s/0.7/. For a good introduction, see http://www.daml.org/services/daml-s/0.7/daml-s.html.

One important point that you should understand is that *all* the Semantic Web languages take advantage of the other languages beneath them in the so-called layer cake or stack diagram of the Semantic Web. All the languages use XML syntax, at least for interchange purposes. Figure 8.12 displays a stack used in a particular domain namespace (the namespace itself can be composed of additional namespaces). We see that XML is at the bottom of the stack. XML furnishes the base syntax for interoperability on the Web. Above it is XML Schema, which provides a database-like structuring capability for Web objects, comparable to database schemas.

The next layer is the RDF/S layer, which provides a simple language for expressing ontology concepts and relations and their instances, and again is in XML syntax. Above it is DAML+OIL or OWL, which enable defining a much more expressive ontology and which in turn use the RDF/S level for representing instances of the ontology constructs. Both DAML+OIL and OWL also directly use XML Schema data types. It should be emphasized that although all of these layers are expressed in XML syntax, you still need to use specific interpreters to understand the particular language in order to really take advantage of what that language offers. For example, though all RDF/S, DAML+OIL, and OWL files can be validated as being in legitimate XML syntax, only RDF/S, DAML+OIL, or OWL interpreters can interpret those respective layers, with this slight qualification: In general, the higher language interpreters can correctly interpret every layer below its language level. So, an OWL interpreter will be able to use any embedded or referenced RDF/S or XML Schema data type construct, in addition to OWL-specific code.[23]

Finally, at the top are reasoning and proof methods, and the so-called "web of trust" layer, which uses automated proof, as well as security and identity features that are still relatively less understood and so, less mature as technologies. At the very top of the stack, we see "Intelligent" domain applications; these are applications that can utilize all of the Semantic Web layers and hence display more "intelligent" behavior or offer more "intelligent" services.

We will not say much more about DAML+OIL, since it is a language that is fairly comparable to OWL and that is expected to be superseded by OWL. Instead, we focus our discussion on OWL. For a feature comparison of XML, RDF/S, DAML+OIL, and portions of OWL, we refer the interested reader to the DAML site (http://www.daml.org/language/features.html) and to Gil and Ratnakar (2002).

---

[23]This is not quite the whole story, since as we will see in the section on OWL, which has three levels of language representation, some language levels of OWL do not treat the underlying RDF/S level in the same way.

- **Trust: Proof + Security + Identity**
- **Reasoning/Proof Methods**
- **OWL, DAML+OIL: Ontologies**
- **RDF Schema: Ontologies**
- **RDF: Instances**
- **XML Schema: Encodings of Data Elements & Descriptions via:**
  - **Define Types, Elements, Content Models, Structures, Local Usage Constraints: structural, cardinality, datatyping**
- **XML: Base Documents**

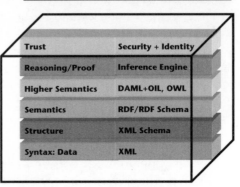

Domain Namespace

Figure 8.12 Stack architecture for the Semantic Web.

OWL

Web Ontology Language (sometimes referred to as Ontology Web Language) is the most expressive of the ontology languages currently defined or being defined for the Semantic Web. Unlike DAML+OIL, OWL is originating as a World Wide Web Consortium (W3C) sponsored language (http://www.w3 .org/2001/sw/WebOnt/). The W3C's Web Ontology Working Group was formed in November 2001, and the first official version of OWL is anticipated to be available in early 2003.

The OWL developers began with DAML+OIL as the initial candidate for an expressive Web ontology language, and evaluated DAML+OIL with respect to its known problems and the sufficiency of its semantic expressivity for developing ontologies usable on the Web. Initially, use cases were developed to drive out requirements, then the requirements for an ontology language were codified.[24] An abstract syntax and semantics, then the full language syntax (at least, up to this point; there are still some issues under discussion), and its semantics were defined.[25]

OWL has three levels of language: OWL Lite, OWL DL (for description logic), and OWL Full. These three levels are in increasing order of expressivity. The higher levels of the language contain the lower levels and so are said to extend the lower levels. A valid conclusion in OWL Lite is still a valid conclusion in

---

[24]Heflin et al. (2002).

[25]The important documents are a feature synopsis of OWL, McGuinness and van Harmelen (2002); the OWL guide, Smith et al. (2002); the OWL v1.0 language reference, Dean et al. (2002); OWL abstract syntax and semantics, Patel-Schneider et al. (2002); OWL test cases, Carroll and De Roo (2002). An additional semantics document may be developed.

OWL DL and OWL Full, and a valid conclusion in OWL DL is a valid conclusion in OWL Full, but not necessarily in OWL Lite. A valid conclusion in OWL Full is not necessarily a valid conclusion in either OWL DL or OWL Lite. Table 8.10 depicts the levels of language in OWL.

Overview of OWL

OWL builds on the conception and design of DAML+OIL. Similar to DAML+OIL, OWL has classes (and subclasses), properties (and subproperties), property restrictions, and both class and property individuals. Like DAML+OIL, OWL allows for class information and data-type information (from XML Schema), defines class constructs such as *subClassOf, disjointWith*, permits the boolean combination of class expressions (*intersectionOf, unionOf, complementOf*), as well as enumerated (listed) classes. OWL also has quantifier forms. The universal quantifier (All) is present as *owl:allValuesFrom* as a restriction (*owl:Restriction)* on (*owl:onProperty)* a specific property (property name identified by a URI): For each instance of the class or data type so restricted, every value for the specified property must belong to the instance. The existential quantifier (*some*) is present as *owl:someValuesFrom*: For each instance of the class of data type so restricted, at least one value for the specified property must belong to the instance.

Some differences between OWL and DAML+OIL include the following:

- Additions to RDF/S since the definition of DAML+OIL were included.

- Qualified restrictions in DAML+OIL were removed from OWL (http://www.daml.org/language/features.html).

- Some semantically equivalent forms were renamed (for example: daml:hasClass is renamed owl:someValuesFrom).

- Various synonyms of RDF/S classes and properties that were in DAML+OIL were removed from OWL.

- Daml:disjointUnionOf was removed because it can be derived from other OWL constructs.

- Owl:symmetricProperty was added.

- Owl:functionalProperty and owl:inverseFunctionalProperty act as global cardinality restrictions. The former is equivalent to an owl:maxCardinality restriction of 1.

- Daml:equivalentTo is now owl:sameAs (with sameClassAs favored because it is a subproperty of rdfs:subClassOf). Note that there are comparable similarity constructs for properties and individuals: samePropertyAs and sameIndividualAs, respectively.

- The namespace is now http://www.w3.org/2002/07/owl.

Table 8.10 OWL Language Levels

LANGUAGE LEVEL	DESCRIPTION
OWL Full	The complete OWL. For example, a class can be considered both as a collection of individuals and an individual itself.
OWL DL (description logic)	Slightly constrained OWL. Properties cannot be individuals, for example. More expressive cardinality constraints.
OWL Lite	A simpler language, but one that is more expressive than RDF/S. Simple cardinality constraints only (0 or 1).

OWL can be viewed as a collection of RDF triples, but those triples that use the OWL vocabulary have a specific OWL-defined meaning. If a given RDF graph (or subgraph) instantiates the OWL specification, then OWL provides a semantic interpretation for the components of that graph or subgraph. Other portions of the RDF graph that do not follow the OWL specification have no OWL semantic interpretation—though, of course, they will have an RDF interpretation.

OWL Lite

OWL Lite enables you to define an ontology of classes and properties and the instances (individuals) of those classes and properties. This and all OWL levels use the *rdfs:subClassOf* relation to defined classes that are subclasses of other classes and that thus inherit those parent classes properties, forming a subsumption hierarchy (or equivalently, as we've seen, a subclass taxonomy), with multiple parents allowed for child classes. Properties can be defined using the *owl:objectProperty* (for asserting relations between elements of distinct classes) or *owl:datatypeProperty* (for asserting relations between class elements and XML data types), *owl:subproperty*, *owl:domain*, and *owl:range* constructs.

A *domain* of a given property is the class for which the first argument of the property is specified; a *range* of a given property is the class for which the second argument of the property is specified. Think of the relation/property *hasFather(Child, Father)*: *Child* is the domain of the property *hasFather*, *Father* is the range of the property *hasFather*. This simply means that any instance/individual in the domain must be a member of the Child class; any instance in the range must be a member of the Father class. If there were a defined inverse property *fatherOf(Father, Child)*, then the domain of *fatherOf* would be *Father*; the range would be *Child*. OWL Lite also enables you to constrain the range of properties using the quantifier expressions *allValuesFrom* and *someValuesFrom* (expressions described in the preceding text).

OWL DL

OWL DL extends OWL Lite by permitting cardinality restrictions that are not limited to 0 or 1. Also, you can define classes based on specific property values using the *hasValue* construct. At the OWL DL level, you can create *class expressions* using boolean combinators (set operators) such as *unionOf*, *intersectionOf*, and *complementOf*. Furthermore, classes can be enumerated (listed) using the *oneOf* construct or specified to be disjoint using *disjointWith* construct.

OWL Full

OWL Full extends OWL DL by permitting classes to be treated simultaneously as both collections and individuals (instances). Also, a given *datatypeProperty* can be specified as being *inverseFunctional*, thus enabling, for example, the specification of a string as a unique key.

Summary

In this chapter, you have been given a solid but necessarily brief introduction to ontologies. We looked at what ontologies are and gave some examples and definitions. We reviewed notions that are important for discussing ontologies, such as the roles of syntax, structure, semantics, and pragmatics in the definition and use of ontologies. We looked at important concepts for ontologies and ontological engineering, such as extension and intension, the difference between labels (terms) and concepts (meaning), the levels every ontology has (meta and object levels; upper, middle, and lower or domain levels), and the distinction between a class (concept) and an instance (individual). We saw that knowledge representation languages are important for ontologies, as is logic (propositional, predicate, and higher logics). Finally, we discussed some ontology management tools and some of the Semantic Web ontology languages that are emerging, such as RDF/S, DAML+OIL, and OWL. You have been given wide, foundational knowledge about ontologies and are now prepared to dig deeper technically into these topics, if you so desire.

But what's the bottom line here? What are the real values for using ontologies? The real value of using ontologies and the Semantic Web is that you are able to express for the first time the semantics of your data, your document collections, and your systems using the same semantic resource and that resource is machine-interpretable: ontologies. Furthermore, you can reuse what you've previously developed, bring in ontologies in different or related domains created by others, extend yours and theirs, make the extensions available to other departments within your company (or your trading consortium or supply chain), and really begin to establish enterprise- or community-wide common semantics.

From our discussion of semantic mapping and merging, we now understand that this does *not* require a common semantics or common model (a *monolithic ontology* in our terminology) across the enterprise or community, but instead a set (or probably more accurately, a lattice) of integrated ontologies: upper, middle, and domain (or subdomain) levels integrated logically and thus *not* all in the same namespace and all contexts *not* the same, and all applications *not* using the same portions of the lattice of ontologies. Instead, ontologies across the board—upper modules, middle modules, domain modules, context modules, application modules—are coherently used (and reused!) across the enterprise or community, but according to the requirements of applications, which ultimately means, according to end-user needs, whoever the specific end users are, and in fact *all* end users in your enterprise or community.

With the widespread development and adoption of ontologies, which explicitly represent domain and cross-domain knowledge, we will have enabled our information technology to move upward—if not a quantum leap, then at least a major step—toward having our machines interact with us at our human conceptual level, not forcing us human beings to interact at the machine level. We predict that the rise in productivity at exchanging *meaning* with our machines, rather than semantically uninterpreted data, will be no less than revolutionary for information technology as a whole.

CHAPTER 9

Crafting Your Company's Roadmap to the Semantic Web

"We are drowning in information, and starved for knowledge."
—**John Naisbitt,** *MegaTrends,* **Warner Books, 1982**

I n this book, we have given you a strategic view and understanding of the Semantic Web, XML, Web services, RDF, taxonomies, and ontologies. Each of these technologies can (and some do) have entire books dedicated to them that delve into the technical details. In Chapter 2, we provided you with practical examples of how Semantic Web technologies can be used in your organization. It is the purpose of this chapter to show you how you can steer your company to take advantage of these technologies now so that you can begin reaping the rewards of the Semantic Web today and prepare your organization for the future. This chapter focuses on three areas: diagnosing the problems of information management, providing an architectural vision for your company, and showing you how to get there.

The Typical Organization: Overwhelmed with Information

The most significant problem today for the typical organization is that information management is haphazard. One problem is the sheer volume of information coming in—from a wide variety of information sources. Complicating the problem are the various formats of the data (paper, email, and a wide variety of multiple electronic media formats). Because of the magnitude of the information coming in from various sources, it is difficult to manage. The typical organization is composed of people like the one shown in Figure 9.1—overwhelmed with information. Combined with the lack of a cohesive information-management vision, the typical organization has lots of information, but little knowledge.

Figure 9.2 shows the typical knowledge process in an organization. The capture process is the first stage in information management. First, a human being in the organization takes information from somewhere (newspaper, radio, Internet, database, phone call, customer contact, email) and brings it to the organization in some way (1). Many times, this is where the process stops. The individual may simply bring it to the organization vocally—by mentioning the information to someone. The individual may send it via email to someone, where it is lost in the plethora of emails that overwhelm the organization. If the data isn't lost in this way, the individual writes a paper or presentation, or writes a status report.

Figure 9.1 Our own information management challenges.

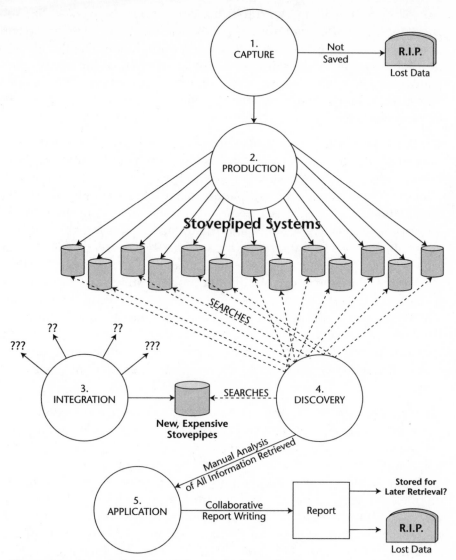

Figure 9.2 Knowledge process in a typical organization.

The second stage, if it gets that far, is production (2), where the data is put into a database, recorded to a digital file, or indexed into a search engine. Entering information is always the first step, but the problem is that each division, group, or project in the company enters the information into different systems. Assuming that there is only one database per project, and assuming a division has 10 projects, there may be 10 different software systems containing data in a division. In a company with four divisions, there are now 40 different software systems containing information. Now add a financial database with your invoices, bills, and collections information to that total. Finally, add your corporate human resources database (assuming there is only one). You now have many data sources that are individual stovepipes in your organization. Stovepipe systems perform a specific task at the expense of trapping the data and robbing the organization of business agility in adapting to new situations.

The third stage of the process may or may not be integration (3), depending on the complexity of your information architecture. Because all of your information systems are stovepiped, there is usually no good way to combine the integrated systems into a coherent picture. That is, any attempt to combine this information in any way is a tedious process, involving data conversions, incompatible software systems, and frustrated systems integrators. There is no repeatable process for integrating the systems, because each database and software system is designed differently and has different interfaces to talk to them. Add to that the complexity of different programming languages used to communicate with each software system, different operating systems and hardware platforms. As a result, there is usually little or no integration of these databases, because it is prohibitively difficult and expensive. When there is an integration solution, organizations usually pay a systems integrator big money to create a very expensive stovepiped system that integrates with your other systems.

The fourth stage of the process is searching—"discovery" of your corporation's internal resources (4). This is haphazard and time-consuming, because it involves so many different systems. You may have to log in to 40 databases and search engines, and manually compare and contrast the information you find into a big picture or coherent thought. Even the results from search engines are usually based on keywords and boolean logic, providing the searcher with results that may or may not be relevant. This is the most wasteful part of the process in person-hours. A study conducted by A. T. Kearney, a subsidiary of EDS, concluded that "lack of efficient publishing capabilities for digital content costs organizations $750 billion annually, as knowledge workers waste time seeking information necessary for them to do their jobs."[1]

Next, there is the application of the search results (5). After the tedious search process, the result is usually a presentation or paper report. Many times, this process of creating the report involves several people. The approval process is done by manual reviews and is slow. After this new product is created, the information may or may not be filed anywhere; it may be emailed into never-never land. If it is filed, perhaps it is filed onto a Web server that may or may

---

[1] "Study Shows $750 Billion Waste of Time," http://www.knowledgeboard.com/cgi-bin/item.cgi?id=44235.

not be indexed by one of your corporate search engines. Later, how do we know what version of the document we have? If this new document is integrated into one of our stovepiped corporate databases, there is no way to tell if the information has been superseded, which parts of the document are authoritative, and if the document has been approved by the organization. Lastly, there is information reuse—the ability months or years later to discover, refine, annotate, and incorporate past knowledge.

If any of these challenges seem at all familiar to you, you are ready for the Semantic Web. A smart company will leverage the Semantic Web technologies we have discussed in this book to craft an information architecture vision touching every part of the organization life cycle. We discuss this life cycle in the next section.

The Knowledge-Centric Organization: Where We Need to Be

A knowledge-centric organization will incorporate Semantic Web technologies into every part of the work life cycle, including production, presentation, analysis, dissemination, archiving, reuse, annotation, searches, and versioning. In this section we talk about how our knowledge process can be—in sharp contrast to the chaotic process of the previous section.

Discovery and Production

The discovery and production phase is where an individual receives information and would like to produce this as knowledge in his or her organization. This can be a repeatable process, as shown in Figure 9.3, and should be an integral part of your corporate workflow process. This is an area where organizations should be aggressive in capturing information, because the effectiveness of reuse will be directly proportional to the quantity and quality of information captured. When the individual gathers the information, he or she should perform due diligence to make certain that the information is valid. With any new piece of information, it is important that it is marked up with XML, using a relevant corporate schema. Once that is done, the individual should digitally sign the XML document using the XML Signature specification to provide strong assurance that the individual verified the validity of the information. The next step is the annotation process, where the individual may want to use RDF to annotate the new information with his or her notes or comments, adding to the XML document, but without breaking the digital signature seal of the original material. After this annotation is finished, the author should digitally sign the annotation with XML signature. Those RDF annotations are how you can make those connections to the corporate ontology and taxonomy.

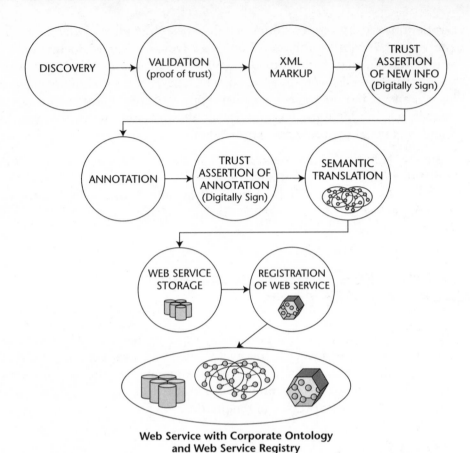

**Web Service with Corporate Ontology
and Web Service Registry**

Figure 9.3 The discovery and production process.

The next step is quite important. Before the information can be integrated into the system, the information must be mapped to topics in the taxonomy and entities in the corporate ontology so that pieces of the information can be compared to other pieces of information in your corporate knowledge base. For example, it is logical to ask the following questions: Who is the person that authored this document? What department does he or she work in? Is the individual an expert on this topic? Is this topic in our corporate taxonomy? As we've seen in Chapter 7, the taxonomy is ordinarily a partial projection of or mapping from the underlying ontology. Once this is done, it is time to store the information in an application with a Web service interface. If this is a new Web service, the Web service should be registered in the corporate registry, along with its taxonomic classifications.

The result of the discovery and production process is that the information coming into your organization is marked up with standard XML markup, the original data has been digitally signed to show assurance of trust, it has been annotated with an author's comments, it has been mapped to your corporate ontology, and it has been published to a Web service and registered in a Web service registry. Because it has been marked up with XML, standard techniques and technologies can be used to store it and style its presentation. Because it is mapped to your corporate ontology, the new information can be associated and compared with other information in your organization. Because the original information is digitally signed, anyone looking at the information will have assurance of its validity. Because author annotations are added and also digitally signed, there is tracking of who found the information and their comments. Because it is stored in a Web service, any software program can communicate with it easily using open standards. Finally, because the Web service is registered in a registry, people and programs in your organization can discover your Web service based on its name or taxonomic classification.

Search and Retrieval

Because data is stored in an easily accessible format (Web services) and is associated with an ontology and a taxonomy, retrieval of information is much easier than the haphazard process described in our earlier "typical organization" section. Integration with all Web services in the organization is easy—they all have a SOAP interface, and since all Web services are registered in a corporate Web service registry, it is easy for an application to find what it is looking for. Because all information is linked with an ontology and taxonomy, searches will provide results that otherwise would be unseen. Figure 9.4 provides a view of the types of searches that can be done with such an infrastructure.

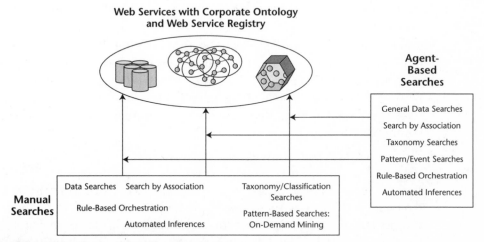

Figure 9.4 The search and retrieval process.

Because of the hard work that was done in the discovery and production process, our search and retrieval process is simpler and provides important functionality:

Discovery of knowledge via taxonomies.   Because each Web service can be classified in various taxonomies, taxonomic searches can be done across the Web services of an organization. A good example would be, "I'm looking for all Web services classified in the corporate taxonomy as related to 'Coal Mining.'"

Web service-based data searches.   Using standard SOAP interfaces, any application can query Web services in the enterprise.

Search by association.   Because our data is mapped into an ontology, semantic searches can be made across the entire knowledge base. We have traditionally left associations out of the search equation. This is the newfound power and possibly the killer app of the Semantic Web—mining associations. A good example of such a search would be, "I would like to perform a query on all relatives of the terrorist Mohammad Atta, their closest friends, and their closest friends' friends." In the world of electronic commerce, associations offer additional buying opportunities to customers. For example, if a potential customer searches for a particular machine or commodity, once that product's representation is found in the ontology, its associations can be selectively displayed—as related equipment, components, and services.

Pattern-based searches.   Because all data can be semantically linked by relationships in the ontology, patterns that would only be seen in the past—by old data mining techniques that did not directly utilize meaning—can now be dynamically found with semantic searches. An example of such a search would be, "Of all grocery stores listed in our corporate ontology, which stores have had revenue growth combined with an increased demand for orange juice?"

Manual and agent-based searches.   Although all of the searches can be manual, software agents can be equipped with rules to continually search the knowledge base and provide you with up-to-the-second results and alerts. An example of such an agent rule-based query would be, "Alert me via pager/email whenever a new document is registered discussing a new computer virus."

Rule-based orchestration queries.   Because Web services can be combined to provide modular functionality, rules can be used in order to combine various searches from different Web services to perform complicated tasks. An example of such a query would be, "Find me the lead engineer of the top-performing project in the company. Based on his favorite vacation spot from his response in the Human Resources survey, book him two tickets to that location next week, grant him vacation time, and cancel all of his work-related appointments."

Automated inference support. Because the corporate ontology explicitly represents concepts and their relationships in a logical and machine-interpretable form, automated inference over the ontology and its knowledge bases becomes possible. Given a specific query, an ontology-based inference engine can perform deduction and other forms of automated reasoning to generate the possible implications of the query, thus returning much more meaningful results. In addition, of course, the inference engine may discover inconsistencies or even contradictions in the ontology or knowledge bases. As the corporate ontology and the knowledge bases it spans are elaborated over time, more complicated automated reasoning can be performed (for example, induction of new knowledge based on old knowledge, the incorporation of probabilistic techniques). This automated inference itself can be considered a Web service or set of Web services, and utilized by software agents or human users.

A business process that supports the production process in the previous section will have benefits that will touch nearly every facet of your organization with these types of searches, allowing you to tap the knowledge you already have—but didn't know you had. To continue taking advantage of this knowledge after the search process, the conclusions from the new knowledge gained from your searches also need to be stored and saved for future use. The next section addresses this process.

Application of Results

Finally, the last production stage of the knowledge-centric organization's knowledge process is the application of results. If an entirely new product has been created (a new report, for example), the responsible person should use the production process, shown in the earlier section *Discovery and Production*. Part of the ontology mapping portion of that section would be the process of associating the new product with information gleaned from the other searches.

Another application in the last stage of the knowledge process may be simple data annotation. This process is shown in Figure 9.5. Based on the information your employees find in the step, it is possible that they will want to annotate the information they find. Of course, much like the production process, the author of the annotation should digitally sign the annotation. Before the new annotation items are added, version control should be added to the document, and it should be republished into the data federation.

Using the process shown in the upcoming section *Create Your Organization's Strategy* not only affects the outcome of your current work, it affects *information reuse*—being able to use that information at a later date. If an organization has a content management and workflow process that includes version control, annotation, and trust assertions, it will be easier to find information and apply the conclusions that were made earlier.

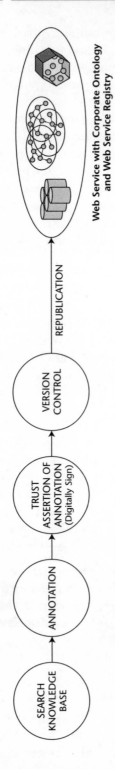

Figure 9.5 Application of results: Annotation and republication.

From discovery and production, to search and application, the corporate knowledge base needs to be a central part of your organization. The result will be that every aspect of your organization will benefit.

TIP At this point, if you haven't already, you may want to read Chapter 2, "The Business Case for the Semantic Web." This will give you some practical ideas of how the processes discussed in this section could affect your business.

How Do We Get There?

At this point in the book, we have described the Semantic Web, discussed practical applications of Semantic Web technologies, given overviews of the key technologies involved, and in the previous section, described processes that need to be in place to realize the vision. Most companies need to change their process in order to take advantage of Semantic Web technologies. Luckily, these changes can be implemented gradually over time, and your organization can easily evolve into a knowledge-centric organization. The most challenging aspect may not be the technology; it may be changing the mind-set of your employees. Leading cultural change may be the greatest challenge for some companies. Changing behavior and the ways that all levels think about accessing, integrating, and leveraging knowledge is critical. Any change plan must include comprehensive actions to address change at the organizational (culture), individual, and process levels.

If you are responsible for leading information technology change in your organization, you may be wondering, "Where do I start?"

Prepare for Change

At the beginning, you will need to be prepared to make changes in your organization. You also must determine who the stakeholders are that are impacted by the change, and how to lead them through the change process. To do this, you will need to define a clear purpose and set clear goals and milestones:

- **Establish and be able to convey your purpose.** To prepare for change in your organization, you will need to first develop your vision so that it can be communicated appropriately. Develop a clear purpose for changing your information management process in your organization. What is the clear and compelling business case for change? How will these technologies enable your organization to achieve its business goal? How does this change link to other, broader corporate goals? If you can't clearly answer these questions, your employees surely won't buy into it. A clear, concise, and simple mission statement may help. Chapters 1 and 2 should assist you in crafting the vision.

■ **Set clear goals.**   Based on your vision in Step 1, you will need to set clear goals and milestones specific to your organization. At this point, visionary goals (not technical goals) are what you will need—for example: "Be able to search all project information across the company by second quarter 2004." Look at Chapter 2 of this book for ideas.

■ **Identify stakeholders and develop a change plan for them.**   Identify critical stakeholders who will be impacted by the change. Segment stakeholders into critical groups (e.g., senior management, front-line employees, human resources). This will assist in assessing the unique impact on each group and develop targeted plans to help them work through change. For each stakeholder group, you should assess the impact of the change to them, the core message that will help them move through the change, and the resources or tools that can assist in managing the change. You can assess positive and negative aspects of the change for each group. You may wish to include a change management expert on your core team to address the cultural and organizational change issues identified through this analysis.

■ **Pick a core team that will help communicate the vision.**   At this point, you will need to choose a small management task force that will help you communicate the vision. This task force should be both technical directors and managers. Once you have your purpose and goals in place, you can get the task force on board. Depending on the needs of your organization, you may or may not want to get all management on board at this point. You also should identify an individual in the business (outside of IT, human resources, or other staff groups) to serve as a champion of the change. This leader should be a senior executive who has embraced the change and will help lead the organizational and cultural change efforts to ensure that the company embraces the new technology. It is important that this champion be a business leader, so the change is seen from a business perspective and not just as an "IT" concept.

Only after you do this will you be able to task your organization with the changes.

Begin Learning

At this point, you will need to make a major time investment in understanding the ideas and technologies of this book. This process will be multifaceted, because your management task force will need to understand the reasoning behind the change, but may not want to focus on the technologies. At the same time, your technical staff will need to know the technologies. The following are the steps you will need to take:

1. **Get management up to speed.** Your management (or management task force) will need to understand the high-level concepts of the Semantic Web, the purpose behind it, and the core business benefits it brings. This book was written with management in mind, so this may help them. Management may not want to focus on some of the technical details, but it is important that they understand the "whats" and the "whys"—not necessarily the "hows" —so they may want to understand the Semantic Web vision and application (Chapters 1 and 2 of this book). Your chief technology officer, if you have one, will need to have a very good understanding of it all.

2. **Get your technical staff started.** The details of the technologies of this book will be important for your technical staff to master, and you will need to make a considerable investment in training them in these technologies. Some of the chapters in this book are a good start, but your staff needs to get into the gory details that haven't been addressed here. Learning will be a journey, because some of these technologies are still evolving. If they can focus on the key technologies of this book and get involved in looking at the status of the standards and implementations of the technologies, they will be well equipped to begin helping you change. The essential focus areas of your technical staff should be as follows:

   - **XML (Chapters 3 and 6).** As this is the basis for all Semantic Web technologies, much emphasis will need to be placed on learning XML and its related technologies. If you are already using XML, you should focus on data typing (like in XML Schema), namespaces, and linking documents to more semantic data via RDDL (what we call creating a "semantic chain").

   - **Web Services (Chapter 4).** Web services are the key to interoperability and will be very important for your technical staff to learn. Web services wrap all the functions that manipulate your XML data in a language and platform-neutral manner.

   - **RDF, Taxonomies, and Ontologies (Chapters 5, 7, and 8).** As these are key technologies of the Semantic Web, it will be important for your technical staff to understand them. Only after your technical staff has a good understanding and grasp of these technologies can your organization leverage the "killer apps" of association mining and semantic searches. In a nutshell, think of using RDF as semantic glue to link your XML marked-up documents to your taxonomy (directory tree) and ontology (formal class model showing relationships). So, a document will be XML inside, RDF outside, filed in a branch of the taxonomy and related to classes in the ontology.

Remember, learning is and should be a continuous process. Once your management and technical staff have a good understanding of the vision and the technologies, it is time for you to plan your strategy.

Create Your Organization's Strategy

Now that you have management and the technical staff on board, it is time to tailor a knowledge management strategy for your organization. Here are the things that you will undoubtedly have to task your organization to do:

1. **Set detailed technical goals.**   Once your management and technical staff are on board, it is time to meet with them and determine the technical goals that you want to achieve. These are most likely the goals that you will want to implement:

   - **Mark up your documents in XML.**   This will be essential and will most likely be your first step. At first, your technical staff should come up with XML schemas to define your formats. After you do this, all new document development should have XML markup. It is important that your data content be separate from your presentation, and style sheets can be used to add presentation to content later. Tools will be helpful in accomplishing this goal—many tools are available that will help your employees author new documents in this manner. Depending on your legacy data, you may want to determine whether or not to mark up old documents. (If not, one solution may be to create Web service interfaces to existing databases of data.)

   - **Expose your applications as Web services.**   To take advantage of interoperability and advanced concepts such as Web service orchestration, you will need your technical staff to expose your application's interfaces as self-describing "knowledge objects." The way to think about access to your data is with a goal of delivering small, modular data building blocks (like LEGOs) that can be assembled by the using organization.

   - **Build Web service orchestration tools.**   Once your Web services are in place, have your technical staff focus on how they can be used together in Web service orchestration to accomplish complex tasks.

   - **Establish a corporate registry.**   An internal UDDI or ebXML registry will be important in allowing your applications to register themselves and query for Web services. Publishing the WSDL for your Web service applications will allow applications to dynamically discover the APIs of your applications.

   - **Build ontologies.**   Because XML merely provides facilities and syntax for specifying a data structure that can be semantically processed, higher-level semantic constructs will need to be overlaid on your XML marked-up documents. Ontologies constitute these semantic constructs. Ontologies can be difficult and time-consuming to build, since they represent the semantics of domains, though the difficulty and costs are coming down drastically. By definition, ontologies are intended to be reusable, and with the emergence of Semantic Web ontology languages such as RDF/S and OWL, more and more ontologies are being created, and these can be incorporated over time into your own ontologies. These ontologies are upper ontologies, middle ontologies, and domain ontologies. They can be brought into your company and refined by you, saving you creation costs, enabling you to structure your knowledge coherently, and helping you to establish or participate in wider community semantics. Also, some ontology tools are emerging that try to "induce" (generalize) the concepts and relationships of a potential ontology from huge document collections. These can help you get a handle on the domains of interest to your company, provide candidates for your growing ontology, and assist the ontologists and domain experts who are building and maintaining your ontologies. Finally, once you have built or acquired ontologies, you can consider using automated inference tools that can work on those ontologies and their knowledge bases. These can be intelligent Web services in their own right or can assist or interoperate with other services and applications, to help bring your information technology closer to human conceptual levels, greatly increasing your corporate productivity levels.

- **Use tools that will help your production process.**   Tools that allow your employees to annotate and sign documents with version control will be very helpful. These tools must be flexible to fit into your workflow process and take advantage of XML technologies (RDF, XTM, XSLT, XML Signature). These tools must be able to annotate, assert trust, and help you with document markup.

- **Integrate search tools.**   You will want to build or buy search tools that allow your employees to do searches of your documents (semantic searches based on your ontology, Web service searches, association searches). You may want to build or buy agents that can be programmed to automatically perform rule-based searches.

- **Use an enterprise portal as a catalyst for knowledge engineering.** Enterprise portals are natural aggregation points. A portal effort is an opportunity to integrate knowledge management into the organization and can be your organization's user interface to your search tools and Web services that you have developed.

2. **Develop a plan with a workflow change strategy.**   In accomplishing the preceding goals, you will need to look at the current workflow process and be able to communicate (and document) how it must be changed. You may want to invest in workflow products that incorporate these technologies into your production process. Once you've thought about these things, it is time for the next step.

3. **Set appropriate staff in place.**   At this point, you may want to consider creating an ontology department, a data production department, and a Web service deployment department that work together in order to accomplish some of your goals.

4. **Set a schedule.**   At this point, you are ready to set a schedule to implement these changes. If some of the work can be done behind the scenes without impacting the employees, this should be done first (such as creating Web service interfaces to existing applications). Make certain that you do this work (ontology planning, Web service, production planning) with your staff (last bullet) before change impacts your regular employees. Once your employees' processes will have to change, be ready to unveil a change in their workflow process. Incorporate this into the schedule.

Move Out!

Now, it's time to implement your schedule. At this point, you may want to communicate your plans to the company, starting with your reasons behind doing this and your high-level goals. Explain to them that specialized staff is working behind the scenes in order to accomplish these goals and make a smooth work transition. When the time is ready, schedule training to help your regular employees adapt to the new process.

General George S. Patton once said, "Accept the challenges so that you can feel the exhilaration of victory." The road to change may be rocky, and you will certainly be challenged along the way. With an intelligent plan and an incremental process, it is extremely doable, and it will be worth it when you get there.

Summary

This chapter presented a vision of where the typical organization is—and where we need to be to become a knowledge-centric organization in leveraging the technologies of the Semantic Web. In doing so, we have defined a knowledge-centric process and a how-to roadmap for crafting your company's roadmap to the Semantic Web.

References

Ahmed, K., D. Ayers, M. Birbeck, J. Cousins, D. Dodds, J. Lubell, M. Nic, D. Rivers-Moore, A. Watt, R. Worden, and A. Wrightson. 2001. *XML Meta Data*. Birmingham, UK: Wrox Press, Ltd.

Allegro Common Lisp. http://franz.com/. . .

Alter, J. 2002. "Actually, the Database Is God." *Newsweek*. (November 4, 2002). Available at http://stacks.msnbc.com/news/826637.asp.

Baader, F., and B. Hollunder. 1991. "KRIS: Knowledge Representation and Inference System." In *Special Issue on Implemented Knowledge Representation and Reasoning Systems, SIGART Bulletin* 2, no. 3 (June 1991): 108–113.

Bechhofer, S., J. Broekstra, S. Decker, M. Erdmann, D. Fensel, C. Goble, F. van Harmelen, I. Horrocks, M. Klein, D. McGuinness, E. Motta, P. Patel-Schneider, S. Staab, and R. Studer. 2000. "An Informal Description of Standard OIL and Instance OIL." White paper. (November 28, 2000.) Available at http://www.ontoknowledge.org/oil/downl/oil-whitepaper.pdf.

Beckett, D., ed. 2001. "RDF/XML Syntax Specification (Revised)." W3C Working Draft. (December 18, 2001). Available at http://www.w3.org/TR/2001/WD-rdf-syntax-grammar-20011218/.

Berners-Lee, T. 2002. *Weaving the Web*. San Francisco: Harper San Francisco.

Berners-Lee, T. "What the Semantic Web can Represent." Available at http://www.w3.org/DesignIssues/RDFnot.html.

Berners-Lee, T., J. Hendler, and O. Lassila. 2001. "The Semantic Web." *The Scientific American*. (May 2001). Available at http://www.scientificamerican. com/2001/0501issue/0501berners-lee.html.

Biezunski, M., S. Newcomb, and M. Bryan, eds. 2002. "Guide to the Topic Map Standards." Project ISO 13250, ISO/IEC JTC 1/SC34 Information Technology—Document Description and Processing Languages. (June 23, 2002). Available at http://www.y12.doe.gov/sgml/sc34/document/ 0323.htm.

Biezunski, M. 2003. "Introduction to the Topic Maps Paradigm." Chapter 2 in *XML Topic Maps: Creating and Using Topic Maps for the Web*, edited by Jack Park and Sam Hunting. Reading, MA.: Addison-Wesley, 17–33.

Brachman, R. J. 1978. "A Structural Paradigm for Representing Knowledge." Bolt, Baranek, and Newman. BBN Report 3605. Cambridge, MA. Revision of Brachman's Ph.D. thesis. Harvard University. 1977.

Brachman, R. J., and H. Levesque, eds. 1985. *Readings in Knowledge Representation*. Los Altos, CA: Morgan Kaufmann.

Brachman, R. J., and J. G. Schmolze. 1985. "An Overview of the KL-ONE Knowledge Representation System." *Cognitive Science* 9, no. 2: 171–216.

Brickley, D., and R. V. Guha, eds. 2002. "RDF Vocabulary Description Language 1.0: RDF Schema." W3C Working Draft. (April 30, 2002). Available at http://www.w3.org/TR/rdf-schema/.

BusinessWeek. 2002. "The Web Weaver Looks Forward." Interview with Tim Berners-Lee. (March 27, 2002). Available at http://www.businessweek .com/bwdaily/dnflash/mar2002/nf20020327_4579.htm.

Bush, V. 1945. "As We May Think." *The Atlantic*. (July 1945). Available at http://www.theatlantic.com/unbound/flashbks/computer/bushf.htm.

Carroll, J. J., and J. De Roo, eds. "Web Ontology Language (OWL) Test Cases." W3C Working Draft. (October 24, 2002.) http://www.w3.org/TR/ 2002/WD-owl-test-20021024/. (But see http://www.w3.org/2001/sw/ WebOnt/ for more recent versions.)

Casey, M., and M. Austin. 2001. "Semantic Web Methodologies for Spatial Decision Support." University of Maryland, Institute for Systems Research and Department of Civil and Environmental Engineering. (November 2001).

Center for Army Lessons Learned (CALL) Thesaurus. 2002. http://call.army.mil/.

Chappell, D. 2002. "Who Cares about UDDI?" Available at http://www .chappellassoc.com/articles/article_who_cares_UDDI.html.

Chaudri, V., A. Farquhar, R. Fikes, P. D. Karp, and J. P. Rice. 1998. "Open Knowledge Base Connectivity Specification." Specification V. 2.0.31. SRI and Knowledge Systems Laboratory. Stanford University.

Clark, J. C., and M. Makoto. 2001. "RELAX NG Tutorial." December 3, 2001. Available at http://www.oasis-open.org/committees/relax-ng/tutorial.html.

Clark, K. 2002. "TAG Rejects HLink." (October 2, 2002). Available at http://www.xml.com/lpt/a/2002/10/02/deviant.html.

Clark, K. 2002. "Community and Specifications," XML Deviant column at XML.com (October 30, 2002). Available at http://www.xml.com/pub/a/2002/10/30/deviant.html.

Cohen, P. R., R. Schrag, E. Jones, A. Pease, A. Lin, B. Starr, D.Easter, D.Gunning, and M. Burke. 1998."The DARPA High Performance Knowledge Bases Project." *Artificial Intelligence Magazine* 19, no. 4: 25–49. Available at http://reliant.teknowledge.com/HPKB/Publications/AImag.pdf.

Common Logic Standard. http://cl.tamu.edu/.

Cyc. *See* Cycorp and OpenCyc.

Cycorp, Inc. "The CYC Technology." http://www.cyc.com/tech.html.

DAML-ONT. http://www.daml.org/2000/10/daml-ont.html.

DAML+OIL. 2001. http://www.daml.org/2001/03/reference.html.

DAML-S v0.7. http://www.daml.org/services/daml-s/0.7/. Also see http://www.daml.org/services/daml-s/0.7/daml-s.html.

Davis, R., H. Shrobe, and P. Szolovits. 1993. "What Is a Knowledge Representation?" *AI Magazine* (Spring 1993). American Association for Artificial Intelligence.

Dean, M., D. Connolly, F. van Harmelen, J. Hendler, I. Horrocks, D. L. McGuinness, P. Patel-Schneider, F. Stein, and L. A. Stein, eds. 2002. "OWL Web Ontology Language 1.0 Reference." W3C Working Draft 29. (July 2002; November 12, 2002). Latest version is available at http://www.w3.org/TR/owl-ref/.

DeRose, Maler, Orchard. "XML Linking Language (XLink) Version 1.0." Available at http://www.w3.org/TR/xlink/ - W3C Recommendation. (June 27, 2001).

Dowling, W., and J. Gallier. "Linear Time Algorithms for Testing the Satisfiability of Propositional Horn Formulae." *Journal of Logic Programming* 3 (1984): 267–284.

DuCharme, B. 2002. "XLink: Who Cares?" (March 13, 2002). Available at http://www.xml.com/pub/a/2002/03/13/xlink.html.

Ewalt, D. 2002. "The Next Web." *Information Week.* (October 10, 2002). Available at http://www.informationweek.com/story/IWK20021010S0016.

Fahlman, S. 1979. *NETL: A System for Representing and Using Real-World Knowledge.* Cambridge, MA: MIT Press.

Fellbaum, C., ed. 1998. *WordNet: An Electronic Lexical Database*. Cambridge, MA: MIT Press.

Fensel, D. 2002. "Semantic Enabled Web Services." XML-Web Services ONE Conference, (June 7, 2002).

Fensel, Bussler, Ding, Kartseva, Klein, Korotkiy, Omelayenko, Siebes. "Semantic Web Application Areas." *In Proceedings of the 7th International Workshop on Applications of Natural Language to Information Systems*, Stockholm, Sweden, June 27-28, 2002.

Fikes, R. and D. L. McGuinness. 2001. "An Axiomatic Semantics for RDF, RDF Schema, and DAML+OIL." KSL Technical Report KSL-01-01, 2001. Updated October 2001. Available at http://www.ksl.stanford.edu/people/dlm/daml-semantics/abstract-axiomatic-semantics.html.

Foster, Kesselman, Tuecke. 2001. "The Anatomy of the Grid: Enabling Scalable Virtual Organizations." *International J. Supercomputer Applications*. 15, no. 3.

Foundation for Intelligent Physical Agents (FIPA). http://www.fipa.org/.

Freese, E. 2003. "Topic Maps and RDF." Chapter 12 in *XML Topic Maps: Creating and Using Topic Maps for the Web*, edited by Jack Park and Sam Hunting. Reading, MA: Addison-Wesley, 283–325.

Guha, R. V., and R. McCool. 2002. "TAP" presentation. WWW2002.

Garshol, L. M., and G. Moore, eds. 2002a. "The Standard Application Model for Topic Maps." JTC1/SC34: ISO 13250, 2002-07-26. Available at http://www.y12.doe.gov/sgml/sc34/document/0329.htm.

Garshol, L. M., and G. Moore, eds. 2002a. "The XML Topic Maps (XTM) Syntax." JTC1/SC34: ISO 13250, 2002-07-22. Available at http://www.y12.doe.gov/sgml/sc34/document/0328.htm

Gil, Y., and V. Ratnakar 2002. "Markup Languages: Comparison and Examples." USC/Information Sciences Institute, TRELLIS project. Available at http://www.isi.edu/expect/web/semanticweb/comparison.html.

Graham, I. 2000. *Object-Oriented Methods: Principles and Practice*, 3d ed. Reading, MA: Addison-Wesley.

Grice, H. P. 1975. "Logic and Conversation." In *Syntax and Semantics, 3: Speech Acts*, edited by Peter Cole and Jerry Morgan. New York: Academic Press, 305–315.

Gruber, T. 1993. "A Translation Approach to Portable Ontology Specifications." *Knowledge Acquisition* 5: 199–220.

Guarino, N. ed. 1998. Formal Ontology in Information Systems. Amsterdam: IOS Press. Proceedings of the First International Conference (FOIS '98), June 6–8, Trent, Italy.

Guarino, N., and P. Giaretta, 1995. "Ontologies and Knowledge Bases: Towards a Terminological Clarification." In *Towards Very Large Knowledge Bases: Knowledge Building and Knowledge Sharing*, edited by N. Mars. Amsterdam: IOS Press, 25–32.

Hagen, P., H. Manning, and Y. Paul. 2000. "Must Search Stink?" *The Forrester Report.* (June 2000).

Halpin, T. 1995. *Conceptual Schema and Relational Database Design*. Upper Saddle River, NJ: Prentice Hall.

Hayes, P. "RDF Semantics." W3C Working Draft. (November 12, 2002). Available at http://www.w3.org/TR/rdf-mt/.

Heflin, J., R. Volz, and J. Dale, eds. 2002. "Requirements for a Web Ontology Language." W3C Working Draft. (July 8, 2002). Available at http://www.w3.org/TR/webont-req.

Hendler, J., T. Berners-Lee, and E. Miller. 2002. "Integrating Applications on the Semantic Web." *Journal of the Institute of Electrical Engineers of Japan* 122, no. 10 (October): 676–680.

Horrocks, I. 2002. "DAML+OIL: A Description Logic for the Semantic Web." IEEE Intelligent Systems, 2002. Trends and Controversies.

Horrocks, I., and S. Tobies. 2000. Reasoning with Axioms: Theory and Practice. Seventh International Conference on Principles of Knowledge Representation and Reasoning (KR2000), Breckenridge, Colorado, USA, 12-15 April 2000 (KR 2000): pp. 285-296.

ISO 704. "Terminology Work: Principles and Methods." 2d ed.. 2000-11-15.

Jacobs, J., and A. Linden. 2002. Gartner Group, Gartner Research Note T-17-5338, 20. (August 2002).

Knowledge Interchange Format (KIF) Specification. (Draft proposed American National Standard, NCITS.T2/98-004: http://logic.stanford.edu/kif/dpans.html. See also isoKIF, http://cl.tamu.edu/discuss/kif-100101.pdf.

Krill, P. 2000. "Overcoming Information Overload." *InfoWorld.* (January 7, 2000).

Lassila, O., and R. R. Swick, eds. 1999. "Resource Description Framework (RDF) Model and Syntax Specification." W3C Recommendation. February 22, 1999. Available at http://www.w3.org/TR/1999/REC-rdf-syntax-19990222/.

Lenat, D., and R. Guha. "The Evolution of CycL: The Cyc Representation Language." In *Special Issue on Implemented Knowledge Representation and Reasoning Systems, SIGART Bulletin* 2, no. 3 (June 1991): 84–87.

Lenat, D., and R. Guha. 1990. *Building Large Knowledge-Based Systems*. Reading, MA: Addison Wesley.

MacGregor, R. 1991. "Inside the LOOM Description Classifier." In *Special Issue on Implemented Knowledge Representation and Reasoning Systems, SIGART Bulletin* 2, no. 3 (June 1991): 88–92.

MacGregor, R. 1994. A "Description Classifier for the Predicate Calculus." In *Proceedings of the AAAI 1994 National Conference*.

Manola, F., and E. Miller, eds. 2002. "RDF Primer." W3C Working Draft. (March 19, 2002). Available at http://www.w3.org/TR/2002/WD-rdf-primer-20020319/.

McGuinness, D. L., R. Fikes, J. Rice, and S. Wilder. 2000. "An Environment for Merging and Testing Large Ontologies." In *Proceedings of the 7th International. Conference on Principles of Knowledge Representation and Reasoning (KR2000)*, Breckenridge, Colorado, U.S.A. (April 2000). Morgan Kaufmann.

McGuinness, D. L., and F. van Harmelen, eds. 2002. "Feature Synopsis for OWL Lite and OWL." W3C Working Draft. (July 29, 2002). http://www.w3.org/TR/2002/WD-owl-features-20020729/. But see http://www.w3.org/2001/sw/WebOnt/ for more recent versions.

McIllraith, S. 2002. "Semantic Enabled Web Services." XML-Web Services ONE Conference, (June 7, 2002).

Miller, G. A., R. Beckwith, C. Fellbaum, D. Gross, and K. Miller. 1993. "Introduction to WordNet: An On-line Lexical Database." (August 1993). Available at ftp://ftp.cogsci.princeton.edu/pub/wordnet/5papers.pdf.

Milne, A. A. 1996. *The Complete Tales of Winnie the Pooh*. New York: Penguin Putnam.

Minsky, M., ed. 1968. *Semantic Information Processing*. Cambridge, MA: MIT Press.

Minsky, M. 1975. "A Framework for Representing Knowledge." In *The Psychology of Computer Vision*, edited by P. Winston. New York: McGraw-Hill, 211–277.

Mylopoulos, J., and M. L. Brodie, eds. 1989. *Readings in Artificial Intelligence and Databases*. San Mateo, CA: Morgan Kaufman.

Nebel, B. 2001. "Frame-Based Systems." http://cognet.mit.edu/MITECS/Entry/nebel.

Newcomb, S. R., and M. Biezunski. 2002. "A High Level Description of a Draft Reference Model for ISO 13250 Topic Maps." Review Draft. (April 4, 2002). http://www.y12.doe.gov/sgml/sc34/document/0298.htm.

Noy, N. F., R. W. Fergerson, and M. A. Musen. 2000. "The Knowledge Model of Protege-2000: Combining Interoperability and Flexibility." In *2nd International Conference on Knowledge Engineering and Knowledge Management* (EKAW '2000).

OASIS Topic Maps Technical Committees. Published Subjects TC: http://www.oasis-open.org/committees/tm-pubsubj/; XML Vocabulary TC: http://www.oasis-open.org/committees/xmlvoc/; Geography and Language TC: http://www.oasis-open.org/committees/geolang/.

Obrst, L., and H. Liu. 2003. "Knowledge Representation, Ontological Engineering, and Topic Maps." In *XML Topic Maps: Creating and Using Topic Maps for the Web,* edited by Jack Park. Reading, MA: Addison-Wesley.

OIL. http://www.ontoknowledge.org/oil/.

OKBC. http://www.ai.sri.com/~okbc/.

Ontolingua. http://www.ksl.stanford.edu/software/ontolingua/.

OpenCyc. http://www.opencyc.org/.

Orr, W. 2002. "Financial Portals Are Hot, But for Whom?" ABA Banking Online. Available at http://www.banking.com/ABA/tech_portals_0700.asp.

OWL: The Web Ontology Language. http://www.w3.org/2001/sw/WebOnt/.

Park, J., and S. Hunting, eds. 2003. *XML Topic Maps: Creating and Using Topic Maps for the Web.* Reading, MA: Addison-Wesley.

Patel-Schneider, P. F., I. Horrocks, P. Hayes, and F. van Harmelen, eds. Web Ontology Language (OWL) Abstract Syntax and Semantics. W3C Working Draft. November 8, 2002. http://www.w3.org/TR/2002/WD-owl-semantics-20021108/. But see http://www.w3.org/2001/sw/WebOnt/ for more recent versions.

Patel-Schneider, P. F., D. L. McGuinness, R. Brachman, L. A. Resnick, A. Borgida. 1991. "The CLASSIC Knowledge Representation System: Guiding Principles and Implementation Rationale." In *Special Issue on Implemented Knowledge Representation and Reasoning Systems, SIGART Bulletin* 2, no. 3 (June 1991): 108–113.

Patil, R. R., Fikes, P. Patel-Schneider, D. Mckay, T. Finin, T. Gruber, and R. Neches. 1992. "The DARPA Knowledge Sharing Effort: Progress Report." In *Proceedings of Knowledge Representation and Reasoning Conference* (KR-92).

Pemberton, Ishikawa. "HLink: Link Recognition for the XHTML Family." W3C Working Draft 13. (September 2002). Available at http://www.w3.org/TR/hlink.

Pepper, S., and G. Moore, eds. 2001. "XML Topic Maps (XTM) 1.0." TopicMaps.Org Specification. Available at http://www.topicmaps.org/xtm/1.0/.

Protégé. http://protégé.stanford.edu.

Quillian, M. R. 1968. "Semantic Memory." In *Semantic Information Processing*, edited by M. Minsky. Cambridge, MA: MIT Press, 216–270.

Rao, A., and M. Georgeff. 1995. "BDI Agents: From Theory to Practice." In *Proceedings of the First International Conference in Multi-Agents Systems*. San Francisco, 1995.

Rumbaugh, J., M. Blaha, W. Premerlani, F. Eddy, and W. Lorensen. 1991. *Object-Oriented Modeling and Design.* Upper Saddle River, NJ: Prentice Hall.

Schneier, B. 2002. "Cryptogram Monthly Newsletter." (February 15, 2002). Available at http://www.counterpane.com/crypto-gram-0202.html#2.

Swartz, A. 2002. "The Semantic Web in Breadth." Available at http://logicerror.com/semanticWeb-long.

Singh, M. P. 2002. "The Pragmatic Web: Preliminary Thoughts." In *Proceedings of the Database and Information Systems Research for Semantic Web and Enterprises Invitational Workshop.* Sponsored by NSF CISE-IIS-IDM. CoSponsored by EU Thematic Network OntoWeb. (April 3–5, 2002). Amicalola Falls and State Park, GA. Edited by Amit Sheth and Robert Meersman. Available at http://lsdis.cs.uga.edu/SemNSF/Singh-Position.pdf.

Smith, B. 1990. "Towards a History of Speech Act Theory." In *Speech Acts, Meanings, and Intentions: Critical Approaches to the Philosophy of John R. Searle*, edited by A. Burkhardt. Berlin/New York: de Gruyter, 1990, 29–61. Available at http://ontology.buffalo.edu/smith//articles/speechact.html.

Smith, K. "Solutions for Web Services Security: Lessons Learned in a Department of Defense Program," Web Services for the Integrated Enterprise-OMG's Second Workshop on Web Services, Modeling, Architectures, Infrastructures, and Standards. (April 2003). Available at http:/www.omg.org/news/meetings/webservices 2003 usa/.

Smith, M., D. L. McGuinness, R. Volz, and C. Welty, eds. 2002. "Web Ontology Language (OWL) Guide Version 1.0." W3C Working Draft. (November 4, 2002). http://www.w3.org/TR/2002/WD-owl-guide-20021104/. But see http://www.w3.org/2001/sw/WebOnt/ for more recent versions.

Sowa, J. 2001. *Knowledge Representation: Logical, Philosophical, and Computational Foundations.* Pacific Grove, CA: Brooks/Cole.

Special Issue on Implemented Knowledge Representation and Reasoning Systems, SIGART Bulletin 2, No. 3 (June 1991).

Trastour, Bartolini, Gonzales-Castillo. "A Semantic Web Approach to Service Description of Matchmaking of Service." In *Proceedings of the International Semantic Web Working Symposium* (SWWS), Stanford, CA, July 2001.

Troelstra, A. S. 1998. *Concepts and Axioms*. Manuscript.

Ullman, J. D. 1989. *Principles of Database and Knowledge-Base Systems*. Vols. 1 and 2. Rockville, MD: Computer Science Press.

UML. http://www.uml.org/.

Vardi, M. 1998. "Logic in Computer Science: An Algorithmic Approach." Course Notes. Available at http://www.cs.rice.edu/~vardi/sigcse/mv2.ps.gz.

Wreder, K., and Yi Deng. 1998. "Architecture-Centered Enterprise System Development and Integration Based on Distributed Object Technology Standard." © 1998 Institute of Electrical and Electronics Engineers, Inc.

World Wide Web Consortium (W3C). "XForms 1.0 Working Draft." Available at http://www.w3.org/TR/xforms/.

World Wide Web Consortium (W3C). http://www.w3.org/DesignIssues/diagrams/sw-stack-2002.png.

World Wide Web Consortium (W3C). http://www.w3.org/TR/SOAP/.

World Wide Web Consortium (W3C). http://www.w3.org/TR/xlink/ - "XML Linking Language (XLink) Version 1.0." W3C Recommendation. (June 27, 2001).

W3C. "Resource Description Framework (RDF) Model and Syntax Specification." W3C Recommendation. (February 22, 1999).

XML, RDF/S, DAML, OWL Comparison. http://www.daml.org/language/features.html.

XHTML (Extensible Hypertext
Markup Language), 35,
134–136, 143
XInclude language, 132–133, 143
XKMS (XML Key Management
Specification), 80
XLANG, 75
XLink, 127–130, 143
xlink:href attribute, 131
xlink:type attribute, 129–130
XML. *See* Extensible Markup
Language
XML Base language, 133–134, 143
XML Key Management
Specification (XKMS), 80
XML Path Language (XPath), 47,
119–121, 143
XML Schema, 29
XML Signature, 79
XML Topic Maps (XTM), 8, 24
xmlns() method, 131
XMP (Extensible Metadata
Platform), 8

XPointer language, 130–131, 143
XQuery
defined, 29
discussed, 143
expressions, 126–127
Query Working Group, 126
xsi:noNamespaceSchemaLocation
attribute, 37
xsi:schemaLocation attribute, 37
XSL (Extensible Stylesheet
Language), 121, 143
XSLFO (Extensible Stylesheet
Language: Formatting
Objects), 121, 143
XSLT (Extensible Stylesheet
Language Transformation), 49,
60, 121, 143
XTM (XML Topic Maps), 8, 24

Z
zip codes, 30